Mission to Moscow

Edited with an introduction by

David Culbert

Published for the Wisconsin Center for Film and Theater Research by
The University of Wisconsin Press

Published 1980

The University of Wisconsin Press
114 North Murray Street
Madison, Wisconsin 53715

The University of Wisconsin Press, Ltd.
1 Gower Street
London WC1E 6HA, England

First printing

Printed in the United States of America

For LC CIP information see the colophon

ISBN 0-299-08380-2 cloth; 0-299-08384-5 paper

C υ

Publication of this volume has been assisted by a grant from
The Brittingham Fund, Inc.

Contents

Foreword

In donating the Warner Film Library to the Wisconsin Center for Film and Theater Research in 1969, along with the RKO and Monogram film libraries and UA corporate records, United Artists created a truly great resource for the study of American film. Acquired by United Artists in 1957, during a period when the major studios sold off their films for use on television, the Warner library is by far the richest portion of the gift, containing eight hundred sound features, fifteen hundred short subjects, nineteen thousand still negatives, legal files, and press books, in addition to screenplays for the bulk of the Warner Brothers product from 1930 to 1950. For the purposes of this project, the company has granted the Center whatever publication rights it holds to the Warner films. In so doing, UA has provided the Center another opportunity to advance the cause of film scholarship.

Our goal in publishing these Warner Brothers screenplays is to explicate the art of screenwriting during the thirties and forties, the so-called Golden Age of Hollywood. In preparing a critical introduction and annotating the screenplay, the editor of each volume is asked to cover such topics as the development of the screenplay from its source to the final shooting script, differences between the final shooting script and the release print, production information, exploitation and critical reception of the film, its historical importance, its directorial style, and its position within the genre. He is also encouraged to go beyond these guidelines to incorporate supplemental information concerning the studio system of motion picture production.

We could set such an ambitious goal because of the richness of the script files in the Warner Film Library. For many film titles, the files might contain the property (novel, play, short story, or original story idea), research materials, variant drafts of scripts

7

(from story outline to treatment to shooting script), post-production items such as press books and dialogue continuities, and legal records (details of the acquisition of the property, copyright registration, and contracts with actors and directors). Editors of the Wisconsin/Warner Bros. Screenplay Series receive copies of all the materials, along with prints of the films (the most authoritative ones available for reference purposes), to use in preparing the introductions and annotating the final shooting scripts.

In the process of preparing the screenplays for publication, typographical errors were corrected, punctuation and capitalization were modernized, and the format was redesigned to facilitate readability.

Unless otherwise specified, the photographs are frame enlargements taken from a 35-mm print of the film provided by United Artists.

In 1977 Warner Brothers donated the company's production records and distribution records to the University of Southern California and Princeton University, respectively. These materials are now available to researchers and complement the contents of the Warner Film Library donated to the Center by United Artists. Both institutions cooperated with David Culbert in the preparation of this volume, and I am grateful to them for doing so.

Tino Balio
General Editor

Acknowledgments

I owe a great debt to James H. Billington, director, Woodrow Wilson International Center for Scholars, for recognizing film's significance to the study of twentieth-century decision making. In June 1977 Robert Williams and I organized a colloquium at the Wilson Center on the making of *Mission to Moscow*. Participants included Howard Koch, the film's screenwriter, and members of the diplomatic corps who served with Ambassador Joseph E. Davies in Moscow in the 1930s, particularly Elbridge Durbrow and Loy Henderson. Later, Daniel Leab invited me to try out some of my ideas about the film at the University Film Seminars, Museum of Modern Art Film Library.

The following granted me interviews or provided valuable letters: Robert Buckner, Erskine Caldwell, Thomas Cripps, Eleanor Davies Ditzen, Elbridge Durbrow, W. Averell Harriman, David Joravsky, Stuart Kaminsky, Howard Koch, Jay Leyda, John O'Connor, and Zina Voynow. John Dilyard proved an able research assistant; John Scippa increased my understanding of the film's cinematic construction. Ned Comstock and John Hein overcame all sorts of problems to provide materials on short notice.

These institutions have given permission to use archival materials: Manuscript Division of the Library of Congress; William Seymour Theatre Collection of Princeton University; Franklin D. Roosevelt Library; Department of Special Collections, University of Southern California; Washington National Records Center; and Wisconsin Center for Film and Theater Research.

D.C.

Introduction
The Feature Film
as Official Propaganda

David Culbert

The problems the United States faced in creating public support for the Soviet Union during World War II explain the content of *Mission to Moscow*, a notorious example of pro-Soviet special pleading. Indeed the film is propaganda—"the controlled dissemination of deliberately distorted notions in an effort to induce action favorable to predetermined ends of special interest groups"—though propaganda for what at the time seemed a worthy cause. How this feature film was made shows the impossibility of assuming that propaganda is always recognized, that it is something that only Fascists indulge in, or that education protects one from the propagandist.[1]

The story behind this film provides small comfort for those who see conspiracy wherever they look—there is no cast of villains. Instead we find a tale of zeal gone awry, of misplaced enthusiasm, of government officials at cross-purposes, a story of the buck never stopping anywhere. While *Mission to Moscow* may not deserve to be considered a Frankenstein's monster, its wholesale rewriting of history, its use of visual innuendo, and its explicit appeal to facts known to be incorrect make it a significant document of World War II America. It is hard to imagine

1. Michael Choukas, *Propaganda Comes of Age* (Washington: Public Affairs Press, 1965), p. 37; see also Jacques Ellul, *Propaganda: The Formation of Men's Attitudes* (New York: Random House, 1973), pp. v–xviii, 52–90.

a more obvious example of the state's desperate need, in time of total war, to wed the home front to official war aims. All of Hollywood's skills were used to subvert an entertainment medium to sell a message in a risky and highly controversial fashion, though this does not mean that every viewer was persuaded by what he saw.

Widespread distrust of the Soviet Union in the face of a wartime alliance explains why Washington was so receptive to Hollywood films with pro-Soviet themes, such as Sam Goldwyn's *North Star* (1943), MGM's *Song of Russia* (1943), and the official *Battle of Russia* (1943), which was part of Frank Capra's *Why We Fight* series made for the United States Army. "Those fine patriotic citizens the Warner Brothers" (as Joseph E. Davies described them in the prologue) contributed *Mission to Moscow*, releasing it on April 30, 1943. The film purported to be a factual account of Ambassador Davies' service in the Soviet Union, 1936–38.

Many in America had feared the Soviet Union ever since the Bolshevik revolution in 1917. Stories of collectivization, famine, police brutality, and purge trials contributed to the distrust. Stalin had been Hitler's most ardent foe, yet suddenly he signed a nonaggression pact on August 23, 1939. Two years later, the Nazi surprise attack on the Soviet Union made America and Russia partners in a marriage of convenience. Experts of every political persuasion spoke confidently of imminent German victory. Public opinion polls showed that while a majority of those questioned hoped Russia would win, virtually everyone believed the Nazis would gain another quick victory.[2] In such a situation, many feared, Stalin might again make a deal with Hitler. Stalin needed constant reassurance from his reluctant allies, Great Britain and the United States, for American Lend-Lease military equipment simply was not available in the period immediately following the Japanese attack at Pearl Harbor, December 7, 1941.

Mission to Moscow rewrote the internal Soviet history to give

2. Ralph B. Levering, *American Opinion and the Russian Alliance, 1939–1945* (Chapel Hill: University of North Carolina Press, 1976), p. 43.

Stalin such reassurance. The film justified acts of aggression; it created a consistent foreign policy where none existed; and most important, it explained Stalin's liquidation of all conceivable internal opposition through a series of purge trials in the 1930s as necessary to weed out Nazi fifth columnists. Was *Mission to Moscow* a Stalinist tract? If so, did this mean that there were Communists in Hollywood? Such a question was rarely raised in 1943, though four years later it seemed the only question worth asking. By 1947 the Cold War had begun; President Truman had pledged American aid to governments in Europe resisting Communist aggression. And in October 1947 the House Committee on Un-American Activities (HUAC) held hearings in Washington to expose Communist infiltration of Hollywood.

Scriptwriters became the villains. HUAC had no interest in whether *Mission to Moscow* was factually accurate; it wanted to prove that Communists had put propaganda into innocent scripts. Some HUAC sympathizers eagerly ascribed Communist beliefs to Franklin Roosevelt and the New Deal. To prove that *Mission to Moscow* had been ordered by Roosevelt, they felt, would prove that America had been endangered from within by a Communist conspiracy to destroy the country through state-directed programs that limited the rights of the individual and enabled the shiftless to live off their working neighbors through such measures as Social Security and unemployment compensation. Jack Warner promised that no Communists wrote scripts for his company, and *Mission to Moscow* was consigned to oblivion. Warner Brothers made amends with *I Was a Communist for the FBI* (1951), which showed how Soviet spies subverted American steel unions from within.

Best Seller to Caldwell Filmscript

Davies' book *Mission to Moscow* appeared late in 1941 at a time when Americans craved "the truth" about Stalin. Not a writer, he turned to ghost-writers for help. Jay Franklin Carter selected material; Spencer Williams and Stanley Richardson, both journalists in Moscow during the 1930s, put the final product together. In July 1941 Undersecretary of State Sumner Welles gave

13

Introduction

formal approval to publish State Department dispatches.[3] It seems clear that Roosevelt and Davies, reasonably good friends since they had served in Washington together during World War I, talked over the possibility of such a book following the Nazi invasion of Russia in June 1941. An unpublished Davies manuscript indicates Roosevelt asked him, but more probably the president approved Davies' idea rather than the other way around.[4] Davies' assistants selected, from diary entries, personal letters sent home, and official dispatches, only those passages that presented Davies in a favorable light or that met the need in 1941 to portray Russia in a friendly fashion. Davies' real passion while in the Soviet Union—collecting Russian art—was generally ignored. More significant, in the middle of his book Davies added a 1941 postscript admitting that he never realized in 1938 that the purge trials were to rid Russia of fifth columnists; this 1941 hindsight becomes the film's central argument.[5]

Davies' book purported to be strictly factual, a documentary record issued with the State Department's official blessing. Dis-

3. The Welles letter is reprinted following p. 14 in Joseph E. Davies, *Mission to Moscow* (New York: Simon & Schuster, 1941). Davies acknowledges the writing assistance in his author's note, p. xxii. In 1944 Edmund Wilson wrote an essay likening the ambassador's prose to that of Warren G. Harding ("Mr. Joseph E. Davies as a Stylist," *Partisan Review*, reprinted in Wilson, *Classics and Commercials: A Literary Chronicle of the Forties* [New York: Farrar, Straus, 1950], pp. 98–104).

4. Preface, "Missions for Peace," p. 9, Box 109, Joseph E. Davies Papers, Manuscript Division, Library of Congress, Washington, D.C. (hereafter cited as Davies MSS).

5. See documents 1 and 2 in the Appendix. The selection process may be seen by contrasting what is printed and what is not in a letter Davies wrote to Stephen Early, April 4, 1938, regarding the trial of Bukharin. The book makes no mention of a trial but quotes Davies' assertion that communism in practice is nothing but socialism. In the original letter Davies also said: "Here there was no issue left—the guilt had already been determined by the confessions of the accused. . . . There is scarcely a foreign observer who attended the trial but what arrived at the conclusion that while there was a great deal that was untrue; that it was established that there had been a great deal of plotting on the part of many of these defendants to overthrow Stalin. It was a case of the 'outs' against the 'ins'" (Box 3, Stephen Early Papers, Franklin D. Roosevelt Library, Hyde Park, N.Y. [hereafter cited as Early MSS, FDRL]).

patches include official numbers; the permission from Welles appears as a full-page Photostat. Entries are carefully distinguished as to origin: diary, journal, personal letter, or memorandum. The effect suggests a book prepared with scrupulous regard for accuracy.

Reality was something else. Elbridge Durbrow, who served with Davies in Moscow, was amazed to discover, when he saw the book, that he and George Kennan were credited as having been present for Davies' farewell speech to his staff, June 9, 1938, although both had left the Soviet Union months before. At a Washington dinner in the spring of 1942 Durbrow "kidded" one of Davies' "ghosts" for "not having checked his facts carefully." The eleventh printing of the first edition deleted these references, but such mistakes speak poorly for the regard to detail with which the "documentary" account was assembled.[6]

Special publicity preceded the publication of *Mission to Moscow* by Simon and Schuster on December 29, 1941. Selections from the book appeared as the lead article in the *New York Times Magazine* on December 14 (a week after Pearl Harbor); for the *Times* piece Quincy Howe rewrote an introduction to give further point to the Davies material (as he also did for the prologue to the film).[7] The book sold over seven hundred thousand copies in English, was translated into thirteen foreign languages, and quickly appeared in a then-new format, the paperback, costing but twenty-five cents. In October 1942 a special Gallup poll commissioned by Davies showed that readers believed the information about the purge trials to be the book's most important contribution. "This book will last," wrote Franklin Roosevelt in his personal copy.

The decision to turn the best seller into a movie required explicit administration approval, though Jack Warner insisted

6. Durbrow to Culbert, December 13, 1977. But errors remained. Durbrow sent photo copies of pages from the third and eleventh printings of the first edition in which the index still shows Kennan and Durbrow as appearing on pages where their names in the meantime had been deleted. My own copy of the sixth printing of the first edition reveals that as of January 1942 no changes had been made.

7. Howe to Davies, December 1941, Box 97, Davies MSS.

otherwise in his 1947 HUAC testimony. A wartime film with impersonations of Stalin, Churchill, and Roosevelt could scarcely remain a secret to official Washington. Why did Warner Brothers decide to make the film? Robert Buckner, the film's producer, insists that the answer lies with Roosevelt himself:

I knew that F.D.R. had brainwashed him [Davies], and the Warners as well, into making the film; as F.D.R. said in a meeting at the White House: "to show the American mothers and fathers that if their sons are killed in fighting alongside Russians in our common cause, that it was a good cause, and that the Russians are worthy allies." This statement was relayed to me by Harry Warner, head of the studio, who was present when F.D.R. spoke in front of Davies, Litvinov, Harry Hopkins and others.[8]

Howard Koch, the screenwriter, makes a similar claim but insists that Jack Warner, not Harry, was present at the White House.

Other evidence suggests that Davies approached Roosevelt and got the latter's approval, which seems more likely. In 1947 Jack Warner first testified under oath that Davies asked Warner Brothers to make the film. He then changed his testimony to say that Harry Warner read *Mission to Moscow* and afterward contacted Davies (see document 15 in the Appendix). Jack Warner's first story is the one Davies himself gave in a letter he sent HUAC in 1947:

I knew of the great war film in War No. 1 which Warner Bros. had produced in filming Ambassador Gerard's great war book [*My Four Years in Germany*]. They had also fought a bold and courageous fight against the Nazis before Hitler's war and in the production of *Confessions of a Nazi Spy*. . . . I therefore called Harry Warner up and told him of the approaches which were being made to me with reference to filming *Mission to Moscow*. I told him frankly that I would prefer his company should do it.[9]

8. All quotations attributed to Buckner in the Introduction are found in letters from Buckner to Culbert, January 1 and January 14, 1978, almost all of which appear as document 7 in the Appendix.

9. Davies to Chairman, HUAC, June 10, 1947, copy enclosed in Davies to Koch, October 1, 1957, Howard Koch Collection, Wisconsin Center for Film and Theater Research, Madison, Wis.

Since this is the same story given to one of Davies' disgruntled "ghosts" in August 1942, it seems more plausible. Warner Brothers company records include a telegram from Robert Buckner to Jack Warner, June 15, 1942, in which he asks if the proposed film's "main purpose" is "influence upon public psychology for reasons of state." Buckner had just finished reading Davies' book on the train to New York. There he met with Harry Warner and then went to Washington, D.C., for two very long meetings with Davies on June 16 and 17. "Think D and I will get along beautifully—great fellow and very helpful," Buckner wired Jack Warner two days later.[10]

Obviously there is something unsettling about a president's agreeing—or urging—that a pro-Soviet feature film be made, no matter what the political considerations. But Roosevelt never liked to leave a paper chain of documentation if he could avoid it, and we can only be sure that those who made the film did so because they believed it was at the special request of the president. And there is no question that Roosevelt and his staff kept abreast of the film's progress. Davies took *Mission to Moscow* to the White House for a sneak preview on April 21, 1943, and Roosevelt had to give specific authority for Davies to take a print with him to show Stalin in Moscow a month later.

Davies signed a contract with Warner Brothers on July 3, 1942. Not only did he get a good price ($25,000), but he also retained absolute control over the script: "Warner agrees to submit to Owner [Davies] for his approval, a copy of the basic story." Thus given a great deal of authority, he proceeded to use it for all it was worth. Every change, he claimed, was at the personal request of the president. The studio obeyed, and not just for reasons of wartime patriotism. The federal government had the power to declare film production nonessential and deny film stock. This further guaranteed that a major Hollywood studio would perform as directed.[11]

10. George Bye to Jay Franklin Carter, August 3, 1942, Box 3, Early MSS. Buckner to Warner, June 15, June 17, 1942, Box 2085, Warner Brothers Archive, Department of Special Collections, University of Southern California, Los Angeles (hereafter Warner Archive-USC).

11. Davies to Bye, August 11, 1942, Box 3, Early MSS; Edgar Dale, Bureau of

Davies first tried to get Robert Sherwood to prepare the script and, when unsuccessful, turned to Erskine Caldwell, known for his books of social protest (including *You Have Seen Their Faces*) and recently back from reporting the Nazi attack on Russia for magazines and CBS radio. Caldwell arrived in Hollywood on July 9. Buckner says Davies had known Caldwell and insisted on using him, though he was inexperienced as a screenwriter. Caldwell says that "a story editor in the New York office of Warner Bros. offered me the job." [12] Caldwell turned in a draft treatment that covered the purge trials and a brief screenplay taking the story through Davies' interview with Hjalmar Schacht in Berlin (scene 75A in this volume). Caldwell's script was considered unacceptable even by Davies; according to Buckner, the writer was "well paid and excused." The difficulty was the intractability of the material. Davies went to Berlin and Moscow, spoke with a variety of officials, including Stalin, and returned home. His book contains few anecdotes or descriptive passages. How could an inexperienced screenwriter take such material and make it suitable for a feature film?

Caldwell recognized the need for emphasis on collective security and how its failure contributed to the breakdown of the League of Nations. His treatment opened at the League of Nations, included a speech by Haile Selassie, and specified the visual emphasis on Wilson (scenes 22–24). Realizing how cumbersome four or five purge trials would be, he telescoped them into one, even though this meant playing fast and loose with facts familiar to many viewers. In the end the release print fol-

Motion Pictures, Office of War Information, to Iris Barry, Museum of Modern Art Film Library, May 10, 1943, "War Production Board" folder, Central Files, Museum of Modern Art Library, New York; Contract, July 3, 1942, copy in Financial Statements, 43–50, vol. 17, p. 5400, Warner Brothers Archive, William Seymour Theatre Collection, Princeton University Library, Princeton, N.J. (hereafter Warner Archive-Princeton).

12. Caldwell to Culbert, January 14, 1978. Caldwell had been in the Soviet Union with his wife, photographer Margaret Bourke-White, who collaborated on *You Have Seen Their Faces*. See Caldwell, *All-Out on the Road to Smolensk* (New York: Duell, Sloan and Pearce, 1942) and *Moscow under Fire* (New York: Hutchinson, 1942); Jack Warner to Davies, June 30, 1942, Box 2085; Warner to Davies, July 9, 1942, Box 2785, Warner Archive-USC.

lowed almost exactly the order and content of the first seventy-seven scenes as Caldwell had prepared them.

Dialogue and visual effects were another matter. Consider the scene in which Davies agrees to become ambassador to Russia. Imagine having Roosevelt say all of this on screen:

Hitler may propose often, but he'll never accept his own proposition. Hitler is a man possessed. He wants war like a child wants candy. Nothing short of war will appease him for any length of time. However, if Hitler will agree to discuss his grievances over a conference table, I suggest that the first and logical step towards world-wide disarmament will be for all nations, Germany not excepted, to agree to stop the manufacture of any weapon of war which is heavier than that which a man can carry on his shoulder.

Another passage again indicated Caldwell's inability to produce the brief, well-turned phrase. After Davies accepts his mission, Caldwell decided, a scene would take place in the State Department with a "puffing congressman, Hightower, a representative of the old school," an isolationist outraged at the thought of sending an ambassador to "Rooshia." Caldwell added a "filler" scene at a shoeshine stand:

"Mr. Davies," the Negro says, "I hear you're going to some far-off country on the other side of the world. What for, Mr. Davies?"

"I'm going to Russia, Ted," Davies tells him. "The President has asked me to be the ambassador."

"Now ain't that something to talk about!" The Negro shines briskly. "I've heard that them Russians are awfully queer folks, Mr. Davies. I heard it said somewhere that they got tired with the way things was going and just tore up everything by the roots, dropped it in a great big hole in the ground, and started all over again."

"Yes, that's pretty close to what they did, Ted," Davies tells him.

"Well, I declare. Those Russian folks sure must be up-and-doing people. I've felt like doing things like that a heap of times, but somehow I just never seemed to get around to doing anything about it. It takes up-and-doing folks to haul off and do exactly what you feel like doing. Now you take me, Mr. Davies. Only just recently a while back I got to thinking about getting shed of my old woman some way or other, and sort of looking around for a younger one at the same time while I was about it. I sure do admire folks who gets up and *does*."

In the end, Caldwell had provided rough dialogue for the first third of the film, virtually none of which was used in the release print.

The Koch Treatment

Howard Koch then received the assignment. He had no background in Soviet affairs, had never visited the country, and was not particularly interested in politics, except for his admiration of Woodrow Wilson and the principle of collective security. Both were honored in *In Time to Come*, his play that premiered on Broadway on December 28, 1941, with Otto Preminger as producer. The play helps explain the film's explicit praise of Wilson and collective security, both discussed but briefly in Davies' book.[13]

Koch, born in New York in 1902, went to Hollywood from radio, where he had written the script for "The War of the Worlds," the 1938 Orson Welles broadcast. His first screenplay was for *The Sea Hawk* (1940), directed by Michael Curtiz. A skillful craftsman, Koch had just come from helping write *Casablanca* (1942), also directed by Curtiz. Robert Buckner says Koch "was a capable screenwriter, following orders, but with no clear knowledge or convictions of the truth or falsity of the issues involved." Koch received from Davies a copy in English of the 1937 and 1938 purge trials, a copy of *Mission to Moscow*, and a few other basic references.

In late August 1942 he went to work—none too soon as far as Davies was concerned. "I am very much concerned with the script," he wrote Jack Warner on August 31. "It is difficult for me to understand the delay." To mollify Davies, Buckner and Koch went to the Davies camp in the Adirondacks for a long conference on September 7–8.[14] Both now realized that Davies intended not to reign but to rule.

Buckner, born in Virginia in 1906, had served as a European newspaper correspondent and written for *The New Yorker* and

13. *In Time to Come: A Play about Woodrow Wilson* (New York: Dramatist's Play Service, 1942), in particular pp. 57, 92–94. Koch specifically thanks John Huston and John Houseman for help "in research and the writing of this play."

14. Davies to Warner, August 31, September 8, 1942, Box 2085, Warner Archive-USC.

Atlantic Monthly before going to Warner Brothers in 1936 as a writer. As producer he faced endless difficulties in his dealings with Davies, for the latter cared about the approach and content of "his" film and felt an overwhelming desire to control its dramatic construction as well.

Koch, working as fast as he could, followed closely the structure of Caldwell's script and, like Caldwell, realized that for dramatic reasons a series of purge trials would have to be condensed into one. He sent revisions along to Davies but discovered that Davies was increasingly thinking of himself as co-author. On September 23 Davies sent twenty-four single-spaced pages of comments and script changes to Michael Curtiz, the film's director. The timing infuriated both Buckner and Curtiz. They sent a carefully worded joint letter of thanks to Davies, but Buckner told Warner what he really thought:

> This morning Curtiz and I received 24 pages of suggestions, objections, etc. from Davies, which are very disconcerting at this stage of our preparations, since Davies had apparently approved the treatment in all major details in his last talk with me. I think, as we both have suspected, that he is apt to prove very difficult. . . . I think you, Curtiz, Trilling and I should go into this problem early in the week, to prepare ourselves for a stand before Davies arrives here.

On September 30 Buckner tried the art of diplomacy in describing to Davies what became scenes 36–39 in the film:

> I am attaching herewith two copies of our proposed scene between yourself and the President. This scene would be weak and ineffective if enacted between anyone but you two men. I know we discussed this question at great length on my first visit to Washington, when you told me that you felt confident that the President would agree to the scene being presented. As a matter of courtesy we would like to have his consent, and in view of his great personal interest in the picture, which we know to be sincere, we feel very hopeful that he will raise no objections. . . . The scene would be photographed in such a way that the actor playing the President would be minimized by the camera and seen only in shadow or from the back, very much as we did in *Yankee Doodle Dandy*.

Koch also sent a long letter to Davies explaining the script changes he had made. Davies had rejected Caldwell's idea of Davies' being called to the White House from the Supreme Court (scenes 27–38). Koch replaced this with a "very light and informal scene in which our purpose is to capture the audience's interest in the personal life of our characters" on St. Regis Lake. He mentioned that in scenes 40–49 "you will be relieved to know that the milk has been dropped overboard into the Atlantic Ocean," a reference to the Caldwell script where Davies takes an "enormous" ice cream freezer to Russia. He then discussed the other specific changes he had made:

3. In your scene with the President I've worked in much of the actual dialogue which you repeated from your memory of the occasion. . . . [scenes 36–39]
4. The scene with Schacht will embody your suggestions for the ending. . . . [scenes 68–75A]
5. The scene of the women's luncheon at the Molotov dacha to be developed along the lines of my conversation with Mrs. Davies. [cut from release print]
6. I've included the debt question and agree with you that it adds a tangible stake. . . . [cut from release print]
7. I liked your description of the purge prisoner taken by the police in the house next to yours. This will be added to the arrests. I can't tell you much more about the exact material to be included in the purge trial, as I confess I'm still hazy about the problem. [scenes 144–48]

Davies' involvement in the script did not end there. In December 1942 he even dictated dialogue for the Churchill interview (scenes 246–49), though he termed the result "crude and merely included for suggestive purposes." [15]

Warner Brothers assigned Michael Curtiz as director. Curtiz had been born in Hungary in 1888 and enjoyed considerable success as a director for the German Ufa, before coming to Hollywood in 1926. In 1942 he had just completed *Yankee Doodle Dandy*, a screen treatment of George M. Cohan's patriotic

15. Davies to Curtiz, September 23, 1942, Box 98, Davies MSS; Curtiz and Buckner to Davies, October 3, with memorandum, Buckner to Warner, October 3, 1942, Box 2085, Warner Archive-USC; Buckner to Davies, September 30; Koch to Davies, September 27; Davies to Koch, December 4, 1942, all in Box 98, Davies MSS.

songwriting career (Buckner was producer) and *Casablanca* (where Koch had served as a writer). Both films contained explicit appeals to wartime unity, as did *This Is the Army* (1943), an enormously popular stage show featuring seventeen of Irving Berlin's songs. The latter film was already in production while Curtiz finished shooting *Mission to Moscow*.

In some respects Curtiz was an unusual choice for a "message" film, though he had made some films with social themes, notably *Cabin in the Cotton* (1932), about tenant farmers, and *Black Fury* (1935), about conditions in the coalfields. His ability at pacing action swiftly was particularly apparent in two of Errol Flynn's most successful films, *The Charge of the Light Brigade* (1936) and *The Adventures of Robin Hood* (1938). Buckner says that Davies at first "wanted a 'bigger' name," but settled for Curtiz (by 1942 clearly one of Warners' most successful and skillful directors) after discovering how ill-suited his choice of Caldwell as screenwriter had been. "Even after the script was finally written and approved," Buckner says, "Curtiz had to be reminded almost daily of the meaning of the events he was directing."

Surviving documents do not offer much information as to precisely what changes Curtiz made in the film, but his vast experience guaranteed that the production was in capable hands. A perfectionist, Curtiz shot one part of an early scene twelve times. The next day Jack Warner sent a pungent note: "There's a war on! We can't start twelve times on a forty-four-second scene." Curtiz, on November 20, 1942, explained the problem: "Believe me, it is no pleasure to reshoot a take ten and twelve times. Walter Huston broke down eleven times, therefore necessitating these repeats. I wasn't able to overlap because it was one shot." [16]

Buckner claims the statement at the end of the film (sequence 321–26) that Finland was not actually invaded by the Soviet Union in 1939 came at Davies' demand. He "insisted that he had

16. Warner to Curtiz, November 19; Curtiz to Warner, November 20, 1942, Box 2085; for details see the Daily Production and Progress Report, November 18, 1942, Box 1486, which lists the scene, characters on the set, daily hour-by-hour schedule, and the number of takes. Box 1486 has these reports for each shooting day; Warner Archive-USC.

'privileged knowledge' of the facts," Buckner says, and "was often prone to pulling this mysterious knowledge to silence us." Perhaps most startling is Buckner's explanation of how Davies changed the script's approach to the purge trials:

An ambiguity about the guilt or innocence had been purposely suggested by Davies when the script was being written, but when time came to shoot the scene and the guilt or innocence had to be made specific, Davies insisted upon the guilt. I went to the brothers Warner and told them I felt that a great historic mistake was being made. They called a meeting with Davies and myself to settle the point, and Davies made one of the most beautiful poker-play bluffs I have ever witnessed. Instead of answering our questions he asked how much the film had cost to that point. I had the figure at hand, just under one million dollars. Davies said: "All right, let's say one million as a round figure. I will give you the million here and now and will take over the negative of the film from you." He took out a checkbook and pen and prepared to write the check. I don't think he ever would have done so, but the Warners and I knew that with Mrs. Davies' money behind him he could have paid such a sum. The Warners were tempted to call his bluff but they didn't at last, and Davies won his point that the Purge Trials would "make clear" that the victims were guilty as traitors and Trotskyites. At this decision I offered to resign as the producer but Warner would not let me. From this point on relations between Mr. Davies and myself were understandably strained.

Koch's final script, dated October 15, 1942, to January 12, 1943, consists of some 339 scenes, though one was added at Davies' insistence as late as April 15. Much of the film was shot according to this script's dialogue and visual instructions. The final script's purge trial scenes leave no question as to guilt, which raises some doubt about Buckner's story, though final editing and visual touches could make the accused look guilty or innocent, according to someone's wishes.

Others besides Koch and Buckner helped with the script. Three days after signing a contract, Davies met with Soviet Ambassador Maxim Litvinov to discuss the film and the need for Soviet documentary footage. Litvinov wrote Nicholas Napoli, head of the Soviet Artkino, on July 7 that "I shall appreciate it if you will lend them your cooperation and meet as far as possible their requirements, as it is desirable that the film should be a success." Three days later, Napoli (conveniently visiting Hollywood at the time) wrote Davies a letter that could not have been more helpful: "I am putting at their disposal all Artkino's film material and the technical assistance of one of my most qualified associates. . . . I expect to see Colonel Warner personally next Monday and hope to make definite arrangements for Artkino to give every possible assistance." [17]

Davies then invited Litvinov and his English wife, Ivy Low, to the Davies camp before the film went into production. Surviving evidence is silent as to what was decided, but how often does a Soviet ambassador, even in wartime, spend an entire week planning the content of a film in which he is a major character and which will be made by another country?

Davies also kept Roosevelt informed about the progress of the film, meeting with him at the White House in October and November 1942. In early October he cleared the simulation of the president's voice in the production. At the insistence of Ivy Low, he even wired the Litvinovs' daughter in Moscow in an unsuccessful attempt to get her to play herself. Davies and his wife spent much of November–December in Hollywood watching the film being shot—and offering daily suggestions as to how things should be done (see Appendix, documents 4 and 5).

Production

Mission to Moscow went into production on November 10, 1942. Davies tried hard, without success, to get Fredric March to take the lead. In the end Walter Huston played Ambassador Davies, the only public figure in the film not made up to resemble his real-life counterpart. Davies was very unhappy about this situation, though everyone agreed that Huston's handsome appear-

17. Litvinov to Davies, July 7; Napoli to Davies, July 10, 1942, Box 2785. Davies also provided Buckner with his personal motion picture footage, color and black-and-white, from his Moscow years; he sent the Warner Research Department fifty-six photographs to help the art department in creating appropriate sets. Davies to Herman Lissauer, August 26, 1942, Box 1015, all in Warner Archive-USC.

ance would not be aided by giving him a bald head. Davies, still dissatisfied, successfully imposed a personal prologue (shot in Hollywood on January 15) on the release print in which he endorsed the film's veracity. Koch and Buckner thought this weakened the film's appeal but Davies was adamant (see Appendix, document 6).

The other characters posed less of a problem. Ann Harding played Mrs. Davies; Eleanor Parker, a relative newcomer, was Emlen Davies; Litvinov was effectively portrayed by Oscar Homolka, who had a convincing "foreign" accent and looked the part. Both Stalin and Churchill required look-alikes. Manart Kippen, a Brooklyn actor with some stage experience, played a kindly, smiling Stalin. Churchill was portrayed by Dudley Field Malone, a lawyer without prior acting experience. Malone, who had served briefly as third assistant secretary of state under Wilson and taken part in the Scopes Monkey Trial, wrote a number of letters to Roosevelt seeking the part, enclosing photographs to prove that he literally looked like Churchill.

Minor parts were filled with some of Hollywood's dependable character actors, including the chauffeur Freddie, played by George Tobias, and Lord Chilston, played by Lumsden Hare. The Japanese ambassador, Shigemitsu, was Chinese actor Peter Goo Chong. Vladimir Sokoloff was a convincing Kalinin, and Leigh Whipper had a brief appearance as Haile Selassie. The black press heralded this performance, for the role had to be played with dignity, not servility. Konstantin Shayne was superb as Bukharin, the most distinguished of the purge conspirators.

In an unusual gesture for the day, a technical adviser, Jay Leyda, was chosen by Koch to help with details. Leyda complained that "Max Rabinovich has been the *de facto* technical advisor on *Mission to Moscow*—at least on the set—because he always told Mike what Mike wanted to hear, which is the part of my job that I've been very slow in learning." [18] Leyda had

18. Leyda to Buckner, February 2, 1943, reproduced in Koch, *As Time Goes By* (New York: Harcourt Brace Jovanovich, 1979), p. 123. The unit manager for the production felt the same way, describing Curtiz's "find" as "nothing but

worked with Sergei Eisenstein in Moscow in the 1930s. He had been forced out of the Museum of Modern Art Film Library in 1939, he believes, because of accusations that he was a Trotskyite. Leyda feels his role in the film was minimal, largely because of conflicting advice from a number of emigré Russians in Hollywood who had the ear of Curtiz even though they seemed not to have visited Russia since about 1905.[19] Curtiz apparently never realized that Leyda had real credentials for the job. Leyda aided in selecting excellent Soviet newsreel footage, which helped give the film its documentary flavor, though he did not edit the montage sequences. Leyda further complained to Buckner about the music being used: "All the folk tunes will have the flavor of an emigré Russian vaudeville act." Certainly there is no evidence that Leyda had any role in the political content of the film, a charge made at the time but denied by Koch, Buckner, and Leyda himself. And it is surely hard to detect the hand of an alleged Trotskyite in a film that accuses Trotsky of collaborating with Hitler.

Bert Glennon, one of Hollywood's best cameramen, handled the photography. Apparently Curtiz let Glennon do most of the lighting. Many of the scenes in the release print use back or front lighting to heighten sinister or portentous moments, such as when the purge suspects are arrested (scenes 144–48), the opening when Davies is shown in his study in a high angle shot, or the report of the sabotage at Kharkov (scenes 139–41). Glennon did everything he could to add variety to a long section of courtroom testimony (scenes 162–92) that lacks much cinematic interest. The same pattern is apparent: long shot (with voice-over) of entire room; long shot of witness; trucking shot to witness with various medium close-up reaction shots; back shot. The visual interest Glennon gets out of these devices testifies to his expertise.

In the final script Koch could offer no specific directions for several montage sequences employing Soviet and German

an extra" who "has been here in Hollywood for years." Alleborn to T. C. Wright, November 23, 1942, Box 1486, Warner Archive-USC.

19. Interview with Leyda, May 2, 1977.

newsreel footage. All montage work was done by Don Siegel, who had organized a montage department at Warners in 1934. Siegel was a master of montage techniques by the time he worked on *Mission to Moscow*. He began shooting on February 2, 1943, after Curtiz finished his parts of the film. "It will help matters a lot if Mike Curtiz is taken off the picture and Siegel films the balance of the work in the montage as well as any other straight cuts that may be needed," the unit manager reported.[20] Scenes 24–26 had been a montage of spreading Axis aggression in the final Koch script; in the release print this was replaced by excerpts from Leni Riefenstahl's *Triumph of the Will*. Davies' trip to inspect Russian industry (scenes 105–106), cut from the final script, was reinserted in the release print (see Note to the Screenplay 30). And of course the newsreel excerpts about the defeat of the Germans at Stalingrad in February 1943 could not have been described in a "final" script finished a month before. Siegel's contribution to the historical persuasiveness of the film was immense because montage played such a large part and Artkino provided such marvelous Soviet footage. Since the final third of the film was virtually all montage, Siegel's role as director is truly significant.

The same cannot be said for Max Steiner, who provided a bombastic score based mostly on "Meadowlands" (a 1942 jukebox hit), "The Great Gate of Kiev," and similar fare. Steiner was the doyen of Hollywood composers, with the music for *Gone with the Wind* (1939) to his credit. In 1942–43 he scored two other films directed by Curtiz, *Casablanca* and *This Is the Army*. "My theory," Steiner once said, "is that the music should be felt rather than heard. . . . What good is it if you don't notice it?"[21] In *Mission to Moscow* every visual reminder of the Nazis is underscored by a cliché reference (generally played by the trombones) to a Nazi marching song or something vaguely Wagnerian. Such compositional techniques were accepted practice in feature films of the day, but by now *Mission to Moscow* has limited musical interest.

20. Alleborn to Wright, January 26, 1943, Box 1486, Warner Archive-USC.
21. Quoted in Tony Thomas, *Music for the Movies* (South Brunswick, N.J.: A. S. Barnes, 1973), p. 122.

Steiner received higher marks from Margery Morrison, a member of the National Film Music Committee's Preview Committee. She described Steiner's handling of the final montage sequences in an article she wrote for the April 1943 issue of *Film Music Notes:*

A swift glimpse of devastating catastrophe was on the screen with a somber Russian theme as background, then the scene shifted to Madison Square Garden. A huge mass meeting . . . music in low frequencies. Vigorous opposition was registered in high frequencies, discords short and sharp, as various dissidents rose to their feet. . . . This scene had evidently been timed and rehearsed and was being recorded. Then began a rehearsal of music alone. National themes in brief counterpoint battling for supremacy, the blare of "Es braustein Ruf" [*sic*] with the steady swing of Russian rhythm winning to a suspended climax out of which "Taps" emerges. There follows, briefly, a noble sustained theme and a chorale finale.

Fortunately for modern viewers, the sound consists of more than music; the result is a surprisingly complex audio mix. In the montage sequences the voice-overs are especially effective since for each there is an audio as well as a video transition. Only the voice of Roosevelt is so loud (scenes 36–39, 293) as to be obviously improbable for intimate discussions with Davies.

The most significant changes between final script and release print are these: the addition of the personal prologue by Davies before the credits; the reinsertion of the fishing scene on Lake St. Regis; the reinsertion of Davies' trip to inspect Russian industry; the deletion of the meeting of Trotsky and Hitler (scenes 193–95) following the purge trial; the addition of the meeting between Mrs. Molotov and Mrs. Davies in the cosmetics shop (scenes 111–14); and the complete reworking of scenes 295–326, where Davies tours the United States in the fall of 1941 to arouse support for Russia. Like most films, the ending was subject to further revisions beyond the final script. Koch wrote a conclusion in which a Russian boy plows a furrow, developing the biblical image of swords and plowshares. Davies objected strenuously, and got his way. "As you can see," Buckner wrote Davies, "we have gone back to your original suggestion, and have in fact incorporated a large degree of your own dialogue. Everyone feels that your idea of paying a tribute to the valiant dead of all nations, together with the final promise to the unborn generations which will follow us, gives the picture a tremendous strength in the ending."

The final scenes were shot in late March 1943. Still necessary, however, was approval of the government's own censor, the Bureau of Motion Pictures, Office of War Information. OWI staff members read several versions of the script and were pleased by what they saw. In early March BMP head Lowell Mellett and his staff came from Washington for a special screening of the rough cut in Hollywood. It also seems likely that staff members of the Soviet embassy in Washington read the final script, though evidence for this procedure exists only for other pro-Soviet feature films, not *Mission to Moscow*. The OWI demanded no changes in the political content of the script. The film, the official summary stated, "pulls no punches; it answers the propaganda lies of the Axis and its sympathizers with the most powerful propaganda of all: the truth." Indeed, the censor added, *Mission to Moscow* will "make a great contribution" to wartime unity (see Appendix, document 8). The government agency charged with overseeing film content found the finished product a model of what was desirable.

With the release date just two weeks away, Davies demanded a change that infuriated all: Mrs. Davies wanted a bigger part for herself and insisted on adding a scene in a Moscow cosmetics shop between herself (Ann Harding) and the commissar of cosmetics, Mrs. Molotov. "Whole thing petty holdup for private grudge," Buckner wired Jack Warner on April 14. Harding added her bit by at first complaining that she was tired and could not stay late to work on a last-minute addition. On April 15 Curtiz returned to shoot scenes 111–14. Davies refused all last-minute appeals about omitting his personal prologue but did agree to "leave Tukhachevsky in at the trial and promised to defend this scene against criticism." Davies showed the film at the White House on April 21. The next night, near Hollywood, Jack Warner ran a sneak preview before a "working-class audience" and passed along the preview cards to Davies. Every single comment was favorable.[22]

Selling the Product

Warner Brothers went all out on publicity. A gala preview for over four thousand persons in Washington, D.C., made page one of *The Hollywood Reporter* on April 29. "Before a tough, hard-boiled audience of . . . newspaper men," the glowing account began, and then listed many of the prominent journalists and military and political leaders in the audience. Warner Brothers announced an advertising budget of $500,000, a handsome figure by 1943's standards. It seemed that a lot of people liked the film for what it said about wartime unity.

No sooner was the film released on April 30, 1943, however, than a roar of protest developed in some quarters. Daniel Bell's *New Leader*, a pro-Trotsky New York newspaper with a small but vocal national readership, had already published a number of attacks on the film during production, including a smear of Jay Leyda.[23] Now Bell redoubled his efforts.

More damaging was a lengthy letter from philosopher John Dewey published in the *New York Times* on Sunday, May 9, 1943, and reproduced in full in every Hearst paper the following Sunday. Dewey had headed an independent inquiry concerning the Moscow purge trials and had already written to the *Times* in January 1942 to condemn the distortions of Davies' book. The film called forth his special rage. *Mission to Moscow*, he began, "is the first instance in our country of totalitarian propaganda for mass consumption—a propaganda which falsifies history through distortion, omission or pure invention of facts." Dewey

22. Buckner to Davies, March 15, 1943, Box 98, Davies MSS. Koch vigorously defends his own ending in *As Time Goes By*. Nelson Poynter to Buckner, December 3, 1942, Box 16; Mellett to Davies, April 19, 1943, Box 11; both in Lowell Mellett MSS, FDRL; Charles Einfeld to Warner, April 12; Buckner to Warner, April 14; Warner to Davies, April 22, all in Box 2085, Warner Archive-USC.

23. The *New Leader* carried articles condemning the film, generally on p. 1, on the following dates: March 20, April 10, April 24, May 1, May 8, and May 15, 1943; the attack on Leyda and the film appeared on December 26, 1942.

also attacked the ending: "Finally, a sinister totalitarian critique of the parliamentary system is introduced in the film. The traditional isolationism of some American members of Congress before the war is represented as equivalent to pro-nazism. The whole effort is to discredit the American Congress and at the same time to represent the Soviet dictatorship as an advanced democracy."

Arthur Upham Pope answered Dewey in the same place the following Sunday, as he had done in January 1942 in response to Dewey's attack on the Davies book. Pope did not enjoy the academic reputation Dewey did, but he was no hired press agent either. Pope had founded the Committee for National Morale, directed the Institute for Persian Art and Archeology, and had spent some time in Leningrad in 1935. Pope defended both film and book. He insisted that Trotsky really had been in league with the Nazis, that Soviet leaders really had plotted to overthrow their country's government, and besides, in the middle of a war in which Russia was our ally, it was unseemly to argue over content.[24]

Other reviewers dealt with the film's dramatic appeal. Bosley Crowther, critic for the *Times*, called it "the most outspoken picture on a political subject that an American studio has ever made" (April 30, 1943). He noted the heavy reliance on dialogue, making, he felt, for a certain dullness, but he praised the film's "realistic impression of fact." James Agee, in the *Nation* (May 22, 1943), termed it "the first Soviet production to come from a major American studio." It was, he noted, "good to see the conservatives . . . named even for a fraction of their

24. *Time* (May 17, 1943), pp. 19–20, ran an article discussing the Dewey letter. See also Dewey to *New York Times*, January 11, 1942, and Pope to *New York Times*, January 18, 1942. Pope also defended the film in *Soviet Russia Today* (June 1943), pp. 8–9; Koch himself defended the film in a letter to the *New York Times*, June 13, 1943. Dewey had already written to Elmer Davis, head of the OWI, to protest the treatment of Trotsky in the film. "I have talked with Mr. Harry Warner and Mr. Davies," Davis replied, "and am assured by both that the treatment of Trotsky . . . will not be the sort to justify your fears." Davis to Dewey, October 5, 1942, Box 1433, entry 264, RG 208, Office of War Information Records, Washington National Records Center, Suitland, Md.

responsibility for this war." He then added that he neither believed nor disbelieved the claims about the purge trials—an interesting position, given what is now known about the subject.

The New Republic's Manny Farber offered the most skillful
roasting:

> Now I'm ready to vote for the booby prize. Mr. Davies' book was a
> stale, innocuous melange of the fewest and most obvious facts that
> Soviet interpreters . . . had been reporting on Russia for years. . . .
> The movie, as a movie, is the dullest imaginable. . . . To describe
> Davies' tour of heavy industry one device is used five times without
> break—Davies talking to a mechanic, a coal miner, an engineer, a
> farmer—until you expect a flashback to the October Revolution and
> Davies talking to Lenin (obviously like this: "Just what do you think of
> your chances, Mr. Lenin? I'm a capitalist myself"). (May 10, 1943)

Letter-writing campaigns also supported or attacked the film.
Dwight Macdonald sent a letter with initiating signatures from
such persons as Alfred Kazin and Edmund Wilson in which he
attacked a film that "falsifies history and glorifies dictatorship"
(see Appendix, document 9). Macdonald warned that "this
super-production will be seen by at least fifty million Americans
. . . as a documentary record of history." Shortly the defenders
of the film, in a group headed by Herman Shumlin, urged support for something which "far from being untruthful . . . gives
a picture of truth" (see document 10). They added a dire warning: "Many well-intentioned and doubtless patriotic people are
still unaware of the extent and subtlety of Nazi propaganda and
its ceaseless efforts to sow the seeds of disunion in the United
Nations' front."

The publicity certainly affected those who had made the film.
On May 20, Buckner wrote to Jack Warner about his own feelings and those of Curtiz: "We certainly stirred up a hornet's nest
there, didn't we? I have carefully read all the criticisms and most
of those boys are wide open on nearly every point. But at least
we flushed out the Red baiters and the Fascist element in the
press. . . . Mike Curtiz is very upset by all the criticisms and is
taking it personally. I have been holding his hand and reassur-
ing him that life will go on as usual." Warner, in New York,

wrote back that he had encountered people who said "the word 'Moscow' in the title is enough for them." [25]

According to the old Hollywood bromide, "There's no such thing as bad publicity." Not so in the case of *Mission to Moscow*. The film was criticized on two counts—first, it glorified Stalin and presented numerous untruths as fact. Second, many considered it dull. Film as history lesson did not appeal to audiences who loved feature films precisely because they permitted an escape from reality.

What did most American viewers think of *Mission to Moscow*? Estimating audience response to this film is just as difficult as it is for most feature films. The best gauge, box-office gross, is only a rough index. In January 1944 *Variety* listed the top grossers of the season; *Mission to Moscow* was eighty-fourth out of ninety-five. Company accounting records report a U.S. gross of $944,777.55 as of May 27, 1944. Since the production officially cost $1,516,912.93 (not including the cost of prints or advertising and publicity), clearly the film did not make a profit in its initial domestic run.

Overseas business might have been better, but all too soon the Cold War spoiled the market. The company ordered all existing prints destroyed in a notice sent to every exchange in October 1947. A final financial account prepared in 1952 reveals that the film lost just under $600,000. Of course this figure includes having written off over $350,000 in blocked assets from Chinese distribution, the token sale of rights within the Soviet Union for $25,000, and a good deal of padding for "proportion of Production Department overhead." Thus even these official figures cannot be considered the final word on that pesky matter of figuring out exactly how many people see a given film. In Buckner's opinion, the film was "not a disaster" but "it never broke even."

Mission to Moscow, then, was neither the hit of the season nor did it collapse after vocal public criticisms. It was seen by millions of servicemen on posts throughout the country as part of

25. Buckner to Warner, May 20; Warner to Buckner, May 22, 1943, Box 2085, Warner Archive-USC.

the Army Motion Picture Service (whose receipts were not included in commercial grosses), and the film found immense distribution abroad, especially in England and China. Certainly the film was seen by many more persons than its gross would indicate.[26] Equally certain, Warners made no profit from its contribution to the war effort.

The film's impact—its immensely rosy picture of Soviet history and its attitude toward Stalin—was significant because other devices for creating pro-Soviet feeling in the United States seemed to have little success. Poll data as to whether one trusted or distrusted the Soviet Union between March 1942 and December 1943 showed that trust never received more than 51 per cent and that in the spring of 1943 trust was on the downward swing. Such responses can best be explained by specific overseas events; the Roosevelt-Stalin meeting at Tehran in December 1943 is a more plausible reason for increased public trust in Russia, not pro-Soviet films. But such films certainly kept anti-Soviet feeling from getting even larger. The United States Army created a *Why We Fight* series—*The Battle of Russia* was released to commercial distributors in October 1943—because so few inductees understood the basic political events of the 1930s. *Mission to Moscow* filled in the gaps for the uninitiated or the credulous. Certainly to the degree a feature film can change or alter attitudes, *Mission to Moscow* was the most extreme Hollywood attempt to intensify support for the ally least liked by Americans.

The Response Overseas

Supporters of the film claimed that attacks on *Mission to Moscow* did the work of Hitler. They had no way of knowing that Propaganda Minister Joseph Goebbels indeed paid attention to this film's release and the controversy it evoked. Goebbels noted in his diary on May 19, 1943, that the film extolled Stalin so uncritically that it had aroused protest "even" from the American public. A week later he described a report he had received from

26. J. J. Glynn to All Offices, October 23, 1947; detailed financial reports for 1943–44 (monthly) and 1945–52 (yearly) may be found in vol. 17, p. 5400, Warner Archive-Princeton.

a source inside the Soviet Union regarding Davies, back again on a mission to Moscow. Goebbels dismissed Davies as a "dangerous ignoramus" and a "type of salon bolshevik." In other entries for this period Goebbels, incorrectly, assumed that the film's release had been coordinated by Roosevelt to accompany Stalin's announcement that he had dissolved the Comintern, the official organization charged with spreading Communist ideology abroad. In July Goebbels arranged for a harsh attack on Davies and his book to appear in *Das Reich*. "The non-official material, . . . whose authenticity cannot be proven, gives the collection its propaganda worthiness," noted the author, who claimed to have "watched the activities of Ambassador Davies in Moscow at close hand."[27] Goebbels, himself a film enthusiast, was eager to believe that *Mission to Moscow* meant that Roosevelt too had turned a medium of entertainment to promoting the interests of the state.

Finally, the film deserves special attention because of its immense circulation within the Soviet Union, where *Mission to Moscow* seemingly had its greatest impact. Between 1939 and 1945 only twenty-four American films were purchased by the Soviet Union for commercial distribution within its borders. Stalin, himself chief movie censor, personally approved every foreign film before it was distributed to between eleven thousand and twenty-one thousand movie theaters.[28] Joseph Davies went to Moscow in May 1943, taking a print of "his" film with him. Roosevelt agreed that the film might put Stalin in a more pro-American mood. Diplomatic records reveal that Stalin, Vyshinsky, Molotov, and other high-ranking officials sat down and viewed the film when Davies arrived in Moscow for a diplomatic reception.

27. Unpublished *Tagebücher*, May 19, May 23, May 25–26, 1943, pp. 2419–20, 2474, 2476, 2493–94, 2509, 2511–12, all in F12/25, Institut für Zeitgeschichte, Munich, Germany. A bowdlerized version of some of these entries may be found in Louis P. Lochner, ed., *The Goebbels Diaries, 1942–43* (Garden City, N.Y.: Doubleday, 1948); Herman Poerzgen, "Retouched Moscow," *Das Reich*, July 25, 1943.

28. See document 13 in the Appendix. Concerning Stalin's addiction to film and his role as censor, see Nikita Khrushchev, *Khrushchev Remembers* (Boston: Little, Brown, 1970), pp. 318–19.

First-hand accounts differ as to just what Stalin thought of the finished product. Davies wrote Harry Warner that the film was a great success and had been warmly received. One who accompanied Davies on his return mission, and who was on hand for the screening, May 23, 1943, has provided this account: "There approached a group of men who stood for an instant in the broad open doorway before approaching the guests to greet them. In the center of the group was Stalin. There was no fanfare. . . . After dinner there followed, in an adjoining room, with Stalin sitting up front, a showing of the film. . . . Stalin was not there when the lights went on."[29] The American ambassador, William Standley, sent home a harsh report of the film's reception, but, it should be remembered, Standley had already been recalled and bitterly resented Roosevelt's sending Davies as special messenger. The dinner began, Standley noted, with a "long oration" by Davies, followed by the screening. "Stalin was heard to grunt once or twice," he declared. "The glaring discrepancies must have provoked considerable resentment among the Soviet officials present" (see document 12 in the Appendix).

Stalin's personal response to the film remains the subject of conjecture, but his official approval is certain. The film went into commercial distribution within the Soviet Union, though probably minus the Davies prologue, and, if newspaper accounts can be trusted, with the scene about bugging the American embassy omitted.[30] The Russian translation followed the original quite closely; the purge scenes remained intact. The Soviet public had an immense curiosity about the United States, of whom they had heard such terrible things, and a fascination to learn how Hollywood would treat their country and its leaders. The film found tremendous popular acceptance within Russia. It is one of the few examples one can point to of Roosevelt's being able to show Stalin that America had experienced a change of heart and

29. Bartley Patrick Gordon to Elbridge Durbrow, October 12, 1977, in Durbrow to Culbert, December 13, 1977. The Davies letter appears as document 11 in the Appendix.

30. *New York Times,* July 28, 1943. Stefan Sharff, who saw the film in Moscow in 1944, says the Davies prologue was cut.

that friendship and understanding were the new watchwords of the day.

Averell Harriman recalls how much the Russians "loved" *North Star*, MGM's pro-Soviet film with a screenplay by Lillian Hellman; it too was distributed commercially within the Soviet Union. Zina Voynow, Eisenstein's sister-in-law, claims that *Mission to Moscow* was "much appreciated" by the Russian people. She feels the average Russian enjoyed the Hollywood-style characterization of his own country even if it was far removed from actuality. A Russian film official told British representatives in Moscow that *Mission to Moscow* "was naive and made Russians laugh at certain points," but would be distributed commercially because so little was known about America.[31] The intent of the film seemed so painfully obvious.

Mission to Moscow is a curious film, an exception to most of the rules of feature production. If it fits any genre it would be something such as "feature-propaganda" or "feature-documentary." It is a spiritual ancestor of today's docudrama. The film purports to be factually accurate. When Davies himself says he will tell the truth and the credits appear over actual pages from his book, and newsreel footage is intercut along with sections of *Triumph of the Will*, we get an overwhelming feeling that the film is fact—it is a real trip discussing real events. The film becomes a documentary about an American ambassador's journey to Russia; it also justifies the value of a Soviet alliance and legitimizes American participation in World War II.

31. W. Averell Harriman to Culbert, March 14, 1977; telephone interview with Zina Voynow, June 22, 1977. The Soviet government proposed to give decorations to two films, *North Star* and *Mission to Moscow,* that had helped strengthen Soviet-American friendship. The State Department suggested that the Capra-unit *Battle of Russia* would be better since *Mission to Moscow* "aroused undesirable and heated controversy . . . concerning the Soviet Union and Soviet-American relations." Harriman to Secretary of State, January 22, 1944; Secretary of State to Harriman, January 29, 1944, Box 4943, 861.4061, RG 59, Department of State Records, National Archives, Washington, D.C.; "Memorandum of a Meeting with Mr. Andrievsky on 5th July, 1943," Moscow, July 6, 1943, INF 1/630/F. 691/49, Ministry of Information Files of Correspondence, Public Record Office, London, England.

Today's audience should be aware of at least eight major errors in the film:

1. Davies did not correctly predict the outcome of every foreign crisis, 1936–41; his expertise was valued by few.

2. Roosevelt did not consistently promote collective security and was something of an isolationist himself before 1939.

3. The Soviet Union could not be counted on to support the League of Nations by sending an army across hostile territory.

4. The *several* purge trials in reality had nothing to do with a Trotskyite group of fifth columnists working for Hitler.

5. One important reason Stalin signed the Nazi-Soviet pact in August 1939 was to take part of Poland, not merely to give himself time to prepare for Hitler's forthcoming invasion of Russia.

6. The Soviet Union invaded Finland and took territory by force. In the film Davies claims the fault lay with Finnish-Nazi collaborators.

7. Soviet leaders did not look and sound like happy, down-to-earth folks—the sort one might find here at home.

8. Collective security is no surefire cure for war.

Mission to Moscow wants to be accepted as fact, but its facts demand refutation since they go far beyond what might be justified by expediency, poetic license, or dramatic considerations.

By now the film's significance is primarily related to what it says about Washington's involvement in wartime feature film production. Why did the Warner brothers risk their name in making such an extreme film? The answer lies in the desperate plight of Russia and the feeling that perhaps a film of the right sort could make the Soviet Union look better in American eyes. Does not the extreme nature of the film offer compelling evidence of just how critical the Russian situation seemed to Davies, Roosevelt, and the Warner brothers in 1941–42?

Should the state in wartime have the right to distort the truth in the interests of wartime unity? Most would say that, within reason, it does. But this film is not within reason. It suggests why the term propaganda has a pejorative connotation to many. The problem, then, is somehow to define such wartime expedients so as to keep "propaganda" and "lies" from turning into synonyms. The record since 1943 inspires little confidence. Again and again, it seems, when some objective truth is pitted against a worthy cause, truth comes out second.

One of the film's most brilliant sequences is the all-out assault on American isolationists near the end. Here is a piece of manipulation whose devices become apparent only after repeated examination. The combination of aural and visual, plus the pacing that comes from skillful editing, results in a device for stereotyping that is truly remarkable (or terrifying). These scenes force our acceptance of facts that in 1943 were presumably familiar. The result is a brilliant device for analyzing the distortions of the so-called great debate over isolationism and interventionism, the key to all arguments for American participation in World War II.

The propagandist can learn something from *Mission to Moscow* of a more general nature. Effective propaganda reinforces that which is true. The Capra-unit *Battle of Russia* never said a word about the purge trials or Finland; it glossed over the 1939 Nazi-Soviet pact. It emphasized the historic hatred of Russia for Germany and included superb Soviet newsreel footage of the battles around Leningrad and Stalingrad. Extraordinary Soviet heroism—sacrifices that destroyed forever the legend of Nazi invincibility—here is factual evidence for liking an ally no matter what his past record. *Mission to Moscow* touched on these facts but diluted its message by extensive use of look-alike historical figures and a wholesale rewriting of history. Such audacity may entitle the film to a certain amount of interest but does not excuse the willful intent to deceive.

One of the most unsettling aspects of the film's production is what it suggests about the federal government's control over Hollywood in wartime. A mechanism existed—a Hollywood Office of the Bureau of Motion Pictures, Office of War Information—to monitor the content of every single feature film while in production. But the OWI never really had the confidence of Roosevelt and, in the end, the president let an idea of an old friend run away with itself. Davies used his wife's fortune and claims of "inside information" to get his way.

Roosevelt gave little thought to how the film should present its message, and the OWI was, from a practical administrative point of view, powerless to impose its will on the president. OWI officials gloried in what Warner Brothers was doing—the script was praised on several occasions and the release print accepted without criticism. A government agency supposedly charged with the power of censorship turned out to have no real impact when it mattered. A film seen by millions of persons throughout the world, and, presumed by the knowledgeable— including Goebbels and Stalin—to represent administration policy, actually came into being without anyone's giving serious thought to the matter of means and ends. It is a disturbing aspect of how media events occur in the modern world that this is so often the case. In the making of this film independent moral judgment deteriorated, thanks to everyone's easy adjustment to bureaucratic procedures. Those who knew no better did the work; those who did kept silent.

Mission to Moscow is a unique film document, a screen manifesto whose notoriety was apparent in 1943 as it is today. Never has another feature film been made in the United States with such explicit direction from the federal government, particularly Joseph Davies, but also Franklin Roosevelt and the OWI. The result became part of the diplomatic process and a key element in the campaign to sell America on the virtues of an awkward ally. The film performed a real service inside the Soviet Union, but at home it mostly defined limits, in time of war, for acceptable levels of distortion. Emily Dickinson, in a poem about propaganda, advises "Tell all the truth, but tell it slant— / Success in circuit lies." *Mission to Moscow* had plenty of slant, but not enough truth. The film serves as a warning for those who insist that entertainment programming should contain social "messages," the stronger the better. It also should be kept in mind by those who argue that mass media control what we think. There is a limit to what the traffic will bear.

1. "I felt it was my duty to tell the truth." Ambassador Davies himself delivers the prologue.

2. In a documentary touch, the book itself is shown before the credits.

3. *Haile Selassie tells the League of Nations about the Italian invasion of Ethiopia.*

4. *On vacation, Davies, his wife, and daughter are informed of a telephone call from President Roosevelt.*

43

5. "But I'm a capitalist." Davies meets with an off-camera Roosevelt and is asked to go to Russia as ambassador.

6. Hitler Youth march through the train station in Hamburg.

7. *At the Polish-Soviet border, Freddie, the family chauffeur, regards in amazement a beefy female locomotive engineer.*

8. *Davies discusses policy with President Kalinin in Moscow.*

45

9. *Madame Litvinov, commissar of cosmetics, shows Mrs. Davies around her beauty shop. The scene was a last-minute addition.*

10. *Emlen Davies and Tanya Litvinov meet at an ice-skating rink.*

46

11. *A visual hint. Yagoda, Bukharin, and Radek will shortly be arrested by the state and charged with collaborating with the Nazis.*

12. *"Your message is pure bunk," Davies has just told the Japanese ambassador.*

47

13. *The Moscow ballet sequence. Notice the painted backdrop.*

14. *Bukharin testifies to "the monstrousness of our crimes" at the climax of the purge trials.*

15. *Davies visits Paderewski (notice the piano) in Poland.*

16. *Dudley Field Malone as Churchill. Having never smoked, Malone became violently ill from the cigars.*

49

17. *Polite animation. The invader's fire burns only from the German (western) side of Poland.*

18. *"What about Finland?" Hecklers confront Davies at Madison Square Garden in 1941.*

19. *"Thank God we're on the right side." Davies meets Litvinov, now Soviet ambassador to the United States.*

20. *"You are your brother's keeper." The world's citizens in silhouette—and all wearing hats—urge an end to war.*

21. *Edward Tinker, Joseph Davies, and Walter Huston at the Davies camp in the Adirondacks. (Photograph courtesy of Mrs. Lowell Ditzen.)*

22. *Official photograph of Davies' 1938 meeting with Stalin, inscribed by the latter. (Photograph courtesy of Mrs. Lowell Ditzen.)*

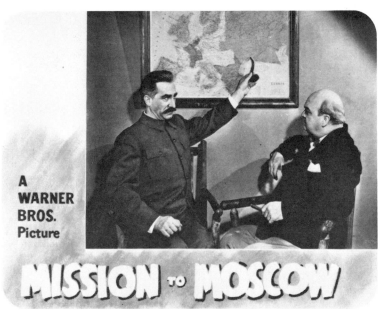

A
WARNER
BROS.
Picture

MISSION TO MOSCOW

23. *Studio card used in theater advertising. Stalin discusses policy with Churchill, although in the film the two never meet.*

24. *Publicity photograph for a moment cut from the release print. Tanya Litvinov receives an award as parachutist. The backdrop is Warner's sound stage.*

53

Mission to Moscow

Screenplay
by
HOWARD KOCH

Mission to Moscow

MAIN AND CREDIT TITLES will be bordered on one side by a pen and scroll and on the other by an unsheathed sword—these to symbolize the two separate ways by which the nations of the world work out their political destinies.

FADE IN

1.   THE BARE SWORD
     now centered on the screen amid the fierce, consuming flames of a forge. A heavy anvil beats down on the steel, bending it to its will. The metal flattens and twists into an indefinable shape.[1]

                                              DISSOLVE TO:

2.   A MINIATURE PLOWSHARE   (INSERT)
     forged from the sword. A pen, reaching into the SHOT, dips into the plowshare, and now we see that it is an inkwell on a desk. The CAMERA MOVES close enough to read its inscription:
                      WOODROW WILSON
           PRESIDENT OF THE UNITED STATES
                            TO
                    JOSEPH E. DAVIES
           COMMISSIONER OF CORPORATIONS
     "They shall beat their swords into plow shares."
                                              Isaiah 2:4

     INSERT   MANUSCRIPT PAGE
     in bold, clear handwriting under the heading:
                    "MISSION TO MOSCOW"
                          Foreword

The CAMERA MATS DOWN to the first paragraph:

> In the fire of war and revolution was forged a new
> Russian government that promised to promote the
> welfare of its people and the cause of world peace.
> How well that promise was kept is of special import
> at this hour when Russia is an ally in the struggle
> against a common enemy who would destroy all we
> value in life. So without prejudice or partisanship I
> offer to my fellow Americans the facts as I saw them
> . . . (a hand writes with the pen) while United
> States ambassador to the Soviet Union.[2]

3.   CLOSE SHOT   JOSEPH E. DAVIES
    who speaks directly to the audience.

    DAVIES:
> No leaders of a nation have been so misrepresented
> and misunderstood as those in the Soviet govern-
> ment during those critical years between the two
> world wars. I hope that my book will help to correct
> that misunderstanding in presenting Russia and its
> people in their gallant struggle to preserve the
> peace until ruthless aggression made war inevita-
> ble. The events of which I speak may be said to
> have begun on an historic day in June of 1936 . . .[3]

4.   STOCK SHOT   LEAGUE OF NATIONS BUILDING   DAY

    DAVIES' VOICE (OVER SCENE):
> . . . in the Palace of the League of Nations at
> Geneva . . .

5.   FULL SHOT   (FROM ABOVE) INT. LEAGUE OF NATIONS
    BUILDING
    The circular hall is filled with members of the League
    assembly, their secretaries, uniformed guards, news
    correspondents, etc.

DAVIES' VOICE (OVER SCENE):

A little man of great dignity is making a plea to the delegates of fifty-two nations that are members of the League. It is His Majesty, Haile Selassie, Emperor of Ethiopia . . .

6.   MED. SHOT   HAILE SELASSIE

on the speakers' dais, facing the League members below. He is wearing a tropical white tunic and a black cape. Seated in back of him are the president and secretary of the League of Nations. A tense quiet grips the room as the emperor speaks with simple, moving sincerity.

SELASSIE:

—And I, who have led my people into battle, my army without arms—I have come here to tell you that the issue before the assembly is not merely Italian aggression against my country—it is a question of the very existence of the League. It is a choice between the rule of law and the rule of force . . .

7.   CLOSE SHOT   A PLACARD

with the printed words Reserved for Italian Press. The CAMERA PULLS BACK to show the Italian news correspondents listening with repressed excitement. Some of them are making notes, others watching closely the delegates' reaction to the speech. They comment acidly among themselves.

ITALIAN REPORTERS:

Fermatelo! Non l'ascoltate! E pazzo!

SELASSIE'S VOICE (OVER SCENE):

That is why I refused all proposals to my personal advantage made to me by the Italian government if only I would betray my people and the covenant of the League. I was defending the cause of all small peoples who are threatened with aggression.

8.   MED. SHOT   GERMAN PRESS BOX
Typical Prussian faces—stony and inflexible—are intently following the speech. Their comments, half-
aloud, are contemptuous.

GERMAN REPORTERS:
Was meint er!? Beobacht ihn! Er schaut uns an!

SELASSIE'S VOICE (OVER SCENE):
It is my duty to inform the governments assembled
in Geneva, responsible as they are for the lives of
millions of men, women, and children, of the
deadly peril which overshadows them. Ethiopia is
but the first to fall before this Fascist barbarism.
Who knows which country will be next?

9.   CLOSE SHOT   A PLAQUE INSCRIBED "RESERVED FOR
FRENCH DELEGATES"

10.   MED. PANNING SHOT
over the faces of the French delegates.

SELASSIE'S VOICE (OVER SCENE):
And what has become of the promises made to me?

THE CAMERA COMES TO REST ON:

11.   MED. CLOSE SHOT   PIERRE LAVAL
His expression is surly, his eyes shifty. (NOTE: Laval did
not attend this meeting, but since he was the first to sell
out Ethiopia by a secret agreement with Italy, I believe
we can take this factual liberty.)[4] Two of his confreres
murmur hostilely, glaring toward Selassie.

FRENCH REPORTERS:
C'etait a notre adresse! Le petit renard noir!

SELASSIE'S VOICE (OVER SCENE):
In violation of the Covenant a certain government
considered that the European situation made it im-
perative at any price to obtain the friendship of their

Axis neighbors, Germany and Italy. The price paid was the abandonment of Ethiopia to the greed of the Italian government.

12.   OMITTED
(NOTE: We will see Litvinov for the first time when he rises to make his speech.)

13.   CLOSE SHOT   HAILE SELASSIE
A tragic appeal in his face. His voice is filled with emotion that he endeavors to restrain.

SELASSIE:
Am I now to be left deserted and forgotten? (Pause.) If a strong government finds that it can, with impunity, destroy a weak people, then the hour has struck for that weak people to appeal to the League of Nations to give judgment in all freedom. God and history will remember your judgment.

The emperor bows slightly and then with great dignity turns, steps down from the dais.

14.   FULL SHOT   ASSEMBLY
There is a scattering of applause as the Emperor Selassie walks down the aisle to his seat. This cautious tribute acts as a signal for a counter-demonstration—boos and hisses from the press boxes of Italy, Germany, and Japan.

15.   MED. CLOSE SHOT   PRESIDENT PAUL VAN ZEELAND
now standing at the dais and rapping his gavel until the uproar dies down.[5] A voice addresses him OVER SCENE.

LITVINOV'S VOICE:
Mr. President . . .

PRESIDENT VAN ZEELAND:
Mr. Litvinov, first delegate of the Union of Soviet Socialist Republics, wishes to address the assembly.

16.   MED. SHOT   SHOOTING TOWARD LITVINOV

LITVINOV:
> Gentlemen, need I remind you the League was formed with one great ideal—to protect the rights of all its member nations—both large and small . . . Mine is perhaps the largest, and we fear no aggressor. But we are here to uphold the principle of collective security for even the smallest nation . . .

17.   MED. LONG SHOT   GERMAN, ITALIAN, AND JAPANESE PRESS SECTION
They begin to murmur knowingly among themselves, disrespectful of Litvinov's words.

LITVINOV (raising his voice over the gathering murmurs):
> This ideal of maintaining a peaceful world through united strength is now being threatened seriously for the first time. The eyes of the world are upon us.

18.   MED. SHOT   SOUTH AMERICAN SECTION   DELEGATE VAN DE WATER in the foreground.

LITVINOV:
> Our decision and our actions now may decide the course of human history for the next thousand years.

A shout of approval from Van de Water for Litvinov's words. This brings an increasing roar of disapproval from the Axis press boxes.

19.   MED. SHOT   PRESIDENT VAN ZEELAND
rapping frantically for order.

20.   MED. SHOT   LITVINOV
facing the hostile press boxes defiantly.

LITVINOV:
> Can you not understand that peace is indivisible?

21.   FULL SHOT   THE ASSEMBLY
The blunt honesty of Litvinov's speech has stirred the members, each according to his interests. There is a growing murmur of comment, an activity as they turn in their seats to comment to each other. Van Zeeland raps for order.

22.   MED. SHOT   THE AXIS SECTION   PANNING
Their derision and distaste for Litvinov's speech is clearly obvious. Two or three of them get up with their portfolios and begin to walk out. The CAMERA MOVES with them as the speaker's voice continues with strong feeling.

LITVINOV'S VOICE:
There is no security for *any* of us unless there is security for *all*. That was the faith and lifelong work of the great man who created this assembly . . . *The League must live! It must be strong!*

During this dialogue the CAMERA MOVES with the delegates who are leaving, until they finally pass a bronze bust of Woodrow Wilson, set into a niche in the wall. CAMERA HOLDS on this as the delegates walk out of scene, then MOVES UP to the

23.   CLOSE SHOT   PLAQUE BELOW STATUE
The inscription reads simply:
TO THE MEMORY OF
WOODROW WILSON
PRESIDENT OF THE UNITED STATES
FOUNDER OF THE LEAGUE OF NATIONS

Litvinov's dialogue from preceding scene is timed to continue over this SHOT, and CAMERA PANS UP to the face of Woodrow Wilson.

CAMERA PULLS BACK AND INTO:

24.   HIGH LONG SHOT   PULLING BACK   THE ASSEMBLY
PULLING BACK from the statue of Wilson to include the

63

entire assembly as Litvinov finishes speaking. The reaction from the members is mixed but intense, some
approving, others in violent disapproval; a general activity and commotion. OVER THIS PULL-BACK Davies' voice
continues the narration:

DAVIES' VOICE:
The voice of the League founder was still, and the
voice of his followers went unheeded. Soon a disil-
lusioned world began to listen to another voice . . .

LAP DISSOLVE TO:

25.   STOCK SHOT   HITLER
seen in pantomime, making one of his impassioned
speeches. Violence and fanaticism are manifested in his
face and gestures.

DAVIES' VOICE (CONTINUING OVER SCENE):
. . . that proclaimed a new order to take the place
of collective security—collective slavery under the
domination of what he termed a master race. At
first people laughed at this caricature of a man, with
his wild threats and his grandiose plans, but words
became deeds, and the laughter ceased.

26.   MONTAGE OF THE SPREAD OF AXIS AGGRESSION
after the Ethiopian breakdown of the League. These
shots will be selected from available stock material and
given whatever footage is deemed advisable. They
should include the best newsreel records of incidents in
the Spanish civil war and the Japanese invasion of
China, such as delivery of Axis planes and tanks to
Franco; battle scenes in the Spanish war; passage of the
Embargo Act cutting off American aid to the legal government of Spain; American volunteers joining the
Loyalist forces in protest; then the Japanese invasion of
China; the bombing of its cities; the strategic withdrawal
of Chiang Kai-shek into the interior; marching, fighting,
bombing, strafing as the MONTAGE increases in tempo.

From time to time SUPERIMPOSE OVER THESE SHOTS the image of Hitler in frenzied speeches, establishing him as the focal figure in the surge of aggression.

OVER THE MONTAGE Davies' voice interprets the events. His speech will be written after the shots are selected so that we can parallel the action with the words.[6] We follow the MONTAGE with:

27. STOCK SHOT   WHITE HOUSE   WASHINGTON

    DAVIES' VOICE (OVER SCENE):
    Like other Americans, I was only vaguely aware of these ominous events . . .

28. HIGH SHOT   PRESIDENT ROOSEVELT'S STUDY
    The president busy at his desk.

    DAVIES' VOICE (OVER SCENE):
    . . . But there was one man who foresaw what they meant—the president of the United States . . .

29. UPPER CORRIDOR   WHITE HOUSE
    as Davies reaches the top of the stairs and enters the president's study.

    DAVIES' VOICE (OVER SCENE):
    . . . He had called me to the White House just as I was about to leave on a vacation . . .

                                                    WIPE TO:
30–35. OMITTED[7]

    FADE IN
36. EXT. WHITE HOUSE   WASHINGTON   (STOCK)   NIGHT
                                                DISSOLVE TO:

37. INT. THE PRESIDENT'S STUDY
    President Roosevelt, back to the CAMERA, is seated at his desk.[8] Davies is seated facing him. They are at ease, old friends. The clock points to 10:15 P.M. They are having coffee and sandwiches.

ROOSEVELT:

> You know, among her other virtues, Joe, your mother had a remarkable gift of prophecy.

DAVIES (smiles):

> Yes, that's in the Welsh blood. (Puzzledly.) But what reminded you of it?

ROOSEVELT:

> Well, away back in the good old days when you and I were just a couple of young lawyers without clients, she once said to me, "Franklin, if you ever really stir yourself, you'll be president of the United States—and Joe's going to help you."

DAVIES (nods with a chuckle):

> I remember that— (he looks toward a framed picture on the desk) and she wasn't the only one who read your future.

Roosevelt's eyes follow Davies' to the picture.

38.   CLOSE SHOT   AN AUTOGRAPHED PICTURE OF WOODROW WILSON ON ROOSEVELT'S DESK

ROOSEVELT'S VOICE (OVER SCENE; reverently):

> The man who gave us our start, Joe. One of these days the world will catch up with him.

39.   MED. SHOT   THE TWO
They look back at each other and Davies smiles.

DAVIES:

> Well, Boss, I know you didn't pull me away from a fishing trip to talk about old times. You've got something else on your mind.

ROOSEVELT (smiles):

> That's right—I've been plotting against you. (He pauses and puts down his coffee cup, his manner

becomes serious.) Joe—I want you to go to Russia as our ambassador.

DAVIES (taken aback):
Ambassador! (Roosevelt nods.) But Frank, I'm not a diplomat.

ROOSEVELT:
This isn't a job for a diplomat. I want a sound American businessman who will get me the hard-boiled facts behind the most complicated and dangerous situation the world has ever faced.

DAVIES:
That sounds like quite an order.

ROOSEVELT:
It is, Joe . . . You've handled some pretty big questions in your law practice, but this is the biggest question there is—Are we going to be able to keep the peace, or is Europe going to force us into another war?

DAVIES:
Do you think it's as close as that, Frank?

ROOSEVELT:
We're on the verge of the worst disaster in history and I want to do everything in my power to stop it. Whether anything can be done depends on just one man.

DAVIES:
Hitler?

Roosevelt nods and continues, leaning forward in his intensity.

ROOSEVELT:
He seems bent on conquest—not only Europe but the whole world. He tells us that all he wants is

freedom of the seas and access to raw materials. If
he means it, I'll move heaven and earth to see that
his people get their share . . . But I think he's
bluffing, Joe, and I'm going to call his hand.

DAVIES (very interested):
How?

ROOSEVELT:
I want you to go first to Berlin and ask Hitler one
question. If he does get what he says he wants, will
he disarm—along with the rest of us?

DAVIES (responding to the president's fervor):
That ought to smoke him out . . . but what has all
this got to do with Russia?

ROOSEVELT:
She is the big unknown factor in this whole problem. If trouble comes, which side is she going to be
on—ours or Hitler's and Japan's? We've got to
know the *truth*, Joe. How strong is Stalin's regime
and how strong is his army?

DAVIES:
Well, we get enough "expert" opinions about Russia. The question is which to believe.

ROOSEVELT:
It's your job to get me the right answers. No, "job"
is too small a word, Joe. This is a mission.

There is a tense pause as they look at each other for a
moment.

DAVIES:
How would the Russians accept me, Frank? Politically I'm a liberal, but I'm also a capitalist. (Smiles.)
In fact, the attorney for some of the richest men and
largest corporations in the world.

ROOSEVELT:

> That will never influence your judgment—I know
> that, and so will they. (Smiles.) Besides, I'm much
> more interested in your opinion of them than in
> their opinion of you.

A pause as they regard each other soberly, Roosevelt
waiting, Davies weighing the great decision.

ROOSEVELT:

> You don't have to give me an answer tonight. Think
> it over.

DAVIES (slowly):

> No, Frank—you've done that for me. If you think
> I'm the right man, that's good enough for me.

Roosevelt holds out his hand. Davies clasps it.

ROOSEVELT:

> Thanks, Joe. The mission is in good hands.

DAVIES:

> Good night, Boss.

ROOSEVELT (smiles):

> Good night, Mr. Ambassador.

Davies grins and starts away, then suddenly stops and
looks back with concern.

DAVIES:

> This'll be an awful shock to my family. They were
> going to spend the winter in Florida.

On Roosevelt's laughter, we

FADE OUT

FADE IN

40. EXT. NEW YORK DOCK (STOCK) NIGHT
A midnight sailing of a large transatlantic liner, ablaze
with lights. In background the myriad lights of lower
Manhattan's skyscrapers.

41.   EXT. THE DOCK   FULL SHOT
A typical busy sailing-night scene, noisy and exciting with gay parties seeing off friends, baggage being hauled, porters, telegraph messengers calling names or carrying huge boxes of flowers and fruit, etc. In background we see the lighted, canopied gangplank, up which people are walking toward the deck of the liner.

42.   EXT. DECK OF THE LINER   MOVING SHOT
The deck is filled with gay, chattering groups, all the usual noise and activity of sailing night. A neatly blue-uniformed steward or busboy is walking down the deck, striking a triangle.

STEWARD (calling loudly):
    All visitors ashore, please—all visitors ashore.

The ship's whistle coughs deeply one or two impatient blasts. The CAMERA MOVES ON to where the party of the Davieses' friends are coming out on deck from one of the doorways. There are quite a number of them, fifteen or twenty, men, women, and young friends of Emlen. The men are all in dinner jackets and the women in evening clothes with fur coats, as if they had all come from a big farewell party. One or two photographers snap flashlight photos of the Davieses and thank them, while several ship's news reporters press up around Davies.

FIRST REPORTER:
    Another question, Mr. Davies—what's your opinion of the Russian army?

DAVIES (jovially):
    I've never seen it. Ask me when I get back.

SECOND REPORTER:
    Is there any special reason you're going by way of Berlin, Mr. Davies?

DAVIES:

> Sorry—that's all I can tell you, boys. Give me a chance to tell my friends good-bye.

REPORTERS (ad lib):

> Sure—thanks, Mr. Ambassador. Good-bye, sir. Good luck, Mr. Davies. Etc.

Davies turns away to the group in background near the gangway, down which other visitors are going.

43.   MED. GROUP SHOT   AROUND EMLEN

A group of five or six nice-looking young boys of nineteen or twenty, typical well-bred college boys in dinner jackets, are around Emlen. Perhaps also two or three girls of her own age. From their manner it is clear that they are all warmly attached to Emlen.

FIRST YOUNG MAN:

> Gee, Emlen, we're going to miss you like the devil.

EMLEN:

> Thanks, Johnny. I'll send you a picture of me— riding in a moujik or droshky or whatever they call it. (They laugh.)

SECOND YOUNG MAN:

> Look, Emlen—why not get me a job in your father's embassy? I'll bet I'd make a darn good diplomat.

EMLEN:

> A darn good diplomat would have arranged it with Father.

More laughter.

44.   ANOTHER GROUP   AROUND MRS. DAVIES

Mrs. Davies is surrounded by friends, most of them smartly dressed women of her own age. Most of them appear concerned for her, even anxious.[9]

FIRST WOMAN:
    Really, Marjorie, we'll all be worried to death about you in Russia. (The others agree ad lib.)

MRS. DAVIES:
    But *why?* It isn't as though we were going to *Mars*, you know. Personally, I'm as excited as a schoolgirl visiting Paris.

FIRST WOMAN:
    Oh, Paris is different. I doubt if there's even a decent hairdresser in Moscow.

MRS. DAVIES (laughs):
    How dreadful! Then I'll stagger along somehow without one.

45.   ANOTHER GROUP   AROUND DAVIES
    Close by the group of women stands a group of Davies' men friends, around his own age. They appear equally concerned as their wives about this venture, and Davies listens with slightly amused interest.

FIRST FRIEND:
    Now don't let those Russians fool you, Joe. Keep an open mind but don't be influenced.

DAVIES (dryly):
    You think I should look around but not see too much, eh?

FIRST FRIEND:
    No, I don't care what you see. But don't *buy* anything—I mean political ideas.

SECOND FRIEND (anxiously):
    Bill means don't forget you're an American, Joe.

DAVIES (laughs):
    Listen, boys—I've handled a lot of tough cases in my life but I never judged a man until I had studied all the evidence, both for and against him. And

that's exactly how I feel about Russia. How they keep their house is really none of our business.[10] Only one thing matters—what kind of neighbor will they be in case of a fire?

They look at him puzzledly for a moment, but before they can question him further, the steward comes up to the group.

STEWARD:
Please, gentlemen—all visitors ashore. This is the last call.

46.   FULL SHOT   THE ENTIRE GROUP   ON DECK
as the Davieses' friends hasten to tell them quick good-byes, shaking hands, the women kissing—ad libs of "Now *do* write to us," "Bon voyage," "Take care of yourself and keep warm," "Good luck, Joe," etc., as they edge toward the nearby gangway, herded tactfully by a couple of the ship's officers.

47.   FULL SHOT   REVERSE ANGLE   FROM THE DOCK
SHOOTING UP to the deck of the liner as the friends descend the gangway, waving to the Davieses, who wave back gaily. The ship's whistle blows impatiently, and there is the usual commotion on the dock and on the ship of getting under way.

48.   MED. CLOSE THREE SHOT   THE DAVIES FAMILY
as they stand against the ship's rail looking down toward the dock, Davies between his wife and daughter. There is a suspicion of tears in Emlen's eyes.

EMLEN (quietly):
Daddy, I feel as if everybody on earth had suddenly gone away and left me.

MRS. DAVIES:
Yes, so do I, darling.

Davies glances at each of them in turn, smiles gently, and puts an arm around each of them. He is also moved.

DAVIES:

I guess we all feel that way. (He looks out toward the twinkling skyline of New York.) When we come back home again—back to America—every tree, every lamppost, is going to seem like the most beautiful thing in God's world.

49.   MED. LONG REVERSE SHOT (PROCESS)
SHOOTING PAST the three Davieses at the rail in close foreground to what they are watching, the million twinkling lights of New York's skyline in the distance. From somewhere off-scene the ship's orchestra is playing a nostalgic piece, and the deep-throated whistle of the ship salutes the shores it is leaving.

FADE OUT

FADE IN

50.   EXT. HAMBURG HARBOR   LONG HIGH SHOT   (STOCK) DAY
A high aerial shot, if available, of Hamburg harbor in 1936 or thereabouts, with a large transatlantic liner being guided into its dock. OVER THIS WE SUPERIMPOSE THE TITLE:

HAMBURG

DISSOLVE TO:

51.   EXT. HAMBURG RAILROAD STATION   MOVING SHOT   DAY
This is not the front or street facade of the station, but a section of the rear which leads out through the gates to the train platforms. The scene is very active and busy with passengers coming and going, baggage being handled on small trucks, etc. A newsstand with German papers and magazines is doing a brisk trade. The tempo of this entire German sequence is brisk, methodic, extremely efficient. This is the Third Reich, the New Germany of Hitler. Soldiers and sailors, rank and file, are

generously sprinkled among the civilians. There is a babble of voices mixed with the sounds of trains.

Uniformed railroad guards are hustling tardy passengers through one of the iron gates. A whistle blows. The guards immediately close the gates. A fat German citizen and his wife rush up with their luggage and we PAN with them to the gate. They are out of breath and try to open the gate, but the guard stops them brusquely.

MAN:
> Quickly, please—open the gate! That is our train!

GUARD:
> You are too late. (He nods to the clock.)

WOMAN (excitedly):
> But our son has had an accident in Leipzig! We must get to him! Please let us through!

GUARD (shakes his head):
> It is forbidden. The trains of the Third Reich wait for no one.

He turns abruptly away from them. The middle-aged couple watch through the closed gate as the train pulls out.

52.   FULL SHOT   ANOTHER ANGLE   PANNING
Out from the station comes the Davies family, accompanied by three or four semiformally attired Germans, diplomats or local dignitaries, detailed by the government as a usual formality to receive visiting envoys. Their spokesman is one Schufeldt, an undersecretary, suave, bland, somewhat self-important. The crowd of waiting passengers, civilians and military, recognize them as someone of importance and watch them with mild curiosity. Davies and the group advance toward the gates. Davies and his family are observing everything with interest.

53.   CLOSER MOVING SHOT   THE GROUP   FAVORING DAVIES
        AND SCHUFELDT

SCHUFELDT:
>   We are disappointed that you cannot stay in Ham-
>   burg for a few days, Your Excellency. There have
>   been a great many changes here in the last few
>   years.

Davies is looking off to one side.

54.   FULL SHOT   A DETACHMENT OF GERMAN SOLDIERS
They are lined up to one side, waiting for a train, all
wearing battle uniforms and carrying heavy equipment
with rifles.

55.   MOVING SHOT   THE DAVIES GROUP

DAVIES:
>   Yes, we have heard of a few of them.

SCHUFELDT (smiles):
>   Ah, but you should see for yourself, Herr Ambas-
>   sador. The New Germany is a revelation. The
>   people have so many more cultural advantages,
>   and such spirit!

Davies' eyes are still ranging over the crowd as they
walk along.

56.   FULL SHOT   A GROUP OF REFUGEES
Off to another side of the crowd stands a little group of
newly exiled refugees, poor, bedraggled men and
women with one or two children, all with their luggage,
all with big numbered discs pinned to their clothes. Two
uniformed guards are standing near them. The empty
staring eyes of the refugees are watching the Americans.
The German guard are eating big chunks of knackwurst,
which the refugees watch hungrily.[11]

57.   MOVING SHOT   THE DAVIES GROUP

DAVIES:
Really? That's very interesting, Herr Schufeldt.

They continue toward the gate that leads out to the train platform.

58.   ANOTHER ANGLE   FULL SHOT
SHOOTING from the gates as the Davies group approaches. Suddenly from off to one side a company of German youths approaches in a double column, young boys of thirteen or fourteen, all in the uniform of their organization, marching with perfect precision and led by an older youth of nineteen or so. The Davies group pauses to let them pass.[12]

59.   GROUP SHOT   DAVIES, MRS. DAVIES, EMLEN, AND
SCHUFELDT
as the company of young Germans stride past, eyes front, stiff as pokers. Schufeldt glances proudly at the Davieses for their reaction.

SCHUFELDT:
Those are members of our Youth Movement—the Reich's new generation. You could perhaps compare them with your Boy Scouts.

DAVIES (dryly):
Perhaps—

MRS. DAVIES:
I never saw any of our Boy Scouts looking quite so serious.

Davies gives her a quick, amused glance, but Schufeldt takes the remark as a high compliment.

SCHUFELDT:
They realize that the great future of Germany is in their hands.

The German boys finish marching past, and Schufeldt leads the group toward the gates. The Davies family glance at each other. The uniformed guards at the gate salute stiffly as the official party goes through the gates and out to the train platform.

60.   EXT. TRAIN PLATFORM   MOVING SHOT   THE GROUP
The platform is covered by a shed. On one side is a first-class train of the German type with the appropriate lettering. Other passengers and groups are waiting for the train to leave, as the Davies group comes down the platform. Schufeldt and Davies are in front, the others closely following.

SCHUFELDT:
I understand that you expect to have an appointment with Herr Minister Schacht, Your Excellency.

DAVIES:
Yes, I hope to.

SCHUFELDT:
And also with the Führer himself, I believe.

DAVIES (in mild surprise):
You seem very well informed of my schedule, Herr Schufeldt.

SCHUFELDT (smiles faintly):
Thank you . . . (Casually.) We feel gratified, Mr. Ambassador, that you chose to visit us first, before going to your appointment in Russia.

DAVIES (noncommittally):
I'm interested in conditions in both countries. (Puts a leading question very casually.) I understand the Stalin regime is firmly entrenched with the Russian people.

SCHUFELDT (eager to use this opportunity to plant a doubt):
On the surface—yes. (Mysteriously.) But before

very long you may possibly have cause to change your opinion.[13]

Davies looks at him quizzically, surprised at the remark. The German catches the look and suddenly realizes that he may have revealed too much. He covers up hastily.

SCHUFELDT:
Of course, I have nothing definite to base that on, you understand. It is merely a personal opinion.

DAVIES:
I see . . .

SCHUFELDT:
Ah, here is your compartment.

They stop beside one of the first-class carriages, and the rest of the party comes up to them.

61.   GROUP SHOT   ON PLATFORM   BESIDE TRAIN
A typically efficient German conductor hastens up to open the door of the Davieses' compartment for them, impressed by the honor of the occasion.

CONDUCTOR (watch in hand):
The train leaves in forty-three seconds, sir. Your luggage is already inside.

DAVIES:
Thank you. (He turns to the Germans.) You gentlemen have been extremely kind and helpful to us. I wish to thank you for both ourselves and our government.

Schufeldt and the other two Germans respond with polite ad libs as they shake hands, then they bow to Mrs. Davies and Emlen, who also thank them and bid goodbyes, then get into the train. Davies follows them in; the conductor closes the door. The three Germans on the platform doff their hats in a simultaneous movement.

62.   CLOSE SHOT   SCHUFELDT AND THE OTHER TWO GERMANS
They stand politely until the train pulls out. One of
them glances at Schufeldt and speaks with quiet disapproval.

GERMAN:
     You shouldn't have let slip that remark about Rus-
     sia, Schufeldt. He may remember it later.

SCHUFELDT:
     I said nothing— (He smiles slightly.) Anyway, *later*
     it will make no difference.

All three of them smile.

                                                DISSOLVE TO:

63.   INT. THE DAVIESES' COMPARTMENT   ON THE TRAIN
A very neat and spotless compartment with facing seats,
continental style, with a corridor on the far side of the
other door. Mrs. Davies and Emlen are seated opposite
each other at the windows, Davies is seated beside his
wife. All three are looking out the windows at the scene
on the platform as the company of German Youths,
whom we saw before, now march down the platform
outside, singing loudly and precisely the "Horst Wessel" song.[14] We can see them through the windows,
little automatons, on their way to board the train. On
the opposite side of the platform another train pulls into
the station. Its carriages are filled with German soldiers.
They see the Youth company and take up the "Horst
Wessel" with them as they pour out of their train onto
the platform. The vision and feeling of a militant Germany of all ages are tremendously effective. The three
Davieses look around at each other as their train begins
to pull out of the station.

MRS. DAVIES:
     I feel as if we had walked onto the stage of a musical
     comedy.

EMLEN (laughs):
> So did I, Bunny—and not very good music at that.

DAVIES:
> No—nor very good comedy, either.

They look around at him in smiling surprise.

MRS. DAVIES:
> Why, Joe—you know all those little wooden sol-
> diers are funny. Just look at them. (She looks back
> out the window.) They must have been stamped
> out of a machine.

DAVIES (soberly thoughtful):
> No—not *out* of—but *into* one.

His wife's and daughter's faces sober a bit as they look
back at the military scene outside.

64.   REVERSE ANGLE   INTO THE COMPARTMENT OF THE
MOVING TRAIN
The door is opened by a large, very Germanic-looking
businessman, carrying a handbag and a briefcase. He
looks at the empty space, moves in, closes the door,
tosses his bag on the rack overhead, places the briefcase
precisely beside him, and sits down. The Davieses are
not aware of his entrance as they watch the scene outside. The German businessman looks out, sees the boys
marching, and smiles proudly.

GERMAN:
> Ein wunderbarer Anblick, nicht wahr? [15]

The Davies family looks around, a little surprised to see
the stranger in their compartment, but not resentful of
it.

DAVIES:
> Es ist sehr interessant.

GERMAN (to Mrs. Davies):
Sie als deutsche Mutter können stolz darauf sein,
gnädige Frau.

MRS. DAVIES (smiles hesitantly):
I'm very sorry— (She looks at her husband for
help.)

DAVIES:
Meine Frau kennt nicht Deutsch.

GERMAN:
Ah—English?

DAVIES:
No—American. (He offers his open cigarette case.)
Would you care for a cigarette?

GERMAN:
Ah, thank you—yes. (Davies lights for both of them
and the German studies the cigarette apprecia-
tively.) You Americans have very good tobacco.
Ours is terrible— (hastily corrects himself) at the
moment. We intend to improve it very shortly.

DAVIES:
Really? Where will you buy?

The German takes another puff and smiles knowingly.

GERMAN:
I am not so sure we will have to buy from anyone.
Our Führer is a very clever man. He has many
ideas.

MRS. DAVIES (dryly):
And what do you smoke in the meantime?

Davies gives her a quick look, amused but gently re-
proving. The German sighs slightly.

GERMAN:
I would rather not know for sure. (He luxuriates in

another puff and expands with wise importance.) We Germans do not mind a few discomforts now, because we know what is in store for us in the great future life.

EMLEN (innocently, perhaps):
Do you mean on earth—or somewhere else?

The German smiles faintly at her, then replies slowly.

GERMAN:
Shall we say—"somewhere else on earth." [16]

The Davieses glance at each other as the German flips open his copy of the *Berliner-Tageblatt* or *Der Angriff* and begins to read. Suddenly the door is opened by the German conductor whom we saw on the platform. He salutes and bows very obsequiously.

CONDUCTOR:
Your Excellency—Madame—the president of the German State Railways has commanded me to do all I can for your comfort on the trip. Please do not hesitate if there is anything you want.

DAVIES (with a polite nod):
Thank you, Herr Conductor. Everything is fine.

The conductor bows stiffly again, glances a bit puzzledly at the German businessman, closes the door, and exits. But out in the corridor he takes a small wooden panel with clips attached and fastens it to the door of the compartment, then walks away.

65. CLOSE SHOT THE GERMAN BUSINESSMAN
He has seen the panel put on the door and heard the conversation with a strangely puzzled expression. Now he looks at the Davieses, then back to the door, and unobtrusively reaches out to lift up the panel and look at it.

66.   INSERT THE PANEL
        It is of the type used on all European trains for the
        courtesy and convenience of traveling diplomats. It
        reads in German, which DISSOLVES into English:
                DIPLOMATIC
                Do Not Disturb

67.   CLOSE SHOT   THE GERMAN BUSINESSMAN
        His face freezes with embarrassment as he sneaks the
        panel back onto the door, then buries his face into his
        newspaper.

67A.   EXT. GERMAN TRAIN   LONG SHOT   (STOCK)
        as the train speeds along through the busy industrial
        scenery of Germany. (NOTE: There is an excellent STOCK
        SHOT of this in the Julien Bryan material.) [17]

67B.   OMITTED

                                                FADE OUT

        FADE IN
68.   EXT. BERLIN   LONG SHOT   "UNTER DER
        LINDEN" (STOCK)   DAY
        The best possible STOCK SHOT of the famous Unter der
        Linden, taken from the Brandenburg Gate, with street
        traffic. OVER THIS SUPERIMPOSE THE TITLE:
                BERLIN

                                        DISSOLVE TO:

69.   EXT. ENTRANCE TO THE REICHSBANK BUILDING
        The imposing entrance of the German State Bank. Two
        uniformed German guards are near the doorway,
        through which there is a traffic of businessmen, bank-
        ers, a few military men. Above or beside the entrance is
        the carved sign Reichsbank. (Check Research for fully
        correct wording.)

                                    DISSOLVE THROUGH TO:

70.   INT. OFFICE   DR. HJALMAR SCHACHT
A large, well-appointed office befitting the position of the head of the Reichsbank. On the walls are portraits of Hitler, the swastika flag, etc. Schacht is at his desk. His personality is polished steel, suave, gracious, keenly intelligent—the perfect composite of a European industrialist.[18] Davies is seated opposite him.

SCHACHT:
Of course we are greatly honored by your visit, Mr. Ambassador. But—well, frankly, we wondered why you would want first to see me. I am only a banker, not a diplomat.

DAVIES:
You are more than a banker, Herr Schacht. You are the financial brains of Germany. (Schacht smiles and shrugs modestly, but says nothing.) I thought perhaps I would get a clearer picture of conditions here from you than from the gentlemen in your Foreign Office.

SCHACHT (smiles faintly):
Then you are speaking now merely as one businessman to another?

DAVIES:
Yes, Herr Schacht. After thirty years of law I still prefer cold facts to hot air.

Schacht looks surprised for a moment, then laughs.

SCHACHT:
So do I, Herr Davies. What would you like to know? I will answer insofar as I can.

DAVIES:
Why is the greater part of Germany's entire production devoted to armaments?

SCHACHT (pauses a second):
We do not want another war. But unfortunately in

85

Europe the dove of peace must have wings of steel—or be destroyed.

DAVIES (unsatisfied):

I cannot agree with you, Herr Schacht. If a nation wants to live in peace with its neighbors it doesn't keep rattling the saber at them.

SCHACHT (with an ironic smile):

Ah yes, I believe you Americans call it the Good Neighbor policy.[19] But you can *be* a good neighbor only if you *have* good neighbors. France and Great Britain are not. We have suffered greatly by their injustices and can tolerate them no longer.

DAVIES:

That might impress the American people except for one factor in the situation—the belligerent and threatening attitude taken by the leaders of the German Reich in which they threaten what they will do "unless" they have their way.

SCHACHT:

I appreciate your frankness, Herr Davies. I will be equally frank . . . Germany has tried to be friends with France and England, but without success. Words have become useless things. Now we have begun to rearm, purely as a basis for argument.

DAVIES:

That kind of argument will only lead to a fight, Herr Schacht . . . (Schacht shrugs slightly.) We are convinced that a peaceful solution can be found. President Roosevelt is ready to support any further German claims that are based on her legitimate needs or her legal rights . . . on one condition— that her leaders agree to a plan for immediate disarmament.

SCHACHT (guardedly):

What plan, Mr. Ambassador?

DAVIES:
> A very simple one. Mr. Roosevelt proposes that all nations of the world limit their armaments to the weapons a man can carry on his shoulder.

SCHACHT:
> Hmm . . .

He rises, walks thoughtfully to a window nearby. Mr. Davies watches him, trying to appraise his reaction. Schacht's eyes fall on a small factory model, which rests on a nearby table.

71. CLOSE SHOT   THE MODEL
Underneath, a small placard in German, which fades into the English words Proposed New Munitions Plant at Mainz.

SCHACHT'S VOICE (OVER SCENE; obviously sparring for time to think):
> Has the president communicated his proposal to England and France?

72. MED. SHOT   THE ROOM

DAVIES:
> Not yet, but we have every reason to believe that no nation will hold back if Germany gives her consent.

Schacht walks slowly back to his desk. His face reflects a conflict of emotions. Davies rises and leans over the desk in an earnest plea.

DAVIES:
> Herr Schacht, you can't build to destroy and escape destruction yourself. Before it's too late, prevail on your leaders to consider this proposal. You and I both know this is the last good chance on earth of peace. If that chance is lost, your government will have to take the responsibility for the most terrible disaster in history.

Schacht seems impressed and for the first time responds with genuine warmth.

SCHACHT:

Herr Davies, I like your president's proposal. It has the simplicity of genius and I believe it is sincere. I shall take it up with my government. (A little wearily.) However, I must warn you . . . I am *not* the government. If they ask it, I shall give them my favorable opinion. That is all I can promise.

DAVIES (aware that the other man is speaking the truth): I quite understand.

They shake hands. Schacht sees the ambassador to the door, CAMERA MOVING with them.

SCHACHT:

If there is anything I can do for you during your stay here, Herr Davies, please let me know. I shall consider it a favor.

DAVIES:

Thank you . . . (Suddenly.) Yes, there is one favor I would like to ask. Ambassador Dodd[20] has had some difficulty in arranging an appointment for me to see Herr Hitler. I thought perhaps your office—

SCHACHT (indulgently, as if Davies were asking for the moon):

My dear Mr. Ambassador, I am sure our Führer would be delighted to see you, but just now he is a very busy man.

DAVIES:

So is President Roosevelt, Herr Schacht. But he felt this was a matter of extreme importance. I am quite willing to postpone my leaving for Moscow—

SCHACHT (hastily covering up):

Yes, yes, of course. (Considers a second.) I will see what I can do.

DAVIES:
   Thank you.

They bow and Davies goes out. Schacht returns thoughtfully to his desk, picks up the telephone.

SCHACHT:
   Get me Herr Minister von Ribbentrop.

73.   CLOSE SHOT   SCHACHT   AT PHONE
His face is soberly intent as he waits. (Research: Check this for correct form of German address in respect to their official positions.)

SCHACHT:
   Ribbentrop? Schacht speaking. The American Ambassador Davies has just left my office . . . He brings a remarkable offer of disarmament from President Roosevelt . . . nothing larger than a man can carry on his shoulder.

                                                     CUT TO:

74.   CLOSE-UP   VON RIBBENTROP   AT TELEPHONE
He is smiling as he listens. Now he laughs harshly.

VON RIBBENTROP:
   How *simple!* The Americans are very naive . . . (He laughs again at the colossal joke.) And to come with such a plan to you—of all persons! To *you*, Herr Schacht! Disarmament!

He roars with laughter.[21]

                                                     CUT TO:

75.   CLOSE-UP   SCHACHT   AT TELEPHONE
His sober expression changes as von Ribbentrop's laughter continues. He smiles hesitantly, then joins in the laughter.

SCHACHT:
   Yes—yes—very amusing! And Davies is also extremely anxious to talk with the Führer.

75A.   CLOSE-UP   VON RIBBENTROP

> VON RIBBENTROP (with an ironic smile):
>> Oh, *is* he indeed? And what do you think of his chances, Herr Schacht?

He laughs again, contemptuous of Davies' presumption.

DISSOLVE TO:

76.   EXT. BERLIN STREET   (PROCESS)   FROM WITHIN A CAR
Davies and an undersecretary from the German Foreign Office, who is escorting him, are seated in the back seat of a large German sedan. They are stopped at a crowded street intersection by a police officer who holds up his hand. Through the car windows we see a huge gathering of people on the street, watching a military parade or demonstration.

77.   LONG SHOT   THE PARADE AND CROWD   (STOCK)
as if from the angle of Davies' car. This is the best possible STOCK SHOT of a Berlin military parade, with mobs of enthused onlookers. Regiments of goose-stepping infantry swing past, a band is playing a German march, the swastika banners are flying everywhere, the crowd is "heiling" and cheering. (NOTE: If we can obtain closer STOCK SHOTS of German heavy artillery on parade they would very usefully emphasize our point here.)

78.   INT.   THE GERMAN CAR   (PROCESS)
with the parade and crowd still visible in background through the windows of the car.

GERMAN DIPLOMAT:
> Today the Führer is reviewing the army. You are very fortunate, Your Excellency.

DAVIES (watching the show):
> Yes, it is quite a privilege.

GERMAN DIPLOMAT (eagerly):
> Can you see everything clearly?

79.   CLOSE-UP DAVIES
He looks out at the parade for a moment before he re-
plies quietly, realizing now the futility of his visit to
Berlin.

DAVIES:
    Perfectly . . .

80.   EXT. LONG SHOT THE PARADE AND CROWD (STOCK)
as the German army continues to sweep past in all its
pomp and power. In foreground just beyond the car,
the German civilians in the crowd outstretch their right
hands in the Nazi salute, cheering the soldiers.
                                    SLOW DISSOLVE TO:

80A.   EXT. CLOSE SHOT MOVING WHEELS ON A TRAIN NIGHT
The fast-moving wheels of a German train, or the
locomotive's whirling pistons. OVER THIS SHOT we hear
Davies' voice in commentary.

DAVIES' VOICE (off-scene):
    I waited two full weeks in Berlin to tell Hitler my
    president's offer—but he would not see me—and I
    left for Moscow, knowing that the first part of my
    mission was unavailing . . . that Germany had al-
    ready turned her back to peace and her face to
    war—
                                    FADE OUT

    FADE IN
81.   EXT. RUSSIAN-POLISH BORDER STATION EARLY MORNING
An archway of wood bears the Russian inscription sig-
nifying this is the border station of Negoreloye. It is
early morning with a hazy ground mist still partly
obscuring the background. The customs and military
officers are examining the papers of travelers who are
passing through the archway toward the Russian train
waiting beyond, only a section of which is visible. Two
or more armed Soviet guards stand watching the activity with impassive faces.

The Davies group approaches the archway on foot, followed by porters with their luggage. They are accompanied by Loy Henderson, the chargé d'affaires, and Colonel Faymonville,[22] military attaché of the American embassy in Moscow, who have come down to the border to meet the new ambassador and escort him back to Moscow. All three of the Davieses are impressed by this dramatic moment of their actual entry upon Soviet soil. They pause near the arch, while the Soviet border officials stand quickly and smile in a friendly way of greeting. Naturally the Davieses are permitted to pass the customs without formality or examination. They are all wearing coats against the early morning cold. Davies and Henderson glance up at the border sign, then at each other.

HENDERSON:
Shall we cross the border, sir?

DAVIES (smiles):
Well, you're the chargé d'affaires, Henderson— lead on.

They start through the border archway.

82. EXT. RUSSIAN STATION PLATFORM
as the Davies group advances down the platform toward the waiting train, only a section of which is visible. Steam and the mist still partly obscure the details of the scene. From the station there may be the SOUND of accordion music playing a Russian song. A detachment of Soviet soldiers is drawn up on the platform as the guard of honor. A handsome young Major Kamenev stands in front of the line. At his crisp command the soldiers present arms as the Davieses approach and pause.

DAVIES (quietly):
A smart-looking bunch of soldiers, Colonel Faymonville.

FAYMONVILLE:

> Yes, sir—and good fighting men, too. Someday somebody's going to get a great shock out of this Russian army.[23]

83.   GROUP SHOT   ON THE PLATFORM
Major Kamenev detaches himself from the company of troops, crosses toward the American group, halts smartly, and salutes the ambassador's party.

KAMENEV:

> Major Kamenev, Your Excellency. May I welcome you to Russia in the name of my government. (Extends his hand.)

DAVIES (smiles, shakes hands):

> Thank you, Major Kamenev. (Introducing.) My wife and daughter.

Kamenev bows to them in turn, touching his cap. Mrs. Davies smiles and Emlen is impressed by the handsome young officer.

KAMENEV:

> Your train will be ready in a few minutes. (He glances to where a Russian woman is standing with a covered tray.) Would you care for a little refreshment perhaps?

DAVIES:

> Oh, splendid! All we had for breakfast was some ersatz eggs.[24]

They laugh.

MRS. DAVIES:

> This is very kind of you indeed.

He smiles, the women comes up, removes the white napkin that covers the tray, revealing an appetizing assortment of Russian sandwiches, hot tea, etc. The Davies family help themselves.

EMLEN:
Our first Russian meal!

MRS. DAVIES:
And *excellent*. What *is* this?

KAMENEV:
The little fish? We call it Volga Sprousa, madame. And this is vichina—a great favorite of ours.

DAVIES (eating):
Mmmm— You know, I think I'm going to like this country. (They laugh.)

84–85. OMITTED

86. CLOSE-UP EMLEN
looking at Major Kamenev.

EMLEN:
Y-yes, so do I, Daddy.

MRS. DAVIES (who has seen where Emlen is looking):
Em-len . . .

Emlen looks around at her mother innocently. They smile.

87. MED. CLOSE TWO SHOT MR. AND MRS. DAVIES
As they eat and drink the tea, they look around the interesting scene on the platform, listening to the gay music, watching the Soviet soldiers. Suddenly Davies' face becomes serious and he leans slightly toward his wife, confidentially.

DAVIES:
Marjorie, I wouldn't admit it to anyone else, but this business of being an ambassador scares me a little.

MRS. DAVIES (smiles):
Nonsense. You behave as though you've been one for years.

DAVIES (hopefully):
> You really think so?

Mrs. Davies nods and takes another sip of tea from her glass.

DAVIES (still uncertain):
> I like meeting people and exchanging ideas—but the part that bothers me is all this protocol formality—the diplomatic language they'll expect me to use.

MRS. DAVIES (with a wifely smile of encouragement):
> Then stick to Joe Davies language. I have a hunch they'll understand it even better.

DAVIES (his face lights up):
> You know, I'm kind of glad I brought you along.

He presses her arm and she smiles fondly at him.

CUT TO:

88. MED. MOVING SHOT DOWN THE PLATFORM
Freddie is coming down the platform carrying some luggage and a woolen lap robe. Walking beside him is a friendly Soviet official who has helped him through the customs gate. Freddie is looking around with much interest, eating a sandwich.

FREDDIE:
> So this is Russia, huh? (The Russian nods with a friendly smile.) Well, where's the caviar?

SOVIET OFFICIAL (nods to Freddie's sandwich):
> You are eating some now.

89. CLOSE-UP A GIRL IN WINDOW OF LOCOMOTIVE
This is only a section, the window of the cab of a Soviet locomotive, nothing else. A good-looking girl of twenty-five or so is leaning casually in the window, smiling down at them.[25] She wears a cap and the proper outfit. She lifts a hand to them in a friendly salute.

90.   MED. SHOT   FREDDIE AND OFFICIAL
Freddie stares back at the girl, open mouthed, then
turns to the Soviet man who has exchanged a word or
two in Russian with the girl in the cab.

FREDDIE:
    Say—do you let *girls* ride with your engineers?

SOVIET OFFICIAL:
    She IS the engineer.

He walks on, as Freddie stares back in amazement at the
girl. His face brightens with interest, but he is confused
as he walks away with another backward look. The train
whistles as the girl engineer gaily pulls the cord.

                                              FADE OUT

FADE IN
91.   EXT. MOSCOW   DAY
ANGLE SHOT   A HUGE STAR OF LEADED RED GLASS
SILHOUETTED AGAINST THE SKY
The whistle fades into the chimes of many bells. The
CAMERA PULLS DOWN and we see that the star is aloft a
belfry in which the chimes are striking the hour. We
show enough of the building to identify the belfry as
one of the Kremlin towers.

92.   ANGLE SHOT FROM ABOVE   THE HUGE KREMLIN GATE
flanked by an elite guard of Red Army soldiers. They
stand stiffly at attention as a large Packard car, with
police escort, enters the gate. On each side of the hood
flies a small American flag.

                                          DISSOLVE TO:

93.   INT. THE KREMLIN   FRONT CORRIDOR   PANNING SHOT
A very plain but impressive high-vaulted hallway. The
diplomatic procession enters the SHOT—first the two
Russian escorts, then the ambassador and Henderson,
followed by Colonel Faymonville and Spendler, all for-
mally dressed except Faymonville, who is in uniform.

94.   CLOSE TRUCKING SHOT   DAVIES AND HENDERSON
as they turn into another corridor.

DAVIES:
> No wonder Napoleon got lost trying to find the
> Russian army.

FAYMONVILLE (amused):
> Yes, it could have hid for years, right here in the
> Kremlin.

HENDERSON (smiles):
> The Soviet leaders have the same genius for being
> hard to reach.

DAVIES (nervously):
> I dread this formality, Henderson. I feel like a fish
> out of water.

By now they are passing a series of doors, evidently the
government offices. Barkov opens the door of an office
for the ambassador and his staff to enter.

BARKOV:
> This way, Mr. Ambassador.

95.   INT. PRESIDENT KALININ'S ANTEROOM   FULL SHOT
As Davies and party enter the room, the waiting Russian
officials rise. They include Kalinin, Vyshinsky, Krestinsky, and subordinate officials who remain in the
background. President Kalinin is a small man, simple in
manner, kindly.

BARKOV:
> The representative of the United States of America,
> Mr. Joseph Davies . . . The president of the Soviet
> Union, Mr. Kalinin.

They shake hands cordially.

KALININ:
> I am happy to meet you, Mr. Davies.

DAVIES:
　Thank you. I wish to give you my credentials.

KALININ (bows as he takes them):
　Thank you . . . May I present Mr. Krestinsky, first assistant to the commissar for foreign affairs.

Krestinsky bows slightly and they repeat each other's names in greeting. Kalinin turns to Vyshinsky, a distinguished jurist.

KALININ:
　And the procurator general of the USSR, Mr. Vyshinsky.[26]

DAVIES (as they shake hands):
　A pleasure, sir. We've heard of your great legal work, even in America.

VYSHINSKY (smiles):
　Thank you, Mr. Davies. May I return the compliment.

As Kalinin turns to greet Henderson, there is handshaking all around among the two official parties. This takes place in the background, the CAMERA REMAINING on Davies and Krestinsky.

KRESTINSKY:
　My chief, Mr. Litvinov, asks me to express his regrets that he is not here personally to greet you. He is still at Geneva.

DAVIES:
　I have a great admiration for Mr. Litvinov, and will look forward to meeting him.

Having shaken hands with the other members of the American embassy staff, Kalinin turns back to Davies.

KALININ:
　Mr. Davies, it is customary to make a formal speech

upon occasions like this, but with your permission, we shall talk what is on our minds instead of what is down on paper.

DAVIES:
That would suit me much better. (He grins as Kalinin leads him toward a door.) I think I've forgotten my speech, anyway.

Kalinin smiles back and the others in the room chuckle as they look at each other. The friendly informality of the meeting is an auspicious beginning.

WIPE TO:

96.   INT. PRESIDENT KALININ'S PRIVATE OFFICE
A small, simple room, simply furnished. As they sit at opposite sides of the desk Kalinin offers Davies a box of cigarettes. The atmosphere is easy and relaxed.

KALININ:
My favorite vice—American cigarettes.

DAVIES (smiles and takes one):
Spasibo.

KALININ (surprised):
You speak Russian!

DAVIES:
That one word is my entire vocabulary.

Kalinin chuckles as Davies snaps his lighter and holds it for him. They sit back comfortably.

DAVIES:
You and your people make me feel very much at home, Mr. President.

KALININ:
So? I am glad.

DAVIES:
You see, I'm not a professional diplomat. The only language I know is to say what I think.

KALININ (beams):
     Excellent! Then you and my people will speak the
     same language.

DAVIES:
     In that sense—yes, sir. But one thing I must make
     clear, Mr. President. I'm a product of a different
     system from yours. I believe in individualism as we
     practice it in America.

KALININ (nods with a friendly smile):
     We know your record, Mr. Ambassador, and we
     believe you're an honest man.

DAVIES:
     I can assure you, Mr. President, that my purpose in
     coming here is to see all things with an open mind,
     and report them faithfully to Washington.

KALININ (nods):
     I believe you. All we ask is that you see as much as
     you can of what we are trying to do before you form
     your conclusions.[27]

DAVIES:
     And that's what my president wants. That's why he
     sent me.

KALININ:
     A very great man, your president—with a deep
     sympathy for mankind.[28]

DAVIES:
     Thank you, sir. That is true. His greatest concern is
     to keep the world at peace.

A weary, troubled look comes over the Soviet president's face.

KALININ:
     Ah, yes—peace—

He half-turns to look at a large globe of the world on a
stand nearby.

KALININ (sadly):
There is room enough for all of us to live in peace.

He touches the globe, turns it slowly as Davies watches.

97. CLOSE SHOT   THE SLOWLY REVOLVING GLOBE
England, then France become the center of our vision as
Kalinin's finger brushes over them softly.

KALININ'S VOICE (OVER SCENE):
If only the other nations will see—and see in *time*.

Now the turning globe reveals Germany on top.

DAVIES' VOICE (OVER SCENE):
And if they should not? If war comes, what about
Russia?

With these words, the vast territory of Russia moves
before our eyes on the revolving globe.

KALININ'S VOICE (OVER SCENE; quietly, simply):
We are prepared to defend ourselves.
DISSOLVE TO:

97A.   EXT. BRITISH EMBASSY   MOSCOW   DAY

97B.   INSERT   CLOSE SHOT   BRITISH EMBLEM ON DOORWAY
with the words Embassy of Great Britain.
DISSOLVE TO:

97C.   MED. CLOSE SHOT   A CUE
is taking aim at a ball on a billiard table. The cue strikes
the ball.

97D.   FULL SHOT   THE GAME ROOM
in the basement of the British embassy. It is a very attractive and comfortable oak-paneled room with a huge
hearth and comfortable leather chairs on one end, the
billiard table and a dart set on the other. On the mantle
are ornamental ale mugs, trophies, etc. Displayed on
the wall are some very good English hunting prints.

Playing billiards are the four ambassadors—Davies, Coulondre of France, Grzybowski of Poland, and their host, Lord Chilston, who has just made a difficult three-cushion shot.[29]

DAVIES:
>A nice shot, Lord Chilston.

COULONDRE (in a joking vein):
>Why shouldn't he be good? He's down here practicing all the while . . . (Obviously trying to rattle Chilston, who is taking aim for the next shot.) Who else but the English would think of converting the embassy basement into a billiard room?

Chilston makes the shot—again perfect.

CHILSTON (looks up at Coulondre):
>Apparently the French have only room for a wine cellar.

COULONDRE:
>Touché.

The others laugh. Chilston is again taking aim.

DAVIES:
>What do you feature at the Polish embassy, Mr. Grzybowski?

GRZYBOWSKI:
>Our house is very small, Mr. Davies. We are Stalin's stepchildren.

Chilston's shot misses this time. Coulondre steps up to the table confidently, cue in hand.

COULONDRE:
>Now, my dear Chilston, you will see how that shot *should* be made.

CHILSTON:
>Yes?

They all watch as Coulondre aims and shoots. The ball caroms from cushion to cushion, not hitting any ball whatsoever. They all laugh. Chilston puts his cue back in the rack, the others following suit.

CHILSTON:
I want you gentlemen to try some new ale I just had shipped in.

COULONDRE (humorously):
I need something to cool me off.

Chilston and Coulondre walk toward the other end of the room, Davies and Grzybowski pairing off behind them.

97E.   TRUCKING SHOT   DAVIES AND GRZYBOWSKI

GRZYBOWSKI:
What a pity you weren't assigned to Warsaw, Mr. Davies. You would enjoy the social life there much more than here . . . (Smiles.) We have a saying: "A Russian is merely an unfinished Pole."

97F.   MED. SHOT   FIREPLACE END OF THE ROOM

CHILSTON:
Sit down, gentlemen.

DAVIES:
I looked forward to this visit, Lord Chilston, not only to get acquainted, but also to become better informed about Russia.

Chilston casually walks over to a wall socket, where he pulls out the plug for the telephone extension.

CHILSTON:
One can't be too careful, you know . . . (Notices Davies' expression and smiles.) Oh, you'll be doing the same before long. There are very large ears in Moscow—perhaps because those in power feel none too secure.

DAVIES:

But I was under the impression that the country is strongly behind the present government.

GRZYBOWSKI:

Don't be deceived by their propaganda, Mr. Davies. These Russians are experts at dressing their windows for foreign diplomats.

DAVIES:

Do you mean the new five-year plan isn't working out?

GRZYBOWSKI (shrugs expressively):

Five years—ten—fifteen . . . They will always be the same Russians—full of great plans and small fulfillment.

Davies, surprised by this attitude of hostility, looks toward the others for clarification.

COULONDRE:

Most of our colleagues feel that way, Davies, but I don't entirely agree with them.

CHILSTON:

I think we shouldn't belittle the many fine works the Soviets have accomplished—but—well, there are more things going on in Russia than meet the eye, my friend.

Davies looks at him for a moment thoughtfully, then smiles slightly.

DAVIES:

Maybe I should take the eyes around and meet the things.[30]

DISSOLVE TO:

98.   MED. SHOT   MOLOTOV'S OFFICE
Molotov is at his desk. On one side of him is seated Maxim Litvinov. Molotov is at the telephone.

MOLOTOV:
. . . Please ask him to come in.

He hangs up and rises. Litvinov makes a motion as if to follow.

MOLOTOV:
No, don't go, it is Ambassador Davies.

LITVINOV:
Ah, yes.

Molotov crosses to the door, which is opened by a clerk who ushers in Mr. Davies. Molotov shakes hands with his visitor.

MOLOTOV:
Welcome home, Mr. Ambassador.

DAVIES:
Thank you.

MOLOTOV (as they cross toward the desk):
Mr. Litvinov is here with me. He just came back from Geneva and he's anxious to meet you.

99.   MED. SHOT   AT THE DESK
Litvinov rises, smiling as Molotov and Davies walk into the SHOT.

LITVINOV (shakes Davies' hand warmly):
Mr. Davies.

DAVIES:
Mr. Litvinov . . . This is a great pleasure.

MOLOTOV:
Please sit down, gentlemen. (He sits behind the desk as the others take chairs.) Tell us about your trip, Mr. Davies.

DAVIES (to Molotov):
First I want to thank you for making it possible.

MOLOTOV:

We only wish more of our foreign guests were that interested to see what we're doing.

LITVINOV:

What were your impressions, Mr. Davies?

DAVIES:

Most of all, I was amazed at the boldness and imagination behind such a vast industrial development. I can think of no other period in history where so much has been done in so short a time.

LITVINOV:

This is very gratifying to us.

DAVIES (smiles):

Naturally I saw things on the other side, too—things that weren't working and some things I didn't like.

MOLOTOV:

Oh, yes, we make mistakes. Our method is experimental—trial and error. We hope you will let us study your criticisms.

DAVIES:

Of course . . . Oh, there was one thing that made me very curious. I noticed in many factories that your installations were not fixed in cement—they were movable.

Litvinov and Molotov exchange glances.

MOLOTOV:

That's in case it is ever necessary to move them in back of the Urals.

DAVIES (gravely):

I see.

DISSOLVE TO:

100.   [EXT. AMERICAN EMBASSY]³¹

DAVIES:

> Don't stay too long. Remember, we've got a date
> tonight.

MRS. DAVIES:

> As if I'd forget my first diplomatic ball. (Half seri-
> ous.) Joe, will there be all sorts of mysterious in-
> trigues going on in alcoves and corners?

DAVIES (dryly):

> Oh, no doubt. Some beautiful brunette named Vera
> will probably offer you the plans of Yokohama, for a
> pair of silk stockings.

They go out, Spadebeard saluting as he opens the door.

101.   MED. SHOT   AT THE CAR
as Freddie holds the door for Mr. and Mrs. Davies.

MRS. DAVIES:

> Good morning, Freddie. How did you rest?

FREDDIE:

> Good morning, Mrs. Davies. With one eye open.

DAVIES (laughs, then gets into the car after his wife):

> Freddie, drop me off at the embassy, then take Mrs.
> Davies to this address. (Gives him a slip of paper.) I
> can't pronounce it.

FREDDIE:

> Yes, sir— (glances at the slip) and I can't read it, sir.

DAVIES:

> Ask the Gay Pay Oo boys.

He nods back to the car behind theirs, which has started
its motor. Mrs. Davies glances back uncomfortably.

MRS. DAVIES:

> I cannot get used to being followed everywhere I
> go.

FREDDIE (climbing into his seat):
> What I can't figure out, ma'am, is whether they're protecting us or watching us.

DAVIES (smiles):
> Probably a little bit of both.

The car pulls out of the driveway. CAMERA HOLDS on the spot and we see the police car follow closely after them, with its three OGPU boys.

DISSOLVE TO:

102.   CLOSE SHOT   DOORWAY OF U.S. EMBASSY OFFICE
with the proper inscription and insignia on the impressive double doorway.

DISSOLVE THROUGH TO:

103.   FULL SHOT   INT. ANTEROOM OF THE EMBASSY
People seated waiting to see the ambassador—members of the staff—secretaries walking to and fro. An air of quiet activity. An embassy undersecretary (whom we recognize as Spendler from the Kremlin scene) emerges from one door and crosses toward another. His manner indicates urgency.

104.   MED. SHOT   OFFICE OF THE AMBASSADOR
Davies sits at a desk in one corner of the room. Henderson is with him, going over the business of the day.

HENDERSON (as he hands Davies a stack of papers):
> More applications for American passports, sir. I've written my comments on the margins.

DAVIES (looks thoughtfully at the stack):
> The pile gets bigger every day. It reminds me of animals scurrying for shelter before a storm.

Spendler walks into the SHOT. He is an employee of the embassy, but not an American, and speaks with a slightly foreign accent. (He had a prototype in reality, but his actions here are not intended to be based upon an actual incident.) Davies and Henderson look up, noticing his air of controlled excitement.

SPENDLER:
Please—forgive my interrupting, Mr. Ambassador—but something has happened that I thought you should know about at once!

DAVIES:
Yes?

SPENDLER (lowers his voice confidentially):
Yesterday, the workmen who are repairing the Italian embassy found dictograph wiring in the rafters. I think we should make an immediate examination. The Kremlin may be recording every word we say![32]

DAVIES (calmly):
Maybe they had a reason with the Italians. We all know the rumors that certain embassies here in Moscow are hotbeds of foreign agents.

SPENDLER (surprised at this calm attitude):
But *eavesdropping*, sir! It's an open affront to one's international rights.

DAVIES:
Let's give them the benefit of the doubt, Spendler. Anyway, I say nothing outside the Kremlin about Russia that I wouldn't say to Stalin's face. (He pauses.) Do *you?*

SPENDLER (uncomfortably):
Well, that's putting it a bit stiffly, sir—

DAVIES (severely):
Then stop gossiping and stop listening to it. We're here in a sense as guests of the Soviet government, and I'm going to believe they trust the United States as a friend until they prove otherwise. Is that clear?

SPENDLER (flustered):
Yes, sir—but if there *were* microphones—

DAVIES:

>   Then *let* 'em hear. We'll be friends that much faster! (He glances around the room and ceiling.) And if they *haven't* got microphones I'm not going to insult them by ripping up the walls to find out. (He pauses and grins.) Anyway, it's much too expensive.

Henderson laughs, and even Spendler has to smile.

HENDERSON:

>   And besides, sir—we examined these rooms thoroughly two years ago.

Davies looks at him in very amused surprise.

DISSOLVE TO:

105.   STOCK SHOT   MOSCOW BUSINESS THOROUGHFARE
Modern office buildings, stores, etc. Street teeming with traffic.

105A.   MED. SHOT   STREET
The Davies car pulls up to the curb, the Gay Pay Oo car still behind it. Freddie gets out to open the door for Mrs. Davies. In the meantime the American ambassador's car attracts the attention of people passing in the street. Urchins run up to peer through the car windows at Mrs. Davies, who smiles and waves at them. Freddie has to hoist a couple of the boys off the running board before he can open the door.

FREDDIE (good-naturedly):

>   All right, kids, skedaddle. Please. (Timidly trying his Russian.) Pozhaluista.

The youngsters howl at Freddie's Russian accent. He now opens the door and Mrs. Davies steps out of the car.

MRS. DAVIES (to Freddie; laughing):

>   They seem to have a healthy curiosity.[33]

110

FREDDIE (grins):
I guess they never heard about private property.

Mrs. Davies turns to one small youngster who still leans over the hood, eyeing the American flag with a dreamy fascination. She looks at him for a moment, then walks over, puts an arm around his shoulders, lifts one of the flags from its standard, and presents it to the child. His face registers astonishment and delight at this incredible good luck. He marches off holding his prize, with the other urchins forming an impromptu cheering parade behind him. Mrs. Davies and Freddie look after them with amused smiles, then she turns toward the door of a building which is opposite.

MRS. DAVIES:
Freddie, I won't need the car until it's time to get Emlen at the rink.

FREDDIE:
Yes, Mrs. Davies.

She walks toward the door of a building.

WIPE TO:

106–110. OMITTED

111.   CLOSE SHOT   A WINDOW
with Russian lettering:
USSR COSMETIC FACTORY

112.   OMITTED
The CAMERA PULLS BACK and PANS TO:

113.   CLOSE SHOT   A FANCY AND VERY ATTRACTIVE DISPLAY OF
COSMETICS
containing lipstick, creams, soaps, perfume, and pow-der.

MRS. DAVIES' VOICE (OVER SCENE):
What an attractive display! That might be in a Fifth Avenue window in New York.

114.   MED. SHOT   MADAME MOLOTOV'S OFFICE
Simple and very modern. The two women are standing
in front of the display in a corner of the room. Madame
Molotov is dressed in a very simple dress.

MADAME MOLOTOV:
>Thank you, Mrs. Davies. When I became commis-
>sar of the cosmetic industry, I went to Paris to study
>their methods.

MRS. DAVIES:
>But I didn't realize that luxury trades were encour-
>aged in the Soviet Union.

MADAME MOLOTOV (smiles):
>We discovered feminine beauty was not a luxury.

MRS. DAVIES:
>I guess women are no different the world over.
>Primarily, they want to please their men.

Crossing to the desk, Madame Molotov picks up a telephone, speaks a few words in Russian: "Please bring the
tea now." She puts down the receiver.

MRS. DAVIES (taking a chair):
>I'm curious to know how the wife of the premier
>has the time to run a large industry.

MADAME MOLOTOV:
>Many of the commissars' wives have some work of
>their own. We prefer that to merely social duties.

MRS. DAVIES:
>So do I. For a number of years I ran my father's
>plant. Now I enjoy helping my husband in his
>work.

MADAME MOLOTOV:
>An American woman managing a business! (Sud-
>denly they see the humor and both laugh.) Here we
>had the impression American women were orna-

mental and not useful, and you thought that our women were useful and not ornamental.

MRS. DAVIES:
I guess we were both wrong.

MADAME MOLOTOV (with deep sincerity):
I think we have much in common, Mrs. Davies.

MRS. DAVIES:
That is a very nice compliment.

MADAME MOLOTOV:
You must come out to our dacha and we will talk over some more of our problems.

At this moment a wholesome, intelligent-appearing young girl dressed in a white smock comes into the room, wheeling a samovar and tea service. Through the opened door we see girls with packing boxes and hear factory sounds.

MADAME MOLOTOV:
Marya, I would like you to meet Mrs. Davies, wife of the American ambassador.

MRS. DAVIES:
How-do-you-do, Marya.

MARYA (forming her words very precisely):
How - do - you - do . . .

MRS. DAVIES (surprised):
Where did you learn to speak English?

MARYA:
To night school.

MADAME MOLOTOV:
At night school, Marya.

MARYA (shaking her head; smiling as she begins to pour the tea):
It is so easy to forget, Mrs. Davies.

MRS. DAVIES:
> I think you do wonderfully. (To both of them.) How proud I'd be if I did as well with Russian!

They both laugh.

MADAME MOLOTOV:
> Perhaps some day we shall all speak the same language.

115.   OMITTED

DISSOLVE TO:

115A.   EXT. RUSSIAN COUNTRY SCENE   WINTER   (STOCK)   DAY
If available from stock, a beautiful scene of the heavily wooded countryside a few miles from Moscow, in the midst of winter. The ground and the fir trees are blanketed in snow. (If a STOCK SHOT from Russian film is not found, we can probably match the locale very closely from domestic sources.)

WIPE TO:

115B.   EXT. A COUNTRY ROAD
A section of a road through the snow, with a few fir trees and leafless beeches in background. Along the road comes a horse-drawn Russian sleigh, or troika. We hear the musical jingling of sleigh bells, which are attached to the harness. As it draws nearer the CAMERA, we see three people riding in the sleigh; Major Kamenev is driving, with Emlen sitting between him and Bob Grosjean, an American. All three are warmly clad for the expedition. They are very gay and laughing.

115C.   MED. MOVING SHOT   THE SLEIGH   (PROCESS)
against a process background of snow and trees that match as closely as possible the preceding scenes. Emlen, very attractively dressed in a skating outfit, is partly covered by a heavy bearskin rug. She is greatly impressed by the beauty of the Russian winter scene.

EMLEN:

> Why, it's just like Wisconsin, Bob! The very same trees—even the hills!

GROSJEAN (smiles and nods):

> This reminds me of a Russian story I read as a kid. All we need is a wolf running behind the sleigh.

EMLEN (dryly):

> Then why don't you?

KAMENEV (not getting the joke):

> There are no wolves near Moscow, Miss Davies. You are as safe as if you were inside the embassy.

EMLEN (with a sidelong look at Grosjean):

> Well, I'm not yet sure that isn't where I met one.

Grosjean laughs and Kamenev looks at them quizzically.

EMLEN:

> I lived all my childhood in a snow country like this, Major Kamenev—and it makes me very homesick.

KAMENEV (smiles):

> Then you have the "russkaya dusha," Miss Davies—the true Russian soul that loves winter.

EMLEN:

> Thank you, Major.

GROSJEAN (pulling up his collar):

> Me—I'll take the spring.

KAMENEV:

> We have an old army proverb: "Spring is for lovers, summer for farmers, autumn for merchants, and winter for soldiers."

GROSJEAN (puzzledly):

> But how can you fellows fight in the bitter cold?

KAMENEV (with a grim smile):
  It is much more bitter to visitors, my friend—and an enemy is only a visitor to Russia.

As they ride on, Grosjean and Emlen exchange a look of amused understanding. Then suddenly Kamenev sees something ahead and points to draw the attention of the Americans.

KAMENEV:
  Look—up the hill—ahead!

All of them look.

CUT TO:

115D. EXT. SKI RUN LONG SHOT (STOCK)
  A rolling expanse of snow-covered slope, fringed by fir trees. Over the crest of the hill and down the white slope speeds a company of ski troops, clothed in white hooded parkas over their uniforms, and with rifles slung across their backs. (NOTE: There are newsreel shots of this, some very recent ones of United States ski troops, who closely resemble the Soviet ski soldiers.)[34] They race down toward the CAMERA.

115E. FULL SHOT THE SLEIGH
  as Kamenev stops the horse, and all three people watch with much interest the off-scene ski troops. (NOTE: This is a section of road only, matching as closely as possible the general scenery and terrain of the long STOCK SHOT.) Suddenly a group of eight Soviet ski troops speed down the short section of slope which is included in the set, execute a smart "telemark" stop near the sleigh, their whirling skis digging up a cloud of snow. The Soviet soldiers are big, husky, fine-looking young men. One of them is a lieutenant. He grins as he recognizes Kamenev and salutes him in a friendly manner. Their dialogue is all in Russian.

LIEUTENANT:

> Comrade Major Kamenev! Happy to see you again, sir!

KAMENEV:

> Hello, Stanitzyn. Is this your new command?

LIEUTENANT (proudly):

> Yes, Major. The finest regiment in the Army. I could never go back to the cavalry now—it's much too slow after this. (They laugh together.)

115F.   GROUP SHOT   AROUND THE SLEIGH

a wider angle, including Emlen and Grosjean with the others. The young Americans are very interested in the Soviet ski troops, as the lieutenant and Major Kamenev converse in Russian for a moment longer, Kamenev questioning and the lieutenant giving information. Then Kamenev turns to Emlen and Grosjean with a friendly smile.

KAMENEV:

> This is a crack regiment of ski troops, mostly men from Siberia and the Caucasus. They are working out a battle problem with one of our generals.

GROSJEAN (surprised):

> You don't mean there's actually a *general* in charge of your ski troops?

KAMENEV:

> Yes, of course. They are many thousand men.

GROSJEAN (interested):

> I thought it was just a publicity stunt for the newsreels—but this sounds like an army!

Kamenev nods with a slight smile and looks toward the main mass of ski troops on the slopes beyond, off-scene.

KAMENEV:

> Some day perhaps you will hear of this army—and its general . . . His name is Timoshenko.

Kamenev and the lieutenant exchange good-byes in Russian and, as the sleigh drives away, Emlen and Grosjean wave back to the soldiers.

115G.   FULL SHOT   THE EIGHT SKI TROOPS
as they look after the departing sleigh, their strong faces smiling. One or two of them wave in reply. The lieutenant turns back to them, picks up his ski sticks, issues a crisp order in Russian, and they move away across the snow-packed road.

DISSOLVE TO:

116.   EXT. A MOSCOW SKATING RINK   LONG SHOT   DAY
(PROBABLY WITH GLASS BACKGROUND SHOT)   WINTER
A small rink in one of Moscow's parks, with an interesting section of the city beyond, extending to a far distance on the glass painting background, giving a feeling of extensive spaciousness. In middle foreground is the rink, busy with moving skaters of all ages, but mostly young men and women. It is early winter and around the edges of the skating area are several snowbanks, as if from the snow which has been swept from the rink. A small, heavily bundled orchestra is playing a lively tune.

117.   MED. FULL PANNING SHOT   THE SKATERS
A group of skaters in an extended line, holding hands, come speeding toward the CAMERA. Most of them are young Russian men and women, including a couple of soldiers. On one end of the line are Emlen and Paul Grosjean, an attractive and personable young man of twenty-seven or so, an American mining engineer. Emlen is wearing a skating costume, but of Russian style and not conspicuously expensive. The line of skaters laugh and shout as they race over the ice. Then the "anchor man" stops suddenly, braces himself, and swings the line in a "snap-the-whip." Yelling excitedly, the line swings around, and Emlen and Paul are snapped off the far end of the "whip." The CAMERA PANS QUICKLY

with them as they speed alone across the rink at a fast
clip, while the others laugh and yell. As they approach
the edge of the rink Paul tries to stop, but Emlen's hand
slips from his grip and with a loud squeal she races on
alone, then plunges head-foremost into a large snowbank.

118.   MED. FULL SHOT   SNOWBANK   AT EDGE OF RINK
Emlen is almost completely engulfed in the snowbank
as Paul hurries up, grinning. He and two or three other
skaters who are passing by pull Emlen out and help her
to her feet. She is laughing, but is covered with snow.
One of the Russians who has paused to help Paul is a
tall, dark girl with a pleasant face. Her name is Tanya.
As she helps Emlen brush off the wet snow, she offers
friendly advice.

TANYA:
   Tebia by luchshe pit chaiu goriachego prezhde ti
   zamorazhivaesh.

Emlen smiles hesitantly, not understanding, and looks
at Paul for help.

PAUL:
   She says you had better have some hot tea before
   you freeze to death.

Emlen smiles at the Russian girl.

EMLEN:
   Thank you— (Hesitantly tries her Russian.)
   Spasibo—

Tanya smiles back, glances at Paul, and replies in English with a slight accent.

TANYA:
   Are you both Americans? (They nod.) Are you
   married—yes?

Emlen and Paul glance at each other quickly, a bit flus-

119

tered and perhaps secretly a bit pleased. They smile and
shake their heads.

PAUL:

> No. I'm a mining engineer—on a little vacation
> from Stalingrad. (He nods to Emlen.) Her father
> just blackmailed me into being a nursemaid.

EMLEN (gives him a look; then to Tanya):

> Don't you believe it. He's been camping on my
> doorstep for two solid weeks!

Paul laughs and Tanya smiles, then seriously to Emlen:

TANYA:

> I meant that about the tea. May I get it for you?

Emlen thanks her graciously; they turn and skate off
together.

QUICK DISSOLVE TO:

119.   CLOSE SHOT   TEA GLASSES   ON A BUFFET TABLE
as glasses are put down, empty. The table has on it
several items of Russian food, perhaps in a sort of warm-
ing apparatus.

CAMERA PULLS BACK TO:

120.   GROUP SHOT   AT THE TABLE
Emlen and the Russian girl are in the foreground, Paul
and the escort are talking in the background. The orchestra is now playing a very gay and lively tune. Russian couples are dancing on skates to the music, whirling rapidly and cleverly. The other skaters drift up to
watch, until soon there's a good-sized crowd laughing
and clapping in tune with the music, some of them calling gaily in Russian to the dancing couples.

EMLEN (as she watches):

> What do they dance generally in Russia?

GIRL:

> That depends on the kind of dance.

EMLEN:
> At a diplomatic ball?

GIRL:
> Oh, mostly waltzes.

EMLEN:
> I was afraid so. It'll probably be a very dull party. Both Daddy and I get bored at anything formal. But we have to go.

GIRL (looking at Emlen with more interest):
> Your father's in the diplomatic corps?

EMLEN:
> Yes, the American.

GIRL:
> The new ambassador? (Emlen nods.) Of course. The ball is being given for him at Spiridonovka.

EMLEN (surprised):
> How did you know?

GIRL (smiles):
> I live there.

EMLEN:
> What!

GIRL (holds to Emlen):
> I'm glad you're coming, Miss Davies. My name is Tanya Litvinov.

Emlen's mouth opens and closes in mute astonishment as she gives Tanya her hand.

TANYA:
> Tonight we shall play some American fox trots.

DISSOLVE TO:

120A.   FOYER SPIRIDONOVKA 17   NIGHT
The CAMERA PICKS UP Mrs. Litvinov talking with Mr. Davies. In the background late guests are arriving. SOUNDS of the party off-scene.

MRS. LITVINOV:
    . . . Now don't let my husband take up your whole evening with politics. This is your party and I want you to enjoy it.

DAVIES (laughs):
    The funny thing is, Mrs. Litvinov, I find I'm beginning to enjoy *politics*.

MRS. LITVINOV (shakes her head):
    Apparently it's a very contagious disease.

120B.   MED. FULL SHOT   INT. FOYER BALLROOM
    As Madame Litvinov and Davies pause near the doorway, we see Molotov and Madame Molotov just emerging from a group of guests in background. Madame Litvinov turns to greet them.

MADAME LITVINOV:
    It's nice to see you both.

MADAME MOLOTOV:
    Thank you, Ivy.

MADAME LITVINOV:
    Ambassador Davies—may I present the Premier and Madame Molotov? (They smile and nod.)

DAVIES:
    Thank you, the premier and I have already met. (They smile and he turns to Madame Molotov.) Madame Molotov, a pleasure. I visited one of your cosmetic factories on my tour of the Ukraine. It was extremely interesting.

MADAME MOLOTOV (pleased):
    Thank you, Mr. Davies—will you excuse us, please?

The men bow slightly and the two women walk out of SHOT, the CAMERA STAYING with Davies and Molotov.[35]

MOLOTOV:

You know, Mr. Davies, this is the first formal reception the Soviet Union has ever given to a foreign diplomat.

DAVIES:

So I understand, sir. It's a great honor to my country. This is a pleasure.

MOLOTOV:

For us, Mr. Ambassador.

As the two men shake hands the women turn away, talking. Among the arriving guests in the background is a man later identified as Bukharin.

MOLOTOV (warmly):

Mr. Kalinin told me about your visit. Everyone here is very grateful that you are America's representative.

DAVIES:

No one is more grateful than I, Mr. Molotov.

121.   FULL SHOT   THE RECEPTION ROOM   NIGHT
filled with the visiting diplomats in Moscow, their families, and a large number of their official hosts representing various commissariats of the Russian government. The white high-vaulted room with crystal chandeliers ablaze is an impressive setting for the gaily attired company of political and social celebrities, many of whom we identify later in the course of the scene. Women are in evening gown, men in full dress or uniform. Beyond the White Room separated by Gothic arches is a smaller room that contains buffet tables and a well-stocked bar served by "chefs" in tall white hats and coats. On a small balcony at one end of the White Room is the orchestra that is playing American dance music. Some of the guests are dancing, others are lounging in

tapestried chairs and couches. Waiters weave in and out, passing hors d'oeuvres and vodka in cut crystal decanters. All ages and many races and nationalities are represented in this gay and colorful assemblage. (The design of the scene is, first, to show the party on its surface—charming, gay, and friendly—then to suggest the intrigue and corruption under its pleasant exterior.)

THE CAMERA PULLS UP TO:

122.   MED. SHOT   PORTION OF THE DANCE FLOOR
where we see Emlen dancing with a Red Army officer, later identified as Tukhachevsky.[36] Dancing near them are Tanya and Paul Grosjean, who gazes after Emlen with a wistful expression, which Tanya notices.

123.   CLOSE TRUCKING SHOT   TANYA AND PAUL

TANYA:
Don't worry over Emlen, Paul. Marshal Tukhachevsky has a lady love of his own.

PAUL (miserably):
Well, why didn't he bring her?

124.   CLOSE TRUCKING SHOT   EMLEN AND TUKHACHEVSKY
as they dance. Tukhachevsky wears the uniform of a vice-marshal of the Red Army. He is middle-aged, with a face that is somewhat soft and boyish.

TUKHACHEVSKY (in a flattering tone):
. . . And you've read Karl Marx?

EMLEN:
It was required reading in sociology. I can't say I enjoyed it.

TUKHACHEVSKY:
Perhaps if you looked into it again, now that you've been in Russia—

EMLEN (archly):
> Marshal Tukhachevsky, you wouldn't be trying to convert me by any chance?

Tukhachevsky laughs, then changes the subject.

TUKHACHEVSKY:
> Miss Davies, some time I want you and your family to be my guests at the ballet. (Smiles.) On the matter of art, I think we'll find it easier to agree.

At this moment Litvinov and Mrs. Davies dance into the SHOT. Emlen waves at her mother, who smiles and waves back.

125. CLOSE TRUCKING SHOT   MRS. DAVIES AND LITVINOV
as they dance.

MRS. DAVIES:
> . . . I suppose most of us in America still think of European diplomacy as it used to be—intrigues whispered behind a fan.

LITVINOV (smiles):
> Well, we no longer have the fans.

They stop dancing in front of three men (later identified as defendants in the "purge" trial) who immediately turn toward the approaching couple.[37]

LITVINOV:
> Mrs. Davies, may I present Mr. Bukharin, editor of *Izvestia* . . . and Mr. Radek, our most distinguished journalist . . . and Mr. Yagoda, commissar of internal affairs.

They all smile and bow.

BUKHARIN:
> How-do-you-do, Mrs. Davies.

MRS. DAVIES:
> How-do-you-do, gentlemen.

YAGODA (to Mrs. Davies):
> We were all envying Commissar Litvinov his agreeable duty.

MRS. DAVIES (laughs):
> And I was told chivalry was discouraged in Russia.

RADEK:
> My dear Mrs. Davies, you can't discourage human nature.

126.   MED. SHOT   OTHER SECTION OF THE ROOM
Madame Litvinov is talking with Lord and Lady Chilston, the English ambassador and his wife. They are a typical English couple. The vodka has the ambassador in good spirits.[38]

CHILSTON (jokingly):
> Now, Madame Litvinov, as one Englishman to another, won't you admit the whole experiment is rather against human nature?[39]

MADAME LITVINOV:
> *Whose* human nature, Lord Chilston?

The English ambassador gives Madame Litvinov a quick, surprised glance, but she is smiling sweetly at Lady Chilston, who is gushing oil on the troubled waters.

LADY CHILSTON:
> This is such a lovely party, my dear. (Leans closer, whispers.) Who is that distinguished-looking man with the stars on his uniform . . . there talking with Mr. Davies?

MADAME LITVINOV (following her gaze; speaks casually):
> A marshal of the Red Army . . . Timoshenko.

126A.   MED. CLOSE SHOT   DAVIES AND TIMOSHENKO
Each holds a glass in his hand as they talk. Timoshenko

is a striking-looking man, bald, strong, solid. He wears the uniform of a Red Army marshal.

DAVIES:

> From what I've heard, Marshal, the Russian army has been developing an entirely new technique of warfare.

TIMOSHENKO (quietly):

> Only a modern army will be able to fight a modern war, Your Excellency. We have the men—we will soon have the machines—and we have a powerful ally.

DAVIES:

> Who is that?

TIMOSHENKO (with a faint smile):

> General Winter.

DAVIES:

> Winter? I never heard of him.

TIMOSHENKO (dryly):

> Napoleon did . . .[40]

In background, a little farther down the table, Litvinov strolls up to a group of guests during the above dialogue, talks with them for a few seconds, then sees Davies and Timoshenko. He comes over to them in foreground on Davies' last line and places a friendly hand on Timoshenko's shoulder.

LITVINOV:

> I heard in Geneva about your promotion, Timoshenko. Congratulations.

TIMOSHENKO (smiles):

> Thank you.

DAVIES (to Litvinov):

> I've been meaning to ask you about your trip. How are things in Geneva?

As Litvinov shakes his head sadly, Marshal Timoshenko smiles at them slightly and bows with a half-salute.

TIMOSHENKO:
 If you'll excuse me, gentlemen—I'm only a soldier.

They smile and Timoshenko strolls away. Litvinov takes Davies' arm.

LITVINOV:
 Come, let us have a cigar together.

They start toward a corner. The CAMERA PANS AWAY from them and PULLS UP to Tanya, who is talking with Shigemitsu, the Japanese ambassador. He is a lame man with a quiet, ominous charm, but outwardly very friendly.[41]

SHIGEMITSU:
 I hear that you have done some parachute jumping, Miss Litvinov.

TANYA:
 Yes, I'm a student in the reserve corps. We practice every week.

SHIGEMITSU:
 So! Are there a great many of you?

TANYA:
 I'm afraid I really don't know, Mr. Shigemitsu. (Innocently.) How many parachutists do you have in Japan?[42]

Shigemitsu smiles at her counter. At this moment Colonel Faymonville comes up with a friendly smile.

COLONEL FAYMONVILLE (bows):
 Miss Litvinov . . .

TANYA:
 Colonel, do you know Ambassador Shigemitsu?

COLONEL FAYMONVILLE:
> Yes, of course. We met years ago in Tokyo.

Shigemitsu nods with a smile and speaks to Tanya.

SHIGEMITSU:
> Colonel Faymonville is a great student of Japan. He has worked very hard to understand us.

COLONEL FAYMONVILLE:
> Thank you, sir. It is quite a difficult subject. (Turns to Tanya.) Would you care to dance, Miss Litvinov?

TANYA:
> Yes, thank you.

They nod politely to Shigemitsu and turn away together.

CUT TO:

126B.   LADY CHILSTON, VON RIBBENTROP, AND VON SCHULENBERG

LADY CHILSTON:
> I was very surprised to see you here, Herr von Ribbentrop. I had no idea you were in Moscow.

VON RIBBENTROP:
> A matter of business, Lady Chilston. But I miss London very much.[43]

VON SCHULENBERG (laughs):
> Herr von Ribbentrop is extremely partial to you English people.

LADY CHILSTON (a little lacking in enthusiasm):
> Indeed . . .

CUT TO:

127.   MED. SHOT   CORNER OF ALCOVE
Davies is holding a light for Litvinov's cigar.

LITVINOV:
> Since Ethiopia, all the countries in the League are frightened. No one trusts anyone else.

DAVIES:

> Yet here they all seem perfectly friendly and cordial.

LITVINOV:

> On the surface, yes. But how do we know what goes on underneath . . . ? We in Russia have learned to judge our neighbors by what they do, and not by what their representatives say. And what is happening in the world today? Not a very pleasant prospect, Mr. Davies.

At this point the CAMERA TRAVELS "on its own" here and there about the reception, pointing up and illustrating Litvinov's analysis. Thus this room becomes the diplomatic world in miniature. Part of the time Litvinov's voice will continue OVER SCENE when the action is in pantomime; at other times the sound track will follow the CAMERA. At no time will the narration refer specifically, but only by inference to what takes place in the room. Those are merely the concrete and illuminating evidences by which the audience may interpret the general comments of Litvinov.

128. LONG SHOT   THE BUFFET TABLE
(FROM ANGLE OF DAVIES AND LITVINOV)
At one end is the Chinese ambassador, Tsiang Ting-Fu. On the other is the Japanese representative, Shigemitsu, each selecting some hors d'oeuvres. As they finish they look up at the same moment. Their eyes hold for an instant, then they move abruptly off in opposite directions.

LITVINOV'S VOICE (OVER SCENE):

> One nation has already invaded another without provocation or excuse, and contrary to its League obligations.

129. MED. SHOT   LITVINOV AND DAVIES
Litvinov continues his analysis:

LITVINOV:

. . . Still another aggressor is attempting to overthrow the legal government of its neighbor by sending men and equipment to support a revolt.

130.   MED. SHOT   THE WHITE ROOM

The Italian ambassador, Rosso, stands with Molotov on one side, Vyshinsky on the other. A plate of olives is passed by one of the servants. Rosso reaches to take one, then hesitates.

ROSSO:

Italian olives, Mr. Molotov?

MOLOTOV:

No, Spanish.[44]

Rosso draws his hand back. Molotov and Vyshinsky exchange glances.

131.   CLOSE SHOT   GENERAL VON KOESTRICH AND
       VON RIBBENTROP

The military attaché of the German embassy—typically Prussian in appearance—is talking quietly with Ribbentrop. He is at the buffet table, carrying a plate brimming over with cheese and sausages. And now he heaps on top of this a mound of caviar.

LITVINOV'S VOICE (OVER SCENE):

. . . while another aggressor nation with far greater ambitions is building up a vast military machine ready to turn in any direction.

132.   MED. SHOT   DAVIES AND LITVINOV

LITVINOV:

. . . No one knows where the blow will fall. The little nations tremble, trying to walk the tightrope between the great powers. Their only defense is their utter helplessness.

133.   MED. SHOT   THE BUFFET TABLE
A small, rather timid man approaches the table near
General von Koestrich, who is still selecting delicacies
from the table. The newcomer is about to speak to the
German when Lord Chilston appears at the other side of
the table. The little man decides not to speak to either,
but he nods and smiles eagerly at both. They nod back
briefly and he turns and walks quickly out of the SHOT.

LITVINOV'S VOICE (OVER SCENE during this pantomime):
    But whom can they trust? On whom can they de-
    pend? It's the devil's gamble. So they smile on
    everyone and hope for the best. The weaker the
    country, the stronger the smile.

134.   MED. SHOT   DAVIES AND LITVINOV

LITVINOV:
    . . . But what of the great powers who could op-
    pose aggression? (Puffs his cigar angrily.) Instead of
    standing together, they make deals with the
    enemy. They even have a lovely new word for it
    now. They call it appeasement. That is what I've
    had to contend with, my friend.

135.   MED. SHOT
Madame Litvinov talking with Coulondre, the French
ambassador.

MADAME LITVINOV:
    Why aren't you dancing tonight, M'sieur
    Coulondre?

COULONDRE:
    Ah, madame, we have to be so careful these days in
    choosing our partners. The last time—

At this moment he becomes aware of others approaching. He leans over, finishes with a whisper in Madame
Litvinov's ear. She laughs heartily. In the background of

the shot we see Lord Chilston and General von Koestrich now crossing the floor together, each carrying his plate of hors d'oeuvres.[45]

136. MED. SHOT   DAVIES AND LITVINOV

LITVINOV:

. . . And that is not the whole story, Mr. Davies. (Pauses, his expression troubled.) Not all our enemies are outside Russia. They also have agents working in our midst to create havoc and distrust.

DAVIES (in surprise):

Traitors? Your own people?

LITVINOV:

Mr. Davies, you will recall the proud statement made recently by a Fascist general—"We have four columns in front of Madrid and a fifth—inside the city."

Davies looks at him intently a moment and nods, then soberly:

DAVIES:

The fifth column . . . It's hard for most Americans to realize these things, with two great oceans between us and our possible enemies.

LITVINOV (significantly):

Do not rely too much on isolation, my friend. Oceans are not as wide as they used to be.[46]

At this moment Krestinsky, whom we last saw in the Kremlin scene, comes up into SHOT and pauses respectfully a few feet away. He looks intensely serious about something. Litvinov sees him and raises a slightly quizzical eyebrow.

LITVINOV:

Yes, Krestinky?

133

KRESTINSKY:

> I beg your pardon—may I speak to you for a moment?

Litvinov rises and turns to Davies, who also stands.

LITVINOV (smiles):

> Forgive me, Mr. Ambassador—whenever Krestinsky wants to see me, it's business.

DAVIES (smiles):

> Of course, sir.

Litvinov and Krestinsky walk quickly away.[47]

137–39. INT. LITVINOV'S PRIVATE STUDY

> A moderately sized, very comfortable room, lined with bookshelves, a few Russian pictures and framed autographed pictures of international political celebrities. As Litvinov and Krestinsky enter, Molotov is standing beside the desk, speaking on the telephone. Sokolnikov and Grinko stand beside him. Molotov's face is tense, serious.

MOLOTOV:

> Yes—yes, I understand— (Sees Litvinov come up.) It's Kommodov, manager of the magnesium plant at Kharkov. (Back into phone.) Go ahead. What has happened?

WIPE TO:

140. INT. OFFICE MAGNESIUM

PLANT KHARKOV (PROCESS)   NIGHT

> Through the window of the office we see flame and smoke boiling upward from a mass of wreckage. First-aid workers pass by, carrying bodies wrapped in sheets. There is a roar of exploding chemicals and the confusion of shouting rescue workers. The manager, Kommodov, is a strong-faced man of forty. He is streaked with grime and smoke stains.

KOMMODOV:
> There's been an explosion. The plant is completely
> wrecked. Several hundred workers on the night
> shift have been killed. It's impossible to determine
> right away what caused the explosion, but we have
> reasons to believe it was an act of sabotage.

141.   INT. LITVINOV'S STUDY

MOLOTOV (into phone):
> This will be investigated immediately, Kommodov.
> Do not talk with anyone about it until you hear
> from me. I'll expect a report from you later tonight,
> and again in the morning. Give me complete details
> when you call.

He hangs up the telephone, looks at Krestinsky, then at
Litvinov.

MOLOTOV (quietly):
> Sabotage—the plant destroyed.

LITVINOV (his face hardens):
> The fifth since March—and each time a defense in-
> dustry. (Molotov nods.)

KRESTINSKY (anxiously):
> But how are you sure it *was* sabotage, Comrade
> Molotov? Was someone caught?

MOLOTOV (quietly):
> We will know that tomorrow, Krestinsky—[48]

CUT TO:

142.   MED. SHOT   DAVIES
He stands up and starts to rejoin the dancers when the
Japanese ambassador, Shigemitsu, comes up into the
SHOT and joins him. Shigemitsu is smiling as he extends
his hand.

SHIGEMITSU:
> Ah, Mr. Davies—

DAVIES:

Mr. Shigemitsu.

SHIGEMITSU:

My government has asked me to give you a personal message for your president.

DAVIES:

Yes?[49]

SHIGEMITSU (glibly):

Please, tell President Roosevelt that Japan desires only America's good will and cooperation to keep peace in the Pacific . . . (He pauses, but Davies says nothing.) The "China Incident" will soon be settled to our mutual satisfaction. After all, this is a matter of concern only to Greater Asia.

He is still smiling blandly as Davies looks at him intently for a moment.

DAVIES (coldly polite):

Thank you, Mr. Shigemitsu. As the ambassador, I will convey your message to my president. (Now dropping his diplomatic tone, he speaks out bluntly.) But between ourselves, Mr. Shigemitsu, if Japan had wanted peace so passionately, there would *be* no "China Incident."

He turns and walks away, the Japanese ambassador staring after him. The CAMERA PANS with Davies, who walks into the White Room. He passes a group of men who are talking intently. They are the same men we saw previously—Bukharin, Radek, and Yagoda—but this time Marshal Tukhachevsky is with them. The CAMERA STAYS on them for a moment, then PANS TO:

143.   FULL SHOT   THE WHITE ROOM

There is much laughter and conversation. Couples begin to dance again. On its surface, the party seems gayer than ever.

SLOW DISSOLVE TO:

144. EXT. MOSCOW STREET   NIGHT
     IN FRONT OF SPIRIDONOVKA 17
     Distant sound of music from inside the house. Bukharin
     walks down to the curb and motions to a taxi parked a
     short distance from where he stands. He takes out a
     cigarette as the taxi drives up.

145. CLOSE MED. SHOT   BUKHARIN (SHOOTING TOWARD THE
     CAB)

     BUKHARIN (to driver):
         Dmit Rovka 16.

     The driver throws open the back door. Before he enters,
     Bukharin pauses to light his cigarette. As he strikes the
     match he sees a figure in the back seat of the cab. The
     man speaks the moment he is noticed.

     MAN:
         The state prosecutor has some questions to ask you,
         Bukharin. You will come with me.

     An expression of terror crosses Bukharin's face. Then he
     quickly composes himself and finishes lighting his
     cigarette.

     BUKHARIN:
         Very well. (Climbs into the cab.)[50]

                                                      WIPE TO:

146. FULL SHOT   YAGODA'S OUTER OFFICE   DAY
     A secretary—a young man of thirty-five—is seated at a
     desk near a door marked Private—People's Commissar
     of Internal Affairs. The door on the other side of the
     room opens abruptly and two police officers enter from
     the corridor. The secretary looks up in amazement at the
     intrusion. Without any explanation, the two men walk
     past his desk to the door of the private office.

147. CLOSE SHOT   YAGODA
seated at his desk. He is looking up with terror as footsteps approach.

WIPE TO:

148. MED. SHOT   A BOOKSHOP   DAY
having the atmosphere of an ancient and dusty habitat of book lovers. Books are piled carelessly in stalls. A bookseller, advanced in years, with a serene, scholarly face, is handing a wrapped book to Krestinsky (introduced to Davies in the Kremlin scene). A young woman, wearing glasses, who might be a schoolteacher, is turning the pages of a book, but at the same time scrutinizing the transaction with Krestinsky.

BOOKSELLER:
Your change, Mr. Krestinsky.

KRESTINSKY:
Thank you.

At that moment the young woman slams the book shut. At this sound, Krestinsky and the bookseller look up in alarm. Police officers appear from nowhere, converging on the two men.

DISSOLVE TO:

149. CLOSE-UP   A CONDUCTOR OF MUSIC   NIGHT
turning the pages of the score, which is in the foreground and bears the title *Kavkazski Plennik* (The Prisoner of the Caucasus) or (alternate to be determined by available stock footage).
    Ballet music OVER SCENE. CAMERA PANS UP from the conductor, over the orchestra, to:

150. FULL SHOT   THE STAGE   BALLET   (STOCK)
The ballet is in full progress. (The detail shots of this ballet will have to be determined by the best available STOCK SHOTS of the Russian Ballet. The amount of footage for which the performance will be held will be gov-

erned by this and by the director's and cutter's staging
of this entire sequence.)

151.   INT. AMBASSADOR'S BOX   MOSCOW THEATER
in which are seated Mr. and Mrs. Davies, and in back of
them, Emlen and Marshal Tukhachevsky, all intently
watching the ballet. (The men occupy the inside seats of
the box, so that the marshal's seat in the rear is nearest
the exit.)

152.   SINGLE SHOT   THE STAGE   FROM THE DAVIESES' BOX
(PROCESS)
SHOOTING PAST the group in close foreground to the
stage, where the ballerina is dancing, or the troupe with
her, dependent upon the most impressive shots available. Mrs. Davies half-turns to Tukhachevsky and
whispers excitedly.

MRS. DAVIES:
It's a brilliant performance—really dazzling! (He
nods with a polite smile.)

DAVIES (leans toward him):
Who is the ballerina?

TUKHACHEVSKY:
Ulanova. They compare her to Pavlova.

EMLEN (equally thrilled):
I like it even better than the Ballet Russe in New
York.

TUKHACHEVSKY:
This is the *real* Ballet Russe, Miss Davies.

They all smile at Emlen's flustered look, then look back
to the stage, where the music and dancing is continu-
ous.

153.   FULL SHOT   THE STAGE   (STOCK)
held briefly for more of the ballet.

154. DAVIESES' BOX   (SHOOTING FROM THE REAR OVER THE
      SHOULDERS OF EMLEN AND TUKHACHEVSKY)
      Suddenly a man appears from the curtains close to the
      marshal's side. He puts a hand on Tukhachevsky's
      shoulder as he leans down to speak to him.

      MAN (low voice):
          Marshal Tukhachevsky, would you come with me,
          please.

      Tukhachevsky looks up at the man for a moment, then
      nods without replying. He rises very quietly and follows
      the man through the curtain. The Davies group is so
      intent on the ballet that they do not notice the marshal's
      disappearance. Ballet music CONTINUES OVER SCENE.

                                                 CUT TO:

155. MED. SHOT   ANOTHER BOX
      Ambassador Shigemitsu and another Japanese diplomat
      are seated in the box. Shigemitsu glances off-scene with
      concern. His companion looks at him questioningly,
      then Shigemitsu takes out a lighted pencil and draws an
      arrow on the back of his program. The other Japanese
      looks at the arrow and then glances in the direction
      toward which it points.

156. FULL SHOT   THE DAVIESES' BOX   (FROM THE ANGLE OF
      THE JAPANESE)
      Tukhachevsky's chair is empty.

157. MED. SHOT   THE DAVIESES' BOX
      as Emlen, noticing the empty chair, leans over to touch
      her father's arm. Their puzzled glances converge on the
      empty chair.

                                             DISSOLVE TO:

158. MONTAGE   NEWS OF THE ARRESTS   (WITH INSERTS)
      An exciting MONTAGE as the first news of the Soviet
      purge hits the world. This should be given an interest-
      ing arrangement, perhaps with DOUBLE EXPOSURE SHOTS

of the newspaper headlines, stock background shots of the various cities, telegraph wires, cable offices, etc. The total impression desired is one of great international excitement.

The newspaper headlines announce boldly:

(London Daily Mail)
MYSTERY SURROUNDS SOVIET ARRESTS

(Paris Soir [In French])
HIGH RUSSIAN LEADERS IMPRISONED!

(New York Herald Tribune)
PURGE SWEEPS MOSCOW

(Chicago Tribune)
RED ARMY REPORTED MARCHING
ON MOSCOW

(Melbourne Times)
SOVIET PURGE SURROUNDED BY
MYSTERY

The bold word MYSTERY flashes across the MONTAGE in larger and larger type.

159. SERIES OF QUICK SHOTS   (OR CONTINUED MONTAGE) establishing the bewilderment of the rest of the world over the Soviet arrests.

1. NEWSPAPER OFFICE (American)
An excited cable editor is dictating to a cable telegrapher who sends from his machine.

EDITOR:
Tell our man in Moscow to cable at once the meaning of these Soviet arrests!

2. OFFICE OF NEWS AGENCY (London)
Perhaps the Reuter's office. A British newspaper executive is on the telephone.

BRITISHER:
> Give us more information from Moscow. What are
> the charges against the defendants?

3. OFFICE OF FRENCH NEWS AGENCY (Paris)
A French news executive is on the telephone, his eager
assistants beside him.

FRENCHMAN (at telephone; to be translated into French):
> No, no . . . We can do our own guessing . . .
> What we want is the truth . . . Why are these men
> arrested? (To the other man.) They cannot say—the
> censor.

4. GERMAN STATE OFFICE
as an official is giving instructions to a subordinate.

OFFICIAL (in German):
> Try von Schulenburg in Moscow. We must know
> what is behind these arrests . . . And hurry.

OFFICER (in German):
> Yes, sir. (Salutes and turns away.)

160.   MONTAGE OF TELEPHONE EXCHANGES, HIGH-TENSION
       WIRES, SHORT-WAVE TRANSMITTERS, ETC.
       handling a barrage of rapid-fire questions in all lan-
       guages.

VOICES:
> What is happening in Moscow? Have the defend-
> ants been executed? Was ist in Moskau passiert? Is
> Stalin purging the army? Is the Red Army marching
> on Moscow? (In French.) Macht das Russland eine
> Revolution gegen Stalin? Our public demands the
> news.[51]

DISSOLVE TO:

161.   MED. SHOT   DAVIES'S OFFICE AT THE EMBASSY   DAY
       A group of American news correspondents are gathered
       around the ambassador's desk, firing excited questions

and comments at him. Henderson is present, also Colonel Faymonville, the military attaché. The atmosphere of the meeting is tense, electric.

FIRST NEWSPAPERMAN:
    . . . Is it a party feud, Mr. Ambassador, or are these men really guilty of conspiracy against the Soviet government?

DAVIES:
    I'm not a mind reader, Charley, and I haven't any more information than you.

SECOND NEWSPAPERMAN:
    My guess is, they're guilty. I don't know what *of*, but—

THIRD NEWSPAPERMAN (heatedly):
    Men like Bukharin and Tukhachevsky? Don't be foolish, Walter. Those two guys are as solid Soviets as the Kremlin walls!

FOURTH NEWSPAPERMAN:
    Sure! Both of 'em are old friends of Uncle Joe's. And so is Yagoda!

THIRD NEWSPAPERMAN:
    Why it's just as if back home the FBI locked up most of the cabinet, the Supreme Court justices and part of Congress!

DAVIES (breaking in):
    Listen, boys, if you want my advice, don't jump to any wild conclusions until you know the facts. Wait for the trials.

FIRST NEWSPAPERMAN:
    Yes, sir—but in the meantime our newspapers are going crazy and we can't send 'em a line!

DAVIES (dryly):
    Well, at the rate they're inventing it, you don't need

to worry. And maybe when the truth comes out,
you'll find it stranger than fiction.

DISSOLVE TO:

162.   INT. SOVIET MILITARY COURT   DAY
MED. CLOSE SHOT
Vyshinsky, state prosecutor, walks up to the CAMERA,
speaking toward an unseen defendant who is behind
the CAMERA.

VYSHINSKY:

Accused Yagoda, do you admit the conversation
with Pyatakov about putting the Kemerova Chemi-
cal Works out of action?

The CAMERA PULLS BACK to include Yagoda, whom Vyshinsky is questioning.

YAGODA (speaks bluntly, as though the exposure of his
crimes was a matter of complete indifference):
Yes, Citizen Prosecutor. It was part of our plan to
cripple defense industries.

163.   MED. SHOT   THE COURTROOM
Vyshinsky faces Yagoda, who stands in the prisoners'
dock. In the background eight or ten other prisoners are
visible, among whom we recognize Radek, Krestinsky,
and Bukharin. On the platform above them are Judge
Ulrich and three other judges, two of whom are in uniform. Soldiers with bayoneted guns guard the prisoners' box.
Vyshinsky's manner of putting questions is detached
and dispassionate, except for quick flashes of biting sar-
casm or angry thrusts when he is cornering a prisoner
into an unwilling admission.

VYSHINSKY:

Did you consider the fact, in carrying out your purpose, that workers in the factory were bound to be
killed?

144

YAGODA:
> Loss of life was inevitable. Once we determined on our course of action, we couldn't afford to be finicky about sacrificing a few lives.

164. MED. LONG SHOT (SHOOTING TOWARD THE PRISONERS FROM A REVERSE ANGLE)
In the background we see the sections reserved to the press and foreign embassies among the front rows of the spectators of the trial. Directly opposite the prisoners' dock sit Davies, Henderson, and Faymonville. Across an aisle are Count von Schulenberg and General von Koestrich. In another row are some Japanese diplomats, among them Shigemitsu. Behind them are English, French, and Italian representatives. A row with small desks is occupied by the press, among whom we recognize the news correspondents of the previous scene. Everyone in the crowded room is intently following the testimony. Some of them, including Davies, make occasional notes as the trial progresses.

VYSHINSKY (turning toward another prisoner in the dock, who rises when he is addressed):
> Pyatakov, were you equally agreeable to sacrificing the lives of innocent men for the sake of your . . . shall we say, ambitious plans?

PYATAKOV (hesitating):
> Well, that is more or less . . .

VYSHINSKY (interrupts with sudden fury):
> Don't answer me "more or less." I realize it is of course somewhat inconvenient for you to admit these things in public. But there is nothing to be done about it. Did you in effect agree with Yagoda that if workers were to perish as a result of your acts of terrorism, well, let them perish? Yes or no?

PYATAKOV (after a moment's pause):
> Yes.

VYSHINSKY:

> That, at least, is a frank answer . . . Now, Citizen Yagoda, you have admitted that these numerous acts of terrorism and sabotage were part of a general plan to weaken the Soviet Union. Did you help to formulate this program?

YAGODA (after a moment's pause):

> I helped, but in the main, the program was Trotsky's.

A murmur goes up over the courtroom.

165. PAN SHOT   OVER THE DIPLOMATS' SECTION OF SPECTATORS starting with Davies and moving along the row. Glances and whispered conversations are exchanged among the diplomats, all reflecting the serious turn that the trial is taking at this point.

VYSHINKY'S VOICE (OVER SCENE; during this PANNING SHOT):

> Do you make this statement from personal knowledge?

YAGODA'S VOICE (OVER SCENE):

> I didn't see Trotsky, if that's what you mean. He was out of the country.

166. MED. SHOT   VYSHINSKY AND YAGODA
Other prisoners in the background.

VYSHINSKY (dryly):

> Yes, I'm aware of that . . . Then how did you know it was Trotsky's orders you were following?

YAGODA:

> Because he sent us letters of instruction. Besides that, one of us was in direct contact with him.

VYSHINSKY:

> Which one of you?

YAGODA (turns slowly toward a fellow prisoner):
Krestinsky.

Another murmur rises in the courtroom.

167.   CLOSE SHOT   KRESTINSKY
looking ten years older than when we last saw him. He rises as the prosecutor addresses him.

VYSHINSKY'S VOICE (OVER SCENE):
Accused Krestinsky, did you hear the statement Yagoda just made?

KRESTINSKY:
Well . . . most of it.

The CAMERA PULLS UP to a WIDER ANGLE that includes Vyshinsky.

VYSHINSKY (thundering):
Most of it! You're sitting right next to him. Are you hard of hearing?

KRESTINSKY (in a pitiful whisper):
No, I'm not.

VYSHINSKY (turning to Yagoda, points at Krestinsky):
Yagoda, do you recognize this man as the one you referred to in connection with Trotsky?

168.   CLOSE SHOT   DAVIES
his hand over his eyes as though deeply affected by Krestinsky's plight.

YAGODA (OVER SCENE; in a voice intended to show his scorn):
He is the same man, although he seemed quite different at the time.

Davies raises his head, gazes again toward the prisoners' dock.

169. CLOSE SHOT   KRESTINSKY

as seen through Davies' eyes, the way he appeared on the day he greeted the ambassador in Kalinin's office— self-assured, smiling, and authoritative. Then the image fades back to the cringing, hapless figure of Krestinsky in the prisoners' dock.

VYSHINSKY'S VOICE (OVER SCENE):
Were you able to hear *that*, Citizen Krestinsky?

KRESTINSKY (weak voice):
Yes, I heard it.

VYSHINSKY'S VOICE (OVER SCENE):
And is it the truth?

KRESTINSKY:
No, I'm not a Trotskyite. I had nothing to do with him.

170. MED. SHOT   VYSHINSKY AND THE PRISONERS

VYSHINSKY (turning to a prisoner farther down the row, who rises when addressed):
Accused Rosengoltz, you have heard these conflicting statements. Which one is true?

ROSENGOLTZ:
Krestinsky is not telling the truth.

VYSHINSKY:
How do you know?

ROSENGOLTZ:
I was in Krestinsky's office when he told us of Trotsky's program and we discussed ways of carrying it out.

VYSHINSKY (turns back to Krestinsky):
You also heard that, I trust.

KRESTINSKY:
I don't feel very well.

VYSHINSKY (looking closely into Krestinsky's face; speaks very deliberately):

> I can well understand. (Looks up toward the judge.) No further questions, Mr. President.

Krestinsky sinks into his chair as the prosecutor turns away.

ULRICH:

> Then we shall proceed with the examination of Citizen Radek.

171. MED. CLOSE SHOT RADEK

at one end of the prisoners' dock, as he rises to face Vyshinsky, who walks into the SHOT. Radek is self-assured, cheerful, almost debonair.

VYSHINSKY:

> In the preliminary examination, you also admitted participating in this bloc that was to prepare the way for Trotsky's program. Please tell us what that program was, as you understood it.

RADEK:

> Our eventual aim was to take over the government of the Soviet Union.

Again there is a stir among the audience.

172. MED. SHOT DAVIES, HENDERSON, AND FAYMONVILLE

They exchange glances of expectation.

VYSHINSKY'S VOICE (OVER SCENE):

> Quite an ambitious one, Citizen Radek. And just how was this to be accomplished?

RADEK'S VOICE (OVER SCENE):

> We realized that the present government was strongly entrenched with the people, so that our only chance of success would come in the defeat of Russia by some foreign power.

Davies gives an appraising glance in the direction of the
German representatives. The CAMERA PANS with his
glance to von Schulenberg and von Koestrich, who look
tight-lipped and tense, but give no other indication of
what is going on in their minds.

VYSHINSKY'S VOICE (OVER SCENE):
Very interesting. And so it was Trotsky's plan to do
everything possible to weaken this country's defense in the event of war?

RADEK'S VOICE (OVER SCENE):
Yes.

The CAMERA NOW PANS to the row of newspapermen.

SECOND NEWSPAPERMAN (nudges his neighbor and
whispers):
What did I tell you?

VYSHINSKY'S VOICE (OVER SCENE):
A war that he was determined Russia should lose?

RADEK'S VOICE (OVER SCENE):
Yes.

173.   MED. LONG SHOT   (FAVORING RADEK AND VYSHINSKY)
The judges platform visible above them.

VYSHINSKY:
And what was your own attitude toward Russia's
defeat?

RADEK:
I considered it inevitable.

VYSHINSKY (pressing him):
But more than that, you were interested in our los-
ing?

RADEK (hedging):
If you're asking what my feelings were—

VYSHINSKY (snapping):
I'm not interested in your feelings—only in facts.

RADEK:
The facts speak for themselves.

VYSHINSKY:
Meaning that your actions show that you desired to bring about our defeat?

RADEK:
Exactly.

VYSHINSKY:
And these actions of yours were deliberate?

RADEK:
Apart from sleeping, I never in my life committed any undeliberate action.

VYSHINSKY (ironically):
And this was not a dream.

RADEK (smiles):
Unfortunately, no.

VYSHINSKY:
How did Trotsky approach you about helping to carry out his defeatist program?

RADEK:
Never directly—always by letter or through intermediaries.

VYSHINSKY:
When did these contacts begin?

RADEK:
In the autumn of 1934. I was at a diplomatic reception, talking with Citizen Bukharin, when we were approached by Count von—

ULRICH (interrupting; sternly):
> The accused will refrain from mentioning the name of any foreign official.

An excited buzz of conversation fills the courtroom. The president judge raps for order. The noise dies down and Ulrich turns back to Radek.

ULRICH:
> Citizen Radek, you are sufficiently versed in politics to know what testimony is forbidden in open court.

RADEK (to the judge):
> I deeply apologize, Mr. President. It slipped out before I thought.

ULRICH:
> Then be careful in the future. Continue your testimony.

RADEK:
> Well, this unnamed gentleman approached us at the party and began talking very casually . . .

174.   MED. SHOT   THE DIPLOMATS' SECTION   (FAVORING DAVIES)
All listening with tense expressions.

RADEK'S VOICE (OVER SCENE):
> "Mr. Trotsky," he said, "seems to be more interested than the Stalin regime in friendly relations between our two countries." . . . We understood he was sounding us out to find out whether Trotsky had been speaking merely for himself or whether he had any substantial backing in this country.

VYSHINSKY'S VOICE (OVER SCENE):
> What did you tell him?

175.   MED. CLOSE SHOT   VON SCHULENBERG AND VON KOESTRICH
Both looking tense and worried.

RADEK'S VOICE (OVER SCENE):
> That there were certain realistic politicians here, among whom I included myself and Bukharin, who were out of sympathy with the policy of the present government, and were anxious to cooperate with Trotsky in bettering the relations between this other country and ours.

176.   MED. SHOT   (SHOOTING TOWARD PRISONERS'
        DOCK—FAVORING VYSHINSKY AND RADEK)

VYSHINSKY:
> In short, you admit going behind the back of your government to join hands with a traitor who was making overtures to a foreign power?

RADEK:
> Yes, if you want to put it that way.

VYSHINSKY:
> What way would you put it, Citizen Radek?

RADEK:
> At the time, our bloc didn't consider Trotsky as a traitor.

VYSHINSKY:
> I notice you say "at the time." But we'll come to that later. Now I have just one more question . . . What was the country whose representative approached you in connection with Trotsky?

177.   FULL SHOT   THE COURTROOM
The atmosphere is heavy with suspense as Radek pauses. He throws a quick glance in the direction of von Schulenberg, then turns back to face the prosecutor.

RADEK:
> The country is Germany.

VYSHINSKY (quickly, to Ulrich):
> No further questions . . .

At this revelation there is a moment of intense silence, then a loud murmur rises and spreads over the room— this time with an ominous, angry overtone. This demonstration causes a momentary halt in the trial. Even the judges are whispering among themselves, apparently in consultation over the grave nature of the evidence divulged.

178.   CLOSE GROUP SHOT

Von Schulenberg, as he whispers into the ear of Shigemitsu, who leans toward him, nodding his head in agreement with whatever the German is saying. In the next seat General von Koestrich has his head turned, in conversation with Lord Chilston, who is seated in back of him, next to Coulondre.

VON KOESTRICH (scoffing):

. . . As if Germany had any interest in Russia's political quarrels! Obviously, the Stalin government is shaky and they're trying to cover it up by inventing this fantastic foreign plot.

CHILSTON (perplexed):

But these men are on trial for their lives. Why should they give testimony that's bound to convict them?

COULONDRE:

Haven't you an English expression, Chilston— "You might as well be hung for a sheep as a lamb"?

The CAMERA MOVES BACK to include Davies, who is directly across the aisle from von Koestrich.

DAVIES (smiles, as he overhears):

. . . or for a wolf in sheep's clothing.

COULONDRE:

What's your opnion, Mr. Davies?

DAVIES:
Based on twenty years' trial practice, I'd be inclined to believe these confessions.

VON KOESTRICH (with a condescending smile to the others):
As an American lawyer, Mr. Davies can't be expected to understand all the intricacies of European politics.

DAVIES (wryly):
I'm learning.

The implication of Davies' remark brings a smile to Coulondre and Chilston. Von Koestrich turns abruptly away. At this moment we hear the judge's gavel OVER SCENE.

179. CLOSE SHOT   ULRICH
rapping for order. Gradually the room quiets down.

ULRICH:
Court will resume with the questioning of Citizen Bukharin.

180. MED. SHOT   BUKHARIN
as he rises from his chair. In the way he conducts himself through the examination, he gives the impression of complete objectivity and an almost scientific passion for the truth, without regard to personal consequences. Perhaps there is even a shade of exhibitionism in his apparent satisfaction at this public opportunity for self-incrimination. Whatever its psychological basis, his testimony carries complete conviction.

VYSHINSKY'S VOICE (OVER SCENE):
Do you recall the conversation mentioned by Radek at the diplomatic reception?

BUKHARIN:
There were so many conversations, I don't recall

this particular one. But if Radek says it occurred, I have no grounds for not believing him.

Vyshinsky walks into the SHOT, stands facing Bukharin, with the other prisoners in the background.

VYSHINSKY:
Would you mind giving a more direct answer? Did the conversation take place? Yes or no?

BUKHARIN:
I couldn't say no, nor can I deny that it did take place.

VYSHINSKY:
So the answer is neither yes nor no.

BUKHARIN:
Nothing of the kind, because facts exist, regardless of whether they are in anybody's mind. This is a problem of the reality of the outer world.

VYSHINSKY (impatiently):
Citizen Bukharin, would you please answer my questions without giving us a lecture in philosophy?

BUKHARIN (smiles):
The lecture was unintentional.

A titter is heard OVER SCENE from the spectators.

VYSHINSKY:
At any rate, you admit similar conversations?

BUKHARIN:
Yes.

VYSHINSKY:
With representatives of Germany?

BUKHARIN:
Of Germany and Japan.

At the mention of Japan, a new buzz of conversation rises from the courtroom.

181.   MED. SHOT   DIPLOMATIC SECTION   (FAVORING SHIGEMITSU)
Other spectators glance toward the Japanese ambassador, but he appears bland and unruffled.

VYSHINSKY'S VOICE (OVER SCENE):
What was the general purpose of these conversations?

BUKHARIN'S VOICE (OVER SCENE):
To make arrangements by which our bloc would receive help from these two countries in our effort to rise to power.

182.   MED. SHOT   PRISONERS' DOCK   (FAVORING BUKHARIN AND VYSHINSKY)

VYSHINSKY:
So you were working out a deal?

BUKHARIN:
Naturally. Germany and Japan were not going to back us for the sake of Trotsky's beautiful blue eyes.

VYSHINSKY:
What *were* their conditions?

BUKHARIN:
The partition of our country. Japan was to get our maritime province and our guarantee of Siberian oil in the event of war with the United States.

183.   MED. SHOT
Davies, Henderson, and Faymonville exchange significant glances.

VYSHINSKY'S VOICE (OVER SCENE):
And Germany?

The CAMERA PANS along the diplomatic section to where the Axis representatives are seated. The Germans now show the strain of the exposure, but the Japanese give no sign of any emotion.

BUKHARIN'S VOICE (OVER SCENE):
> We agreed to open the border for German expansion to the Ukraine.

A loud murmur of indignation rises from all sides. Suddenly von Schulenberg and von Koestrich get up from their seats.

184.   FULL SHOT   THE COURTROOM
as the German ambassador and his military aide, summoning all their dignity, walk from the room amid an angry buzz of voices from all sides. The judge again raps his gavel for order. Slowly the outburst dies down and Vyshinsky continues his questioning.[52]

VYSHINSKY:
> But first, before you could partition your country to its enemies, you and your bloc, as you call it, had to come into power. How was this to be accomplished?

BUKHARIN:
> Our plan was to seize the Kremlin and set up a military dictatorship financed by the Fascist governments.

VYSHINSKY:
> I see. And you had your Fascist dictator picked out?

BUKHARIN (smiles):
> I'm not sure we were all in agreement on that point.

VYSHINSKY:
> Who were the candidates?

BUKHARIN:
> Naturally, Trotsky was one—but our military leader

was Tukhachevsky, who, I suspect, had ambitions of his own.[53] (Again a murmur rises from the courtroom.)

185.   MED. SHOT   DAVIES, HENDERSON, AND FAYMONVILLE

DAVIES (in an astonished whisper):
   Tukhachevsky!

FAYMONVILLE:
   There's your wolf in sheep's clothing.

VYSHINSKY'S VOICE (OVER SCENE):
   Accused Bukharin, you are aware, of course, that you are confessing to the most serious crimes a citizen can commit against the State?

BUKHARIN'S VOICE (OVER SCENE):
   Yes, Citizen Prosecutor.

186.   MED. SHOT   THE PRESS ROW
where the news correspondents are listening intently and taking down their notes.

VYSHINSKY'S VOICE (OVER SCENE):
   And you make these damaging admissions of your free will? I mean by that—no pressure of any kind has been exerted to make you confess?

BUKHARIN'S VOICE (OVER SCENE):
   None whatsoever. The only pressure came from my own conscience.

187.   CLOSE SHOT   BUKHARIN
as he speaks to the courtroom with deep feeling and sincerity.

BUKHARIN:
   For three months I refused to testify—then I decided to tell everything. Why? Because while in prison I made an entire revaluation of my past. For

when you ask yourself, "If you must die, what are you dying for?" an absolutely black vacuity rises before you with startling vividness.[54]

188.   SERIES OF SHOTS AROUND THE COURTROOM
Davies, the news correspondents, the judges, the other prisoners, and various portions of the spectators, all obviously impressed by Bukharin's moving statement.

BUKHARIN'S VOICE (OVER SCENE; during these SHOTS):
There was nothing to die for if one wanted to die unrepentant. And on the contrary everything positive that glistens in the Soviet Union acquires new dimensions in a man's mind. One has only to weigh the wise leadership of the present government against the sordid, personal ambitions of those who would overthrow it, to realize the monstrousness of our crimes.

189.   MED. CLOSE SHOT

BUKHARIN (with other prisoners in the background visibly affected by his words):
I am about to finish. I am perhaps speaking for the last time in my life. My hope is that this trial may be the last severe lesson in proving to the world the growing menace of Fascist aggression and the awareness and united strength of Russia. It is in the consciousness of this that I await the verdict. What matters is not the personal feelings of a repentant enemy, but the welfare and progress of our country.

WIPE TO:

190.   FULL SHOT   COURTROOM
The commandant of the court is addressing the room.

COMMANDANT:
The court is coming, please rise.

The assembly stands as the judges appear from behind the curtains and walk to their places on the platform. The presiding judge, Ulrich, turns toward the prisoners' dock with a paper in his hand. As he begins to read, klieg lights are thrown full on the prisoners, and a newsreel camera begins to turn. Except for these sounds, the room is breathlessly still during the reading of the verdict.

ULRICH:

> In the name of the Supreme Court of the USSR, we find the accused guilty of organizing a conspiratorial group known as the Trotskyite Bloc whose aim was to overthrow the Soviet state . . .

191.   MED. SHOT   THE DIPLOMATS' SECTION   FAVORING
DAVIES, HENDERSON, AND FAYMONVILLE
all listening intently with their gaze fixed on the prisoners' dock.

ULRICH'S VOICE (OVER SCENE):

> . . . by means of wrecking, terrorist, espionage, and treasonable activities directed to undermine the economic might and defensive power of the Soviet Union, and to assist foreign aggressors in defeating and dismembering Russia . . .

192.   CLOSE TRUCKING SHOT   DOWN THE LINE OF PRISONERS
as they hear their sentence. The klieg spots strike full in their faces. They contort their expressions and try to close their eyes against the blinding light that exposes them as unmercifully as their own confessions.

ULRICH'S VOICE (OVER SCENE):

> On the basis of the aforesaid and guided by the articles 319 and 320 of the Code of Criminal Procedure, we sentence the defendants to the supreme penalty—to be shot with the confiscation of their personal property.

The CAMERA COMES TO REST on Bukharin, who alone faces the glaring light without flinching—a man resigned to his fate.

SLOW DISSOLVE TO:

193.   STOCK SHOT   OSLO, NORWAY

WIPE TO:

194.   EXT. GERMAN EMBASSY   OSLO
with Nazi insignia over its entrance.

WIPE TO:

195.   MED. CLOSE SHOT   LEON TROTSKY   (SEE PHOTOGRAPH FOR DESCRIPTION)
an intense and agitated man. Though he is obviously a suppliant in this scene, he keeps a certain dignity in his plea, appropriate to his position as one of the world's leading revolutionaries.

TROTSKY:
. . . Even though part of our plans have miscarried, Herr von Ribbentrop, there is no reason to turn back from our objective.

CAMERA PULLS BACK to include von Ribbentrop and Heinrich Sahm, the German minister to Norway. The scene takes place in the latter's office, an austere and graceless room. The Germans retain a surface politeness, but underneath this manner is condescension and contempt for the exiled Russian conspirator.

VON RIBBENTROP (smoothly):
We are not changing our objectives, Herr Trotsky—only our methods. There is no place in our program for bungling.

TROTSKY:
There would have been no bungling if I hadn't been forced to leave things to others . . . if I had been in Russia myself.

VON RIBBENTROP (shrugs):
  But you were not there. (With a malicious smile.)
  And now it seems . . . shall we say unlikely that
  you will *ever* be there.

SAHM:
  As a matter of fact, Herr Trotsky, in view of the
  publicity arising from the trials, you may find it
  difficult to stay in Norway.

TROTSKY (nervously):
  That's why we must strike fast. If the German army
  moves at once—

VON RIBBENTROP (sharply):
  Just a moment. The German army will move only
  when it is ready to move. The Führer will decide the
  time and the place.

TROTSKY (for the moment almost hysterical):
  But what about me? What am I to do in the meantime? My following in Russia will fall away—

VON RIBBENTROP (cutting in abruptly):
  I think you slightly overestimate your following,
  Herr Trotsky. At any rate you've had your chance.
  And as far as Germany is concerned, our eventual
  plans neither begin nor end with Russia.

Trotsky looks at von Ribbentrop and meets his cold
stare. Realizing that any personal appeal would fall on
granite, he spares himself any further indignity. He col-
lects himself, rises.

TROTSKY:
  Very well, I quite understand.

Von Ribbentrop remains seated as Sahm escorts Trotsky
to the door, where he turns and bows stiffly.

TROTSKY:
  Good day, gentlemen.

SAHM:
Good day, Herr Trotsky.

Von Ribbentrop merely bows. Sahm closes the door behind Trotsky, walks back to the room. Von Ribbentrop
is lighting a cigarette.

VON RIBBENTROP:
We have no more time for an exile's delusions . . .
Now, how are things progressing here?

SAHM (takes his seat at the desk):
Our plans have been going forward, Herr Minister.
While you're in Oslo, I want you to meet a man
who may be very useful to us. (Picks up the phone.)
Please call Herr Quisling . . .[55]

DISSOLVE TO:

196. LONG SHOT (STOCK) A SKY FILLED WITH PARACHUTE
JUMPERS

197. MED. LONG SHOT (STOCK) PARACHUTISTS LANDING IN A
FIELD (NOT CLOSE ENOUGH TO DISTINGUISH THE
JUMPERS)[56]

198. MED. CLOSE SHOT
Tanya Litvinov, who has just landed, unstrapping her
parachute. In the background other girls, dressed in
paratroop uniforms, unstrapping their parachutes, making their way across the field. (We see none of these girls
actually land their parachutes.)

WIPE TO:

199. LONG SHOT A LINE OF RUSSIAN GIRLS (TANYA CLOSEST
TO THE CAMERA)
receiving parachute medals from a Red Army officer.

199A. CLOSER PANNING SHOT THE LINE OF GIRL PARACHUTISTS
as the officer, a general of the air force, moves slowly
down the line of girl parachutists, all standing rigidly at

attention. They are of various types, Caucasian blondes, the Asiatic type from Turkestan, Uzbeks, but mainly Russians of the usual sort. The general is just pinning a medal upon Tanya.

OFFICER:

Your father must be very proud today, Corporal Litvinov.

TANYA:

Yes, General—but not so much as I.

He smiles and moves on to the next girl in line.[57]

OFFICER:

Where are you from, Comrade?

FIRST GIRL:

The Caucasus, General.

He nods and moves on to pin a medal on the next girl, an Asiatic type.

OFFICER:

And you, Comrade—from Turkestan?

SECOND GIRL:

Yes, General. How did you guess?

They laugh. He passes on to the next girl, a very attractive, strong-faced girl with blonde hair.

OFFICER:

Only the Ukraine gives the Red Army soldiers as handsome as you, Comrade.

THIRD GIRL (smiles):

Thank you, General. (Soberly.) We can also fight when we are needed.

OFFICER (looks at her; quietly):

Yes—but I hope you never shall be.

200. GROUP SHOT   EMLEN, GROSJEAN, AND COLONEL KAMENEV
standing among the spectators, watching the ceremony.

201. MED. CLOSE SHOT   RED ARMY OFFICER
who has just made the presentation, now addresses the
girls.

OFFICER:
Comrades, you have passed your final test, and
now I take pride in welcoming you into the Auxil-
iary Paratroop Corps of the Red Army of the Soviet
Union.

202. CLOSE PANNING SHOT   ALONG THE LINE OF GIRLS
starting with Tanya. Their faces are striking in their ea-
gerness and vitality. As the CAMERA PASSES over them,
several girls can't resist glancing down at their newly
won medals pinned on the front of their uniforms.

OFFICER'S VOICE (OVER SCENE):
Always remember that you are as vital a part of the
Red Army as we men—all the many thousands of
you—pilots, snipers, doctors, nurses, technicians.
Truly ours is an army of the people, united as one
and ready to fight as one, side by side.

203. CLOSE SHOT   THE OFFICER

OFFICER (smiles slowly):
Good luck to you all, and— (he salutes them) long
live Russia!

204. LONG SHOT   THE TROOPS
The girl parachutists respond with a rousing cheer, then
break ranks, eager and excited, congratulating each
other warmly. Tanya disengages herself from her army
friends and crosses toward the hangar.

205. GROUP SHOT   EMLEN, GROSJEAN, AND KAMENEV
among the spectators near the hangar. A small boy is

greeting his sister, who was among the girls receiving the medals. An old man puts an arm around his daughter, who was also among the jumpers. General excitement and congratulations among the group. Tanya comes into the shot and Emlen rushes up to kiss her exuberantly.

EMLEN:
It was wonderful, Tanya, but I held my breath.

GROSJEAN (as he shakes Tanya's hand):
She held mine, too. By the time you hit the ground she nearly had me strangled.

Tanya laughs and turns to Kamenev, who speaks to her in Russian. His tone conveys his admiration and personal interest.

KAMENEV (holding her hand):
Pozdrazhau, Tanyushka.

TANYA (smiles warmly):
Spasibo.

They release hands and the two couples start walking off, chatting as they go.

TANYA:
How nice of you to come.

EMLEN:
Tanya, tell me: What were you thinking when you jumped?

TANYA (casually):
Well, first—whether my chute would open—and then if my nose was shiny.

They all laugh.

DISSOLVE TO:

206. GROUP SHOT THE LITVINOVS AND DAVIESES
standing in the crowd of onlookers.[58]

MRS. DAVIES:
> Ivy, I don't see how on earth you keep so calm with your daughter dropping out of the sky.

LITVINOV (puffing on his cigar):
> That's her British side. She isn't nearly as calm as she pretends.

MRS. LITVINOV (smiles at him):
> And what about you, trying to hide your emotion behind that smoke screen?

They all laugh.

LITVINOV:
> Well, anyway, the Litvinovs are good jumpers. They fall many times, yes . . . but they land always on their feet.

206A.   MED. CLOSE TWO SHOT   DAVIES AND LITVINOV
as they watch the soldiers, Davies' face is soberly thoughtful.

DAVIES (quietly):
> Somehow, seeing these women soldiers brings the terrible threat of war much closer.

LITVINOV:
> My friend, you heard the testimony at the trials. We *are* at war. It is merely undeclared. We have called his hand in Russia before he was ready. Now he will turn to easier game—my guess is Austria and Czechoslovakia.

DAVIES (deeply troubled):
> Is there no way to stop this insanity, when every decent normal person hates the very thought of war?

LITVINOV:
> Yes, there is one way—if the democracies stop feeding Hitler's vanity by making him one concession

after another. They should take a firm stand together. Collective security is still the one hope left.
At Geneva I say that over and over again . . . (with
a weary gesture) but I think only the statue of your
former president listens.

DAVIES:

There's another president who's deeply concerned
over what's happening . . . Maxim, I'm going to
impress upon my government how grave the situation is. Maybe something can be done before it's too
late.

LITVINOV (with a gleam of hope):

Good . . . Mr. Roosevelt can wake the people to
their danger if anyone can.

DISSOLVE TO:

207.   CLOSE SHOT   AMBASSADOR DAVIES
at his desk in the embassy, dictating his communication
to the State Department. As he dictates, the CAMERA
PULLS BACK to include the embassy secretary who is taking down the message.

DAVIES:

. . . There is no longer any question in my mind
that these defendants, under the leadership of
Trotsky, Bukharin, and Tukhachevsky, were guilty
of a conspiracy with the German and Japanese high
commands to pave the way for an attack upon the
Soviet state.

208.   STOCK SHOT   WASHINGTON
(Shot should include the State Department building.)

DAVIES' VOICE (OVER SCENE):

Consequently all of the trials, purges, and liquida-
tions which at first seemed so violent and shocking
to the rest of the world . . .

169

209.   FULL SHOT   THE CODE ROOM   WASHINGTON
showing about eight code machines, each with its own
operator. Surrounding the machines is heavy wire grat-
ing. An armed guard stands at the only entrance. During the decoding of the message two or three messengers deliver other communications to the operators.

DAVIES' VOICE (OVER SCENE):
. . . are now seen clearly as part of a vigorous and
determined effort by the Stalin government to protect itself from not only revolution from within, but
from attack from without. They went to work
thoroughly and ruthlessly to clean out all treason-
able elements—fifth columnists—within the country.

210.   CLOSE SHOT   A MACHINE
over the shoulder of the operator, who is decoding the
Davies communication. First we see the message in its
code form; then as it comes out of the machine we read
the words of Davies that we hear OVER SCENE.

DAVIES' VOICE (continuing OVER SCENE):
When I asked Mr. Litvinov whether the government now felt positive it could rely upon the support and loyalty of the Red Army, he assured me
that the army is unquestionably loyal and that the
position of the Soviet government is actually
strengthened by the purge of its traitors.

211.   MED. SHOT   UNDERSECRETARY OF STATE WELLES
at his desk reading the communication.

DAVIES' VOICE (continuing OVER SCENE):
Mr. Litvinov also stated that the Soviet Union was
prepared to take a strong stand against the aggressor nations if it were in cooperation with France,
England, and the United States.

                                            CUT TO:

212.   MED. SHOT   SECRETARY OF STATE HULL
at his desk reading the communication.

DAVIES' VOICE (continuing OVER SCENE):
> He expressed the hope that the democracies would
> see the necessity of such collective action before
> Germany gets a head start in carrying out its pro-
> jected moves against Austria and Czechoslovakia
> . . . I have the honor to be, sir, respectfully yours,
> Joseph E. Davies.

As Davies' voice concludes, Secretary Hull looks up
thoughtfully from the message, then with a troubled
expression reaches for the telephone on his desk.

SECRETARY HULL:
> Please get me the president.[59]

WIPE TO:

213.   MED. SHOT   (FROM OVER SHOULDER)   PRESIDENT
ROOSEVELT SPEAKING THROUGH A MICROPHONE
(Excerpts taken from his famous Quarantine Speech.)

ROOSEVELT:
> . . . It is because the people in the United States,
> under modern conditions, must for the sake of their
> own future give thought to the rest of the world
> that I, as the responsible executive head of the na-
> tion . . .

CUT TO:

214.   SMALL FAMILY GROUP IN A TYPICAL AMERICAN HOME
listening to the radio.

ROOSEVELT'S VOICE (OVER SCENE):
> . . . wish to speak to you on a subject of definite
> national importance. The present reign of terror in
> international lawlessness began a few years
> ago . . .

CUT TO:

214A. A TAXICAB IN A CITY STREET
A group gathered around listening to the car radio.

ROOSEVELT'S VOICE (OVER SCENE):
. . . It began through the unjustified interference in the internal affairs of other nations or the invasion of alien territory in violation of treaties and has now reached the stage where the very foundation of civilization is seriously threatened . . .

CUT TO:

214B. PORCH OF A FARM HOME
The farmer, his wife, and a hand gathered around a portable radio.

ROOSEVELT'S VOICE (OVER SCENE):
. . . The peace, the freedom, and the security of ninety per cent of the population of the world is being jeopardized by the remaining ten per cent who are threatening a breakdown of all international law and order . . .

CUT TO:

214C. WORKBENCH IN A FACTORY
Workers listening to a small radio.

ROOSEVELT'S VOICE (OVER SCENE):
. . . When an epidemic of physical disease starts to spread, the community approves and joins in a quarantine of the patients in order to protect the health of the community against the spread of the disease . . .

CUT TO:

214D. A WEALTHY CLUB
Members listening with comfortable complacency to a very large radio.

ROOSEVELT'S VOICE (OVER SCENE):
. . . War is a contagion whether it be declared or undeclared. It can engulf states and peoples remote from the original scene of hostilities . . .

As the inference of these words becomes apparent, one of the club members makes a gesture toward the radio which says in effect, "Some more New Deal nonsense." Another member nods his head in agreement and goes back to reading his paper.

CUT TO:

214E. THE PRESIDENT
concluding his speech.

ROOSEVELT:
America hates war. America hopes for peace. Therefore, America actively engages in the search for peace.[60]

FADE OUT

FADE IN

215. THE KREMLIN TOWER
SUPERIMPOSE THE DATELINE MAY 1, 1938
The tower clock begins to strike the hour of nine.

216. STOCK SHOT RED SQUARE IN FRONT OF THE CLOCK TOWER
with the clock still striking. Voroshilov, marshal of the Red Army, rides through the Spassky Gate underneath the tower, mounted on a spirited black horse.

217. FULL SHOT STOCK THE SQUARE
as the marshal rides up to the officer of the day and his mounted guard, who are waiting in front of the reviewing stand. After a few words and salutes are exchanged the huge band (composed of all band units in the Moscow vicinity) strike up the "Internationale."

Voroshilov dismounts, an orderly taking his horse, whereupon he walks toward the reviewing stand on Lenin's tomb. At the same time the officer of the day and the honor guard are riding to one end of the square to give the marshal's order for the start of the parade.

(Check all details against the newsreel footage of this event.)

218. MED. LONG SHOT   THE DIPLOMATIC SECTION OF THE
SPECTATORS' STAND
(Terraced stone benches without backs, directly in front
of the square.) Seated in a front row are Ambassador
and Mrs. Davies, Faymonville, Spendler, Henderson,
Emlen, and Bob Grosjean. In the row in back of them
are Lord Chilston, Coulondre, and the Belgian minister
and his wife. Scattered around the section are the German, Japanese, Italian, Chinese, Latvian, and the other
embassy representatives we have met in the reception
and trial scenes. Also present are the American newspapermen and other press representatives occupying a
row of their own. The seating should be informal and
mobile—people occasionally standing and moving
about. The audience, dressed in light clothes for the
warm spring day, appear in a gala mood fitting the fes-
tive occasion. They crane their necks in every direction
like a circus crowd endeavoring to see all three rings at
the same time.
During the SHOT we hear the stirring band music from
OFF-SCENE.

219. MED. CLOSE   SLOW TRUCKING SHOT
beginning with Grosjean, Emlen, and Faymonville in
that order.

EMLEN (excited):
Bob, wasn't the marshal magnificent on that black
horse!

GROSJEAN (in a chiding tone):
Anyone in a marshal's uniform looks magnificent to
you.

FAYMONVILLE:
Poor old Tukhachevsky! He led the parade last
year.

The CAMERA NOW PASSES over Henderson.

HENDERSON (in slightly humorous vein):
Uneasy lies the head that craves a crown.

The CAMERA NOW COMES TO REST on Mr. and Mrs. Davies, with Chilston, Coulondre, and the Belgian minister and his wife in the close background.

DAVIES (stretching his neck):
I'd like to have three heads and six pair of eyes.

MRS. DAVIES:
Good heavens! Could *anything* be more undiplomatic?

General laughter from the group. Chilston leans over toward Davies.

CHILSTON (gesturing toward their right):
Look over there, my friends.

Mr. and Mrs. Davies gaze in the direction indicated.

220. LONG SHOT STOCK (SHOOTING TOWARD LENIN'S TOMB)
On the tribune of the mausoleum are the high Soviet officials who have just arrived to review the parade. Prominent among them are Stalin, Molotov, Kalinin, and Vyshinsky. (No production shots of this group necessary.)

CHILSTON'S VOICE (OVER SCENE):
This is as near as any of us ever get to Stalin.

COULONDRE'S VOICE (OVER SCENE):
And even that only happens two or three times a year.

221. CLOSE GROUP SHOT (FAVORING MR. AND MRS. DAVIES)

DAVIES (still looking off; meditatively):
It isn't close enough. I'd like to know that man.

Suddenly we hear a blare of trumpets signaling the start of the parade. All eyes turn left.[61]

175

222. STOCK SHOT
A detachment of cavalry, beautifully mounted, opens the parade into Red Square, appearing from the street below. The music of the band is now a spirited march. Following the cavalry come infantry and various mechanized units, including motorcycle, artillery, and tank corps. How much of the military portion of the parade is included will, of course, depend on how long it will hold for. It is suggested that enough be used to give an impressive demonstration, since the appraisal of Russia's military strength is a part of the Davies mission. After this portion of the ground parade:

223. STOCK SHOTS
An airplane demonstration overhead, showing at fairly close range various units of the Soviet air force.

224. MED. SHOT   THE DIPLOMATIC SECTION   (FAVORING MR. AND MRS. DAVIES, FAYMONVILLE, CHILSTON, COULONDRE) heads tilted back, eyes scanning the heavens. The roar of planes overhead.

FAYMONVILLE:
They look more advanced in design than those they used in Spain.

DAVIES:
What I've seen today has convinced me of the Soviet power—in the air and on the ground.

COULONDRE:
You've seen only part of their strength, Mr. Davies. The rest of the parade will show you what is *behind* the military forces.

CHILSTON (with a smug smile):
But in the long run, the strongest power is the one who holds the balance.

DAVIES:
> Perhaps, Lord Chilston— (with a slight smile) but even the best jugglers sometimes miss.

225.   STOCK SHOT   THE AIRPLANES IN THE AIR
over the buildings of Red Square.

226.   MED. SHOT   THE DIPLOMATIC SECTION
as before.

FAYMONVILLE (with excitement in his voice):
> Mr. Ambassador, watch this. I hear a new bomber model is being shown for the first time today.

The group looks up to their left expectantly.

227.   STOCK SHOT   THE SKY
Over the roofs of the historical museum the broad shape of an enormous plane (or pair of planes) appears.

228.   MED. SHOT   ANOTHER PART OF THE DIPLOMATIC SECTION
including some foreign military attachés. All look up with interest at the approaching plane.

229.   CLOSER SHOT   ANOTHER GROUP IN THE DIPLOMATIC
SECTION
with Shigemitsu in the center, flanked by the military attachés of other countries. The others casually follow the passage of the plane across the square (its roar increasing in volume), but Shigemitsu calmly lifts a pair of binoculars to his eyes and holds the plane in its view throughout the crossing, obviously making a study of the new model. No one notices him until Shigemitsu, turning with his binoculars to his right, attracts the attention of his right-hand neighbor, who looks at the binoculars unbelievingly.

WIPE TO:

230.   FULL SHOT (STOCK) RED SQUARE
later that day, featuring the grand opening of the second
section of the parade after the military part is finished.

231.   SERIES OF THE MOST EFFECTIVE STOCK SHOTS
For the industrial, agricultural, and cultural displays the
following are typical of this portion of the parade:
   1. Floats decorated with sheaves of wheat and other
grains. Little girls in representative costumes are dancing on the floats as they pass through the square.
   2. Vehicles bearing model locomotives and tractors
with the factory workers, men and women, marching
in solid groups.
   3. Floral floats of great beauty and intricate designs.
   4. A sports display—men and women swinging In-
dian clubs in time to the music or carrying athletic tab-
leaux.

232.   MED. SHOT DIPLOMATIC SECTION
Many of the diplomats have left; others are leaving. The
Davies group is among those staying to the end. The
Italian ambassador, Count Rosso, who sits beyond
Coulondre, leans over to speak to the American ambas-
sador.

ROSSO:
   Mr. Davies . . .

DAVIES:
   Yes, Count Rosso?

ROSSO (with a gleam of satisfaction that his voice attempts to conceal):
   Were you disappointed in the public reaction to
   your president's Chicago speech?

DAVIES (poker-faced):
   Not particularly. It's only natural that a peace-
   loving people would be a little slow to realize that
   not all other nations are equally desirous of peace.[62]

ROSSO (quickly changing the subject; gestures toward the parade):
>What do you think of today's demonstrations?

DAVIES:
>I'll tell you what I feel—that at least one European nation—with no aggressive intentions—is ready for anything that comes. And I say thank God for it.

FAYMONVILLE:
>Hear, hear!

There is a general mild reaction of applause for Davies' statement from the rest of the group. The Italian ambassador bows stiffly and moves off.

CUT TO:

233. ANOTHER IMPRESSIVE STOCK SHOT
of some part of the parade.

CUT BACK TO:

234. CLOSE TWO SHOT   MR. AND MRS. DAVIES
their eyes glued on the parade.

MRS. DAVIES:
>Joe, I wouldn't have missed this for the world.

DAVIES (with deep humility):
>When we go home, Marjorie, we'll be taking with us a good deal more than we brought.

She presses his hand affectionately.

DISSOLVE TO:

FADE IN

234A. INT. FOYER   SPAZZO HOUSE   FULL SHOT   NIGHT
The Chinese ambassador to Moscow is standing alone in the foyer, wearing his overcoat, his hat in his hand. His face is very serious. The butler who has gone to call Mr. Davies returns with him down the stairway, then exits through a side doorway.

CHINESE AMBASSADOR:

Mr. Davies, please forgive me for calling at this late hour—

Davies smiles cordially and comes up to him with out-stretched hand.

DAVIES:

Of course, Your Excellency—it's always a pleasure to see you.

234B.   CLOSER SHOT   THE TWO
as they shake hands.

DAVIES:

Take off your coat and come into the study.

CHINESE AMBASSADOR:

Thank you, I cannot stay. I am on my way to the hospital. I wish you would come with me. It is very important.

DAVIES:

Oh. Is someone of your family ill?

CHINESE AMBASSADOR (nods, quietly):

My *people* are ill, Mr. Davies—all China is sick of an old disease—Japan.

DAVIES (sympathetic, but still puzzled):

Yes, Mr. Ambassador—their recent atrocities at Shanghai and the *Panay* incident have greatly shocked the American people—but— (He pauses quizzically.)

CHINESE AMBASSADOR:

I want you to see some of those atrocities with your own eyes.

DAVIES (surprised):
Here? In Moscow?

CHINESE AMBASSADOR:
Yes. A trainload of refugees arrived yesterday.

DISSOLVE TO:

234C.   INT. FOYER OF HOSPITAL
It is crowded with Chinese refugees of all ages, many of them wounded and bandaged, huddled against the wall or upon benches; the terror and suffering of their ghastly experience are stamped upon their faces. The Russian hospital attendants and nurses are moving among them, inspecting the case-report cards hung by strings around their necks. There is a low murmur of Russian words as they lead or carry some of the refugees into the various wards.

As Davies and the Chinese ambassador slowly cross the foyer, the CAMERA MOVES with them; once or twice we INTERCUT to the Chinese at whom they look with much pity—a mother and her child, an old couple, pathetic and lost.

234D.   CLOSE TWO SHOT   DAVIES AND THE CHINESE AMBASSADOR
Davies is tremendously shocked and moved by what he sees.

DAVIES (quietly):
And how many others are there like these?

CHINESE AMBASSADOR:
Sixteen million, Mr. Davies—all destitute, homeless, and starving—

Davies shakes his head slowly, bitterly. They continue across the foyer and through the doorway into a ward.

DISSOLVE TO:

234E.   INT. MOSCOW HOSPITAL   NIGHT
TRUCK SHOT   THROUGH A CROWDED WARD
The ward is crowded with beds, in each of which is lying a Chinese victim of Japanese horror. Many of them are bandaged, all are silently staring with fixed eyes

while the Soviet nurses and hospital aides move in and out among the beds trying to make them comfortable. Many of the victims are young children. Davies is staring in impassioned astonishment as he and the Chinese ambassador walk slowly between the twin lane of beds. The Chinese ambassador lifts up the case-report boards, which are attached to the foot of the beds which they pass.

CHINESE AMBASSADOR:

Age, twelve—machine-gun wounds in lung and throat— (They pause at the next bed.) Age, eighty-four—bayonet wound in back—right arm amputated in Nanking— (They move on to the next bed where a girl child lies with eyes heavily bandaged.) Age, seven—shrapnel in both eyes— parents killed—[63]

Davies looks at the child with deep compassion.

234F.   CLOSE SHOT   CHINESE CHILD   IN BED
The sweet-faced girl of seven tries to smile back at the sound of unfamiliar words from the two men. Her eyes and the top of her head are covered by bandages, and in one hand she is holding a dirty and battered Chinese rag doll.

234G.   MOVING SHOT   DAVIES AND THE CHINESE AMBASSADOR
They walk on in tense silence for a few feet, a silence broken only by the low, pathetic whimpering of an injured child. Davies is greatly moved.

CHINESE AMBASSADOR:

And their only crime is that they lived in a town which the Japanese wanted . . .

DAVIES:

It's terrifying . . . but why were these people brought to Moscow?

CHINESE AMBASSADOR:

> Because Russia is our friend, Mr. Davies—as she is the friend of Spain—or of anyone who fights fascism.

As they come opposite a doorway that leads into the anteroom of the operating theater, the Chinese diplomat indicates courteously for Davies to enter with him.

234H. INT. ANTEROOM TO OPERATING THEATER

A room, spotlessly clean, in which the doctors and operating room attendants prepare their work and clean up afterward. Several doctors and nurses move in and out, moving swiftly, busy. Among them is a middle-aged Soviet doctor, still wearing his operating robes and white cap. He is removing his rubber gloves, preparing to wash his hands at a basin. A Soviet nurse helps him change to a fresh outfit during the following scene. The two ambassadors move toward him.

234I. CLOSER SHOT   DR. BOTKIN

He looks up as the diplomats enter the SHOT and greets the Chinese ambassador quietly in Russian. They speak quietly, soberly throughout this scene. Dr. Botkin's voice is restrained, calm, but with a deep personal feeling. He is very tired.

CHINESE AMBASSADOR:

> Dr. Botkin, this is the American ambassador, Mr. Davies. I took the liberty of bringing him with me.

DR. BOTKIN (slowly):

> I am glad you came, Mr. Davies. I have heard that you are an unusual diplomat.

DAVIES:

> In what way, Doctor?

DR. BOTKIN:

> That you see what is really happening, instead of what you want to see.

CHINESE AMBASSADOR:
That is why I asked Mr. Davies to come here.

DAVIES:
I hardly need say I'm appalled by what I've seen here.

DR. BOTKIN:
We have been operating without pause for twenty-one hours—many will die, but all of them are very brave—even the children never cry. (Davies shakes his head, unable to speak.) Mr. Davies, I am only a doctor, but the saving of human life is all I live for—and I see in this tragedy of China the beginning of a bloodbath for all the world.

DAVIES (slowly):
I am terribly afraid you may be right, Doctor—and it must be prevented at any cost.

DR. BOTKIN:
Yes—yes—

CHINESE AMBASSADOR:
The cost is a very simple one, Mr. Davies—only an understanding between our three nations and Great Britain. By uniting our strength now, we could stop Japan and Germany!

DR. BOTKIN (nods):
Yes, the four of us must face this common enemy together—and better soon than late, Mr. Davies.

DAVIES:
I agree with you, Dr. Botkin—and with you, Your Excellency . . . but none are so blind as those who will not see.

A Soviet nurse rolls in a patient on a wheel-cot, pauses beside Dr. Botkin, and asks him quietly in Russian if he is ready for the next operation. Botkin replies wearily (and also in Russian), "Yes, prepare the patient." Then he looks back from the child on the cot to Davies and nods in quiet agreement.

DR. BOTKIN (quietly):
No, none but those who *cannot* see, Mr. Davies.

As his eyes turn back to the child, Davies and the Chinese ambassador also look, and the CAMERA PANS to the little Chinese girl with bandaged eyes whom we saw in the ward. She lies very still beneath the white sheet. The Chinese ambassador comes to her side, and his eyes are moist with emotion as he presses her small hand. He says to her quietly in Chinese, "Be brave, little one. Everything will be all right." The child's lips smile faintly and she whispers back, "I will be brave."

234J. CLOSE SHOT DAVIES
His face is filled with emotion as he looks down at the child, then slowly at what she is clenching so tightly in her hand.

234K. CLOSE SHOT THE CHILD'S HAND
It is still tightly closed upon her little ragdoll.

234L. MED. FULL SHOT THE ROOM
The Russian nurse is also close to tears as she wheels the child on into the operating room. Dr. Botkin turns slowly to Davies.

DR. BOTKIN (quietly):
Thank you for coming to see us, Mr. Davies.

Davies nods, unable to speak. Dr. Botkin nods to the Chinese ambassador, then turns and walks through the doorway into the operating room.

234M. CLOSE-UP DAVIES
as he looks after him.

FADE OUT

235.   CLOSE SHOT   LITVINOV
seated in a chair, finishing an informal talk.

LITVINOV:
. . . And my pleasure at having you here is marred
only by the fact that this is a farewell dinner.

THE CAMERA PULLS BACK to:

236.   MED. SHOT   DINING ROOM   SPIRIDONOVKA 17
on the occasion of a stag dinner given to the departing
ambassador. Besides Davies and Litvinov, those seated
at the round table include Kamenev, Barkov, Faymonville, Henderson, Spendler, and several other embassy
employees not previously seen. Dinner is over, so that
no food appears on the table. The men are smoking
cigars and drinking Russian liqueurs.

LITVINOV (speaking directly and affectionately to
Davies):
You, Mr. Ambassador, have done what no other
foreign diplomat has been known to do in this
country. You have devoted much of your time and
your great energy to the study of this country, los-
ing no opportunity of seeing for yourself anything
worthy of study and observation. We appreciate it
very much. We do not like being just looked at,
gullibly talked of, preferring to be studied, and, of
course, to be properly understood . . . You, Mr.
Ambassador, have done your best to understand
our country, what is going on here, the motives
behind our doings and the aims in front of them. If
you will, as I am sure you will, pass on the results of
your observation and unbiased judgment to your
government and to your country, you will contribute more to the friendly relations between our two
countries than any other diplomat in the history of
the Soviet Union.

As Litvinov stops, the others at the table break out in

applause. After a moment Davies, also still seated, replies to Litvinov.

DAVIES:

> I am deeply moved by your generous remarks, Mr.
> Litvinov. You have commented on the sympathy
> and understanding which exists between your
> country and mine. I believe that is preeminently
> true. It is my belief that both peoples are seeking to
> improve the lot of the common man. That is the end
> toward which we are striving. Our methods are dif-
> ferent. We believe ours to be the best. We concede
> that you have the right to maintain that yours are
> the best. Whether or not your government succeeds
> in all its ultimate aims, the ideas and human forces
> which you have released will have a profound effect
> on the future of the world . . . I came here with an
> objective mind. I am leaving with an objective
> mind, but possibly less objective and more friendly
> because of the kindnesses which you and your gov-
> ernment have extended to me, as the representative
> of my country. (His glance sweeping the table.) In
> conclusion, I want to say to everyone here, I am
> going to miss you very much and I hope to see all of
> you many times again, wherever our paths might
> cross . . . I am sure my American staff will want to
> join me in raising our glasses to you, Mr. Litvinov,
> your associates, and the traditional friendship of
> the peoples of our two countries.

The others at the table rise; they lift their glasses to
Litvinov, who bows and smiles.

AD LIB:

> Mr. Litvinov . . . Mr. Foreign Minister . . . Your
> health . . . Etc., etc.

As the others drink, the secretary enters the SHOT,
hands a slip of paper to Mr. Litvinov.

237.   CLOSE SHOT   LITVINOV
As he reads, his expression becomes more serious—in
contrast to the merriment around him.

FAYMONVILLE'S VOICE (jovially, OVER SCENE):
I suggest a final game of poker, so that we can win
back some of our money from the boss before he
leaves.

HENDERSON'S VOICE (OVER SCENE):
I second the motion.

DAVIES' VOICE (OVER SCENE):
As if I could ever hold my own with you sharks.

Laughter OVER SCENE, which suddenly stops as Litvinov
looks up. He speaks in a grave voice.

LITVINOV:
Gentlemen, I'm sorry to interrupt, but I have some
bad news.

238.   FULL SHOT   THE ROOM
which is now very still, all eyes on Litvinov.

LITVINOV:
I have just received a telephone message from the
Czech minister . . . Hitler has invaded Austria and
German troops are already in Vienna.

The expressions on the faces around the room seem to
say, "It has come."
                                                    WIPE TO:

239.   STOCK SHOTS OF THE GERMAN OCCUPATION OF AUSTRIA
At the end we see the swastika flying over the Viennese
capitol.
                                                 DISSOLVE TO:

240.   MED. SHOT   KALININ'S PRIVATE OFFICE
Davies is making his farewell call on Kalinin and Molotov. He has nearly finished his visit and is about to take
leave of them. All three are standing.

KALININ:

. . . On your first visit here, Mr. Davies, I felt I was welcoming a capable and honest ambassador, but now, more than that, I feel I am saying good-bye to a friend.

DAVIES (as they shake hands):

Thank you, Mr. President. I feel the same way.

MOLOTOV (as Davies turns to say good-bye to him):

I am only sorry that you are not staying with us longer.

DAVIES:

Well, you see, Mr. Molotov, I've done what my president sent me to do. My end of the job is finished.

MOLOTOV:

No one could have been more conscientious in respect to both our countries.

There is the SOUND of a door opening and shutting at the far end of the room. Molotov stops, looks off-scene. The others follow his gaze.

241.   MED. LONG SHOT   STALIN

from their angle as he walks toward the camera. (NOTE: In his book, Mr. Davies describes Stalin as follows: "His demeanor is kindly, his manner almost deprecatingly simple, his personality and expression of reserved strength and poise very marked." In the writer's opinion these characteristics for the part are even more important than physical verisimilitude.)

242.   MED. SHOT   THE GROUP

as Stalin walks directly to Davies, dispensing with the formality of an introduction. The two men shake hands.

STALIN:

Mr. Davies, I am happy to know you.

DAVIES:

Thank you, Mr. Stalin. This is a great pleasure for
me . . . (smiles) also considerable of a surprise.

They all smile at this frankness and the ice is broken.

KALININ:

Gentlemen, won't you please have chairs?

STALIN (as they are seated):

Besides your work here in Moscow, I understand
you have visited many other sections of the Soviet
Union.

DAVIES:

And I've been deeply impressed by what I've
seen—your industrial plants, the development of
your natural resources, and the work being done to
improve living conditions everywhere in your
country. I believe history will record you as a great
builder for the benefit of common men.

STALIN (with sincere modesty):

It is not my achievement, Mr. Davies. Our five-year
plans were conceived by Lenin and carried out by
the people themselves.

DAVIES:

Well, the results hve been a revelation to me. I confess I wasn't prepared for all I've found here. (With
a smile.) You see, Mr. Stalin, I'm a capitalist, as you
probably know.

STALIN (laughingly):

Yes, we know you are a capitalist—there can be no
doubt about that.

They all join in the laughter.

KALININ:

We also know this about you, Mr. Davies—the
worst things you've had to say, you have said to

our faces, the best things you have said to our enemies.

STALIN:

We want you to realize that we feel more friendly toward the government of the United States than any other nation. If there are any matters that are not settled between us, please take them up with Molotov.

DAVIES:

Thank you . . . Well, gentlemen, I know how busy you are. I mustn't take up more of your time.

He rises, and the others follow suit, but Stalin interposes before the ambassador can move toward the door.

STALIN:

Mr. Davies, do you have another appointment?

DAVIES:

No, I don't.

STALIN:

Then please do not hurry away.

The CAMERA PANS with the two men as Stalin leads Davies by the arm toward the door of his own office.

STALIN (as they walk):

There are some things on my mind that I would like you to know—and your great president to know.

WIPE TO:

243. FULL SHOT STALIN'S OFFICE

An austere room with maps on the wall and a large conference table in the middle of the room. We should give the impression here of two men surrounded by the problems of the world. They should be seen at first as very small in contrast with the table at which they are seated. As Stalin talks, the CAMERA PULLS UP to them.

STALIN:

The outlook for European peace is bad—very bad. England and France have allowed Hitler to take Austria without a struggle. They will probably allow him to do the same with Czechoslovakia. They have repudiated their pledges to the League and are throwing the defenseless countries on the mercies of bandits.

DAVIES:

It's clear what they're doing. What I don't understand is *why* they're doing it.

STALIN:

I will tell you why, Mr. Davies, and I will tell you frankly because this is a time for plain words—the reactionary elements in England, represented by the Chamberlain government, have determined upon the deliberate policy of making Germany strong. And at the same time they shout lies in their press about the weakness of the Russian army and disorder in the Soviet Union.

DAVIES:

You mean, Mr. Stalin, that these elements are actually encouraging German aggression?

STALIN:

There is no doubt that their plan is to push Hitler into a war with this country. Then when the combatants exhaust themselves they will step in to make "peace"—yes, the kind of peace that will serve their own interests.

DAVIES:

But I am sure the English people do not approve of such a policy.

STALIN:

In my opinion the present governments of England and France do not represent their people. Finally the Fascist dictators will drive too hard a bargain and the people will call their governments to account—but by then it may be too late.

DAVIES:

Mr. Stalin, may I ask you a very direct question?

STALIN:

Of course.

DAVIES:

If Hitler *does* attack Czechoslovakia and if France and England go to her aid—is Russia willing and ready to join them in war against Germany?

STALIN:

We have a commitment with France to fight in the event they go to the aid of Czechoslovakia. The Soviet Union has never repudiated a treaty obligation. She would not repudiate this one.

DAVIES:

Your past record speaks well for the future.

STALIN:

But we are not going to be put in the position of pulling other people's chestnuts out of the fire. Either we must be able to rely on our mutual guarantees with the other democracies or . . . well, we may be forced to protect ourselves in another way.

DAVIES:

Mr. Stalin, on my way home I'm stopping off in England. May I quote what you have just told me?

STALIN:

If you could convince them and your own government that peace or war is in the balance, you would do us all a great service.

At this point Davies rises and Stalin walks with him slowly toward the door.

DAVIES:

I feel as keenly as you and Mr. Litvinov that collective security is the last bulwark against war.

STALIN:

Litvinov has done all he can to make the world realize it.

DAVIES:

A very great foreign minister . . .

244.   MED. SHOT   AT THE DOOR

DAVIES (earnestly):

Mr. Stalin, a while ago I made the remark that my job was finished. After talking with you, I wonder if it hasn't only begun.

Stalin looks pleased and gratified.

DISSOLVE TO:

245.   STOCK SHOTS   GERMAN ARMY
massing on Czechoslovakia border.

DAVIES' VOICE (OVER SCENE):

Stalin kept his word. When Hitler announced his determination to take Sudetenland, the Soviet government reaffirmed its pledge to fight on the side of France if she went to Czechoslovakia's aid.

245A.   FULL SHOT   HITLER, CHAMBERLAIN, DALADIER,
MUSSOLINI AT MUNICH CONFERENCE

DAVIES' VOICE (OVER SCENE):

But Chamberlain and Daladier turned their backs on Russia. At the Munich conference, they traded part of Czechoslovakia for Hitler's promise to mend his ways and commit no future agression.

245B.   STOCK SHOT   CHAMBERLAIN
as he arrives at London airport. He takes a document from his briefcase, waves it at the cheering crowd.

DAVIES' VOICE (OVER SCENE):
> That pledge was written on a piece of paper signed by Hitler. Chamberlain proclaimed, "This means peace in our time."

245C.   STOCK SHOTS   THE SEIZURE OF THE REMAINDER OF CZECHOSLOVAKIA
German troops moving into Prague.

DAVIES' VOICE (OVER SCENE):
> Hitler's word was good for less than six months. This time he dispensed with conferences. The German army marched into Prague, and Czechoslovakia was swallowed by the German Reich.

245D.   STOCK SHOT   LONDON
showing state buildings, Houses of Parliament, No. 10 Downing Street, etc.

DAVIES' VOICE (NARRATING OVER SCENE):
> Through the regular diplomatic channels, I tried to impress British leaders with the dangers inherent in their policies of appeasing Germany at the sacrifice of a military alliance with the one country Hitler feared. But my warnings failed to bring any real response.

DISSOLVE TO:

246.   STOCK SHOT   A TYPICAL ENGLISH COUNTRY ROAD
with a car driving through.

DAVIES' VOICE (OVER SCENE):
> Finally in desperation I went to a man who was then living in Kent . . .

247.   STOCK SHOT   AN ENGLISH COUNTRY MANOR HOUSE

DAVIES' VOICE (OVER SCENE):
> . . . but who was later to move to No. 10 Downing Street.

248.   MED. SHOT   A TERRACE

overlooking an English country garden. Mrs. Churchill, a charming, patrician Englishwoman, is leading
Ambassador and Mrs. Davies to some chairs on the terrace, chatting with them as they walk.

MRS. CHURCHILL:

Winston is working in the garden but he's expect-
ing you. He's building one of his pet brick walls.

DAVIES:

I wouldn't interrupt his weekend, Mrs. Churchill,
but I'm very anxious to see him.

MRS. CHURCHILL:

We're delighted to have you both. (Motions to a
chair.) Please sit down and I'll call him.

DAVIES:

Let *me* go. I'm familiar with some of his other ac-
complishments but I'd like to see how good a
bricklayer he is.

They all laugh.

MRS. CHURCHILL:

Then follow that path. And please remind him that
Hitler's speech is on the wireless at three o'clock.

Davies nods and starts down the terrace and out of the
shot.

MRS. DAVIES:

I doubt if either of them will remember once they
get started on politics.

MRS. CHURCHILL:

Did you ever stop to think, Mrs. Davies, that men
are always trying to make the world better or worse
while most women are content just to live in it.

Mrs. Davies smiles.

                                              CUT TO:

249. MED. SHOT   A SEQUESTERED CORNER OF THE GARDEN
containing some attractive planting and several rough,
wooden garden chairs. Churchill is working on his brick
wall with trowel and mortar. He is dressed in an old
coat, sports pants, and a shirt open at the neck. An unlit
cigar protrudes from the side of his mouth.

DAVIES' VOICE (OVER SCENE):
You lay those bricks like a professional.

As Davies walks into the SHOT, Churchill turns around,
grinning.

CHURCHILL:
I *am* a professional. I'm only an amateur at politics.
(He comes forward to shake his visitor's hand.)
Well, Davies, it's good to see you again . . . Sit
down.

He motions to a chair. They both take seats.

DAVIES:
It's always nice to be here.

CHURCHILL:
Well, tell me all about Russia.

DAVIES (laughing):
Do you want it in five minutes or do you want me to
stay a week?

CHURCHILL (lighting his cigar):
First, about that Red Army. You hear all sorts of
things. The French general, Gamelin, just made a
statement that it's strong only on paper.

DAVIES:
That's the kind of reckless statement one ally
shouldn't make of another—if he wants to *keep* him
as an ally.

CHURCHILL:
But most of the military observers bring back the
same kind of report.

DAVIES:

There's so much anti-Soviet prejudice in the diplomatic corps that they won't see the truth or, if
they do see, they won't admit it.

CHURCHILL:

Well, what *is* the truth?

DAVIES:

I'm not a soldier, Churchill, but I think it is one of
the finest armies in the world—in morale, in train-
ing and equipment. And I've never seen a Soviet
general whose stomach girth isn't smaller than his
chest. (Smiles.) That's more than you can say for
Gamelin—or Goering, for that matter.

CHURCHILL:

But an army's no better than its second line of defense. How about their industry?

DAVIES:

I've inspected their plants and I know plants. In a
short span of years they've accomplished miracles
in their industrial development. It's my opinion
that if war comes, these people will give a magnificent account of themselves. And it's foolish to un-
derestimate either their strength or their good faith.

CHURCHILL:

Humph . . . (Plays with his trowel for a moment.)
Well, what do you want me to do?

DAVIES:

I can tell you what I'd like to see done—and done
quickly.

CHURCHILL:

Yes?

DAVIES:

My friend, I wish you were helping to build another
wall . . . (gestures toward the brick wall) a solid

wall of military alliances with Russia and with every other country threatened by Germany. That would pin Hitler in and short-circuit his plan of chewing up Europe a piece at a time.

CHURCHILL:

Davies, as you already know, I'm not a member of the government.

DAVIES:

But you have tremendous influence with the English people. Bring home to them the terrible danger we're all in.

CHURCHILL (ironically):

No, I'm an alarmist. I say things people don't like to hear. Nothing short of a major catastrophe would cause my voice to be heard.

DAVIES:

Unless you make it heard, it will be a major catastrophe. If the democracies continue to look down their noses at Russia, do you know what will happen? Just as sure as we're sitting here, they'll drive Stalin into Hitler's arms.[64]

CHURCHILL:

Do you think that's possible?

DAVIES:

Stalin himself implied that in our talk. And I've had information from the most reliable sources that Moscow is getting fed up with the delays of England and France in concluding a military alliance. All they ask is the same guarantee of assistance against Hitler that they're willing to give.

CHURCHILL:

Well, I can't see anything wrong with that. It sounds fair enough. As a matter of fact, I've long been an advocate of a realistic Triple Alliance, including Russia, directed against aggression. In my opinion, we ought to stop all this boggling and settle these negotiations with Moscow.

DAVIES:

If you don't, they'll certainly take Hitler's alternative. These people are realistic, Churchill. They're not going to fight anyone else's war. In the long run they know they'll have to fight Germany, but a temporary nonaggression pact would give them more time to prepare.

CHURCHILL:

And it would be a disaster for us. If Hitler could close his eastern door, he'd be able to fight on one front.

DAVIES:

Exactly. And that front would be against your country and France.

Churchill rises, walks across the corner of the garden and back again, puffing meditatively on his cigar. He turns back to his guest. For the first time, his voice is intense and emotional.

CHURCHILL:

It's that damnable blackmail threat from the air. It ties our government's hands. That's been the trouble all along . . . But what you've said has impressed me tremendously, Davies. We should make this alliance effective, and effective at once. I can't promise too much, but I'll do what I can.

DAVIES:

Then I'm very glad I came.

CHURCHILL:

And what about America? Your government could throw considerable weight behind the other democracies if it weren't for that Neutrality Act.[65]

DAVIES:

> I'm going back there to tell the president and Congress what I've just told you—that unless we stand together against Hitler, we're very apt to have to fight him alone.

Suddenly we hear the unmistakable staccato, hysterical voice of Hitler coming OVER SCENE from the house.

CHURCHILL:

> Speaking of the devil. (They both grin.) Well, we might as well go in and listen.

Davies rises. They start to walk slowly up the path.

CHURCHILL:

> It might give us an idea what he's going to do next, because it will be the exact opposite of what he promises.

The CAMERA STAYS for a moment on the unfinished brick wall.

DISSOLVE TO:

250. STOCK SHOT (LONG) CHURCHILL
speaking to a group of English people, who are listening intently.[66]

DAVIES' VOICE (OVER SCENE):

> Churchill kept *his* word. He made speeches urging an immediate and effective military alliance with the Soviet Union. The English people began to listen, but again, the reactionary government hesitated, compromised, juggled even at the eleventh hour.

251–56. OMITTED

257. STOCK SHOT STALIN AND MOLOTOV
receiving von Ribbentrop in the Kremlin.

DAVIES' VOICE (OVER SCENE):

> Then the bombshell exploded in the face of the world. Stalin and Molotov boldly reversed their policy and signed a mutual nonaggression pact with Germany. Hitler's eastern door was closed, and he turned his eyes toward the west.[67]

258.   STOCK SHOT   THE CAPITOL, WASHINGTON

DAVIES' VOICE (OVER SCENE):

> At this point only one country could possibly swerve Hitler from his course—the United States of America. But our government was powerless to act on behalf of the democracies, with the Neutrality Bill in force, which forbade American aid or supplies to any country at war—regardless of whether that country was the aggressor or the victim of aggression.

259.   STOCK SHOT   STATE DEPARTMENT BUILDING

DAVIES' VOICE (OVER SCENE):

> After making my report to the president on the state of affairs in Europe, he asked me to attend the meeting of a congressional committee that was called to consider the administration's plea for amending the Neutrality Act.

260.   MED. CLOSE SHOT   FIRST CONGRESSMAN
who is the committee spokesman at this meeting. He is self-assured but not pompous.

FIRST CONGRESSMAN:

> . . . But congressional sentiment hasn't changed, Mr. Secretary. Personally I don't advise reopening the question of amending the Neutrality Bill in this session.

261.   FULL SHOT   OFFICE OF THE SECRETARY OF STATE
Mr. Hull is seated at his desk. A committee of a half-

dozen congressional leaders, unidentified to the audience, are scattered about the room. Ambassador Davies sits in a corner at one side of the secretary's desk. He is listening to the remarks of the congressmen with a concerned, and sometimes incredulous, expression. Their attitude in the beginning of the scene is one of only mild interest in the matter under discussion.

SECOND CONGRESSMAN:
> In my judgment, it wouldn't have a chance of passing unless some emergency made it imperative.

THIRD CONGRESSMAN:
> And as a matter of fact, the European situation looks better than it has for some time. Hitler's got Czechoslovakia and Memel. That may keep him quiet.

HULL (remaining patient with an effort):
> Gentlemen, do you really believe Hitler's going to be satisfied with crumbs when he thinks he can grab the whole loaf?

262.   MED. CLOSE SHOT   FOURTH CONGRESSMAN
gazing idly out of a window.

HULL'S VOICE (OVER SCENE):
> According to his own statements, Danzig and the Polish Corridor are next on his list.

CAMERA PANS to the fifth congressman, who is cleaning his fingernails with a pocketknife.

VOICE OF SECOND CONGRESSMAN (OVER SCENE):
> We believe he's bluffing, Mr. Secretary, and this time England and France won't let him get away with it.

CAMERA CONTINUES TO PAN to the sixth congressman, who is idly leafing pages in a book while he listens with only superficial attention.

HULL'S VOICE (OVER SCENE):

Mr. Senator, I don't propose to argue the point with you. It's one opinion against another.

CAMERA NOW PANS to Ambassador Davies as he takes troubled note of these evidences of disinterest on the part of these several congressmen.

HULL'S VOICE (OVER SCENE):

But we have a man here who's just come back from Europe and has observed conditions at first hand. The president has asked Ambassador Davies to give us his views.

263.   MED. SHOT   THE ROOM   FAVORING DAVIES

FIRST CONGRESSMAN:

We'll be glad to hear whatever Mr. Davies has to tell us.

DAVIES:

Well, gentlemen, I hope you'll let me speak frankly. As I sat here listening, I felt like someone returning to another planet, instead of another continent. In Europe they don't ask anymore, "Is there going to be war?" They only ask, "When is war coming?"

SECOND CONGRESSMAN:

And what answer did you hear to that question?

DAVIES:

That unless something is done quickly to change the present course, it will come either before Hindenburg's birthday in August or before the Nuremberg rally in September.

There is a moment of silence over the room. The congressman who has been cleaning his nails stops, looks at Davies.

THIRD CONGRESSMAN:

But that would be within two months!

DAVIES:

Yes. That's why I feel much depends on the action of Congress. By amending the Neutrality Bill, we can serve notice on Hitler that this country is prepared to give material aid to any nation resisting aggression. In my opinion that's the last desperate chance to prevent the outbreak of war.

FIRST CONGRESSMAN:

On what do you base your conviction that war is so close, Mr. Ambassador?

DAVIES:

I visited seventeen European countries and talked to all kinds of people—heads of government, businessmen, and taxicab drivers. Almost all of them were agreed it would come this year. Besides that, I saw enough with my own eyes to convince me that Hitler is getting ready to take the plunge. He can't afford to wait until the other countries catch up in armament. Time is working against him and for his enemies.

SECOND CONGRESSMAN:

In my opinion, Hitler hasn't the economic strength to take on England and France.

DAVIES:

Mr. Senator, may I submit a few facts to test that opinion?

He rises, walks to a large map of Europe on the wall.

264. CLOSE SHOT   DAVIES AT THE MAP

DAVIES:

Here's the territory Germany would control. (Indicates the portions of map as he names them.) All this vast area of Central Europe. He would have access to all the resources from Berlin to Bagdad.

265.   CLOSE SHOT   SIXTH CONGRESSMAN
as he stops turning pages of his book and gives all of his attention to Davies. The CAMERA THEN PANS over the faces of the other congressmen, now all equally attentive and listening with serious expressions.

DAVIES' VOICE (OVER SCENE):
Britain and France with a combined population of 82 million, desperately unprepared, would be confronted with 76 million German, 44 million Italians, having a working agreement with 70 millions in Japan—a total of 190 million people armed to the teeth.

266.   FULL SHOT   THE ROOM

THIRD CONGRESSMAN:
But the British navy could blockade Germany and Italy by sea.

DAVIES:
Hitler has enough submarine and air power to break any blockade. In fact, the shoe might be on the other foot. (Walks back to his chair.) That's not a very pleasant picture, gentlemen, but it's safer to see an enemy reaching for his gun than to find yourself looking in the barrel.

HULL:
Thank you, Mr. Ambassador. (Turns to the others.) I can't add anything to what Mr. Davies said. I can only plead with you to put all party considerations aside—give our president the one chance left to stave off what may be a catastrophe for the whole world.

The congressmen look uncomfortably toward their spokesman, who musters what self-assurance he can.

FIRST CONGRESSMAN:

Mr. Secretary, if we agreed with your premise, it would be our duty to join in amending the Neutrality Act at once. We don't doubt that Mr. Davies is sincere in his convictions, as you are in yours. But we must act in accordance with our own.

HULL:

Then, Mr. Senator, it will be your responsibility for whatever happens. We've done all we can.

FIRST CONGRESSMAN:

We accept that responsibility. We've gone to considerable trouble and expense to get our own information, which assures us that there will be no war in Europe this year.

DISSOLVE TO:

267. A DATELINE   SEPTEMBER 1, 1939
The date DISSOLVES with the terrific roar of cannon as German artillery goes into action against Poland.

268. STOCK SHOT   GERMAN BOMBERS
filling the sky over Poland. (From the first SHOT of war till the next narration no words and no music, only the mounting noise of war mechanisms.)

269. STOCK SHOT   POLISH PEASANTS
running in panic.

270. STOCK SHOT   A CRUMBLING HOUSE
whose walls fall toward the CAMERA.

271. A MAP   GERMANY IN EUROPE
The borders begin to spread outward through Poland,[68] and as the Denmark and Norwegian lines waver and break—

272. STOCK SHOT   PARACHUTE TROOPS

273. STOCK SHOT GERMAN SOLDIERS
marching through peaceful streets in the early morning
light.

274. STOCK SHOT NAZI PENNANT
flapping over the invaders.

275. THE MAP GERMANY IN EUROPE
The borders, now that Denmark and Norway are engulfed, spread toward Holland and Belgium.

276. STOCK SHOT BOMBED ROTTERDAM
as seen from plane.

277. STOCK SHOT BOMBING OF LIEGE, BELGIUM

278. THE MAP GERMANY
The French border weakens and crumbles.

279. STOCK SHOT TANKS
rumbling along a country road.

280. STOCK SHOT TANKS
passing a French signpost.

281. STOCK SHOT A SCENE SHOWING EVACUATION OF DUNKIRK

282. STOCK SHOT HITLER
stepping through the streets of Paris. Although no machines are in sight, the clanking machine noise continues over his steps.

283. THE MAP GERMANY IN EUROPE
As the map absorbs Italy, Spain, the Balkans, and
Greece, the clanking sound dies down, and over the still
map, whose border is slightly pulsating but not changing, Davies' voice is heard:

DAVIES' VOICE:
> And then the conqueror paused, faced with a formidable nation on each side . . .

284. STOCK SHOT DOVER CLIFFS

DAVIES' VOICE:
> Britain, standing anxious, but firm . . .

285. STOCK SHOT SOVIET BORDER GUARDS

DAVIES' VOICE:
> And the Soviet Union, with whom the German Reich was, technically, at peace.

286. STOCK SHOT FOUNDRY

DAVIES' VOICE:
> Soviet industry used every minute of the time it had gained to prepare.

287. MAP SHOWING SOVIET BORDERS EXTENDING OVER PORTION OF FINLAND

DAVIES' VOICE:
> While the Soviet leaders, well knowing Hitler's past record of broken promises, asked Finland's permission to occupy strategic positions against Germany and offered twice the territory in exchange. But Mannerheim, Hitler's friend, refused and the Red Army moved in by force.

288. STOCK SHOT LOADING DOCKS, U.S.A.

DAVIES' VOICE:
> In the meantime, with the Neutrality Act finally amended and the Lend-Lease bill passed, we were rushing supplies to England—in spite of German submarines.

289.   STOCK SHOT   BOMBING OF LONDON

DAVIES' VOICE:

> And a capital that Hitler tried desperately to shake loose withstood his assault from the air . . .

290.   R.A.F. SHOOTING DOWN GERMAN BOMBERS

DAVIES' VOICE:

> . . . then outfought him in the skies and shattered his dream of invading the British Isles.

291.   STOCK SHOT   A PEACEFUL SUMMER LANDSCAPE

DAVIES' VOICE:

> But Hitler *had* to move. He had gone too far to stop, and he chose to attack the country he had solemnly agreed not to attack.

292.   STOCK SHOT   EXPLOSIONS

out of which the date June 22, 1941 comes. The date fades out and German armored divisions advance on Russian soil.[69]

293.   MED. SHOT   PRESIDENT ROOSEVELT'S STUDY   NIGHT

Davies and the president are leaning over a small map that rests on the desk under a lamp. The rest of the room is dark. Except for his hands on the map, the president is mostly in shadow. Unlike the first scene, whose atmosphere was easy and relaxed, this is one of tension and repressed excitement. As Davies talks, his finger is on the map.

DAVIES:

> . . . I was in Smolensk in '38. The city is an important rail center. It will be a serious blow if the Germans take it.

ROOSEVELT:

> I don't see how it can hold out with pincers closing in on both sides.

DAVIES:

> Well, losing a city—or ten cities—isn't losing the war. The Russians will take their losses and go on fighting.

ROOSEVELT:

> How about Moscow? The military experts say it will fall within six weeks.

DAVIES:

> I can only say that I think they're wrong, Boss. I predict the Red Army will amaze the world.

ROOSEVELT:

> I'm glad to hear you say that, Joe. I'm going to ask Congress to extend Lend-Lease aid to Russia. That means, if we're wrong, the stuff will fall into German hands.[70]

DAVIES:

> It's worth the risk. For the first time in months I feel there's a chance of beating Hitler.

ROOSEVELT:

> If only more of our people realized that! There's been so much prejudice stirred up about the Soviet Union that the public haven't been given a chance to know the truth.

There is a moment's pause.

DAVIES:

> Mr. President, a few years ago you called me into this office to give me a job. It was a bigger job than I thought at the time—and I don't think it's over yet. I want to lay those ghosts that our Fascist propagandists have been brewing up about Russia and tell our people the facts. May I have your permission to use my reports to the State Department?

ROOSEVELT (with deep satisfaction):
> You've more than my permission, Joe. You have my blessing.

DAVIES:
> Now the next thing is to get Marjorie's. She made me promise to take a rest . . .

QUICK DISSOLVE TO:

294. LIVING ROOM OF DAVIES' WASHINGTON HOME LATER THAT NIGHT

Mrs. Davies is seated in a chair with some embroidery work. Emlen and Bob Grosjean, now her husband, are playing a game of checkers. Emlen makes a move, but her mind isn't on the game.

EMLEN:
> Do you suppose we'll ever get off to camp?

MRS. DAVIES:
> Maybe we can go next week if your father finishes up his business.

EMLEN:
> We haven't had a family vacation for three years. (To Bob as he jumps three of her men.) You brute!

BOB (sweetly):
> Keep your mind on the game, darling.

Davies walks into the room. He makes an attempt to be casual and cheerful.

DAVIES:
> Hello, Ekay— Hello, son.

BOB:
> Hello, Mr. Davies.

EMLEN:
> Hello, Daddy.

DAVIES (kisses his wife):
Sorry to be so late, darling, but—

EMLEN:
Daddy, *can* we start our vacation next week?

DAVIES:
I'm afraid not. You see, I . . . I've got to make a little trip first.

All three look up at him.

MRS. DAVIES:
Where to, Joe?

DAVIES (still trying to toss it off):
Around the country—New York, Chicago, Toronto, maybe the Coast.

MRS. DAVIES:
What on earth for?

DAVIES:
I've just had a talk with the president and—

MRS. DAVIES:
Joe, you're not going to lecture?

DAVIES:
Not lecture, dear—just speak. Clear up some things about Russia.

MRS. DAVIES:
But you know what the doctor said. Unless you take a real rest—

DAVIES:
Oh, doctors are over-cautious. They're as bad as lawyers. (Changes to serious vein.) Listen, Marjorie, our friends in Russia need help. And that isn't all. We're going to be in this ourselves before long . . . (gestures toward Emlen and Bob, who are listening intently) the children, you, all of us. (Puts

his arm around his wife.) I'm just getting a little head start.

For a moment Mrs. Davies seems about to press her objection further but changes her mind, smiles understandingly, and presses his arm.[71]

DISSOLVE TO:

295.   STOCK SHOT   GERMAN FOOTAGE
A wave of German tanks breaks over Soviet positions. Red Army troops fight desperately but give ground under the sheer weight of the attack. (Again no music—only harsh, mechanized sounds.)

FIRST ISOLATIONIST'S VOICE (OVER SCENE):
Why, Russia's as good as licked! She'll never last out the summer.

296.   CLOSE-UP   FIRST ISOLATIONIST

FIRST ISOLATIONIST:
And then what will happen to the war supplies we're sending her?

297.   STOCK SHOT   CROWD
listening to the isolationist's words.

FIRST ISOLATIONIST'S VOICE (OVER SCENE):
Supplies that *you're* paying for, my fellow citizens, out of your hard-earned taxes.

298.   CLOSE SHOT   SECOND ISOLATIONIST

SECOND ISOLATIONIST:
. . . Another thing about this Joe Stalin. He might change color overnight—from Bolshevik red to the black swastika.

299.   LONG SHOT   DAVIES
speaking from a platform, SHOOTING OVER the backs of an audience. (NOTE: At the beginning, let Davies speak

at a distance as though his voice were at first a small one that grows in volume as his cause gathers strength.)

DAVIES:

> The plain answer is that Premier Stalin and the Soviet government have solemnly pledged they will fight to the end and make no separate peace with Hitler.[72]

300.   STOCK SHOT   RUSSIAN ARTILLERY

firing at the invaders. The Soviet gun crews working with feverish speed.

DAVIES' VOICE (OVER SCENE):
> And the Soviet Union keeps its word!

301.   CLOSE SHOT   THIRD ISOLATIONIST

THIRD ISOLATIONIST (with gesticulations):

> If I had to choose between Hitler and Stalin, I'd a thousand times rather live in a world dominated by a Nazi Hitler than by Red Stalin.

302.   MAP OF EUROPE

The German borders have engulfed most of Europe and are slowly swallowing the vast territory of Russia.

FOURTH ISOLATIONIST'S VOICE (OVER SCENE; speaking in a hollow, prophetic voice):

> We have seen France fall, England bruised and helpless, and now Russia reeling toward defeat. Why throw good money after bad?

303.   MED. SHOT   DAVIES

DAVIES (pleading):

> Russia needs tanks and planes. Russia needs food and strategic metals. Russia needs understanding and encouragement.

304. STOCK SHOTS OF HEROIC RUSSIAN RESISTANCE

Civilians digging breastworks in their streets. Guerrilla snipers shooting Germans from behind trees. Soviet airmen shooting down German bombers. Russian demolition squads blowing up one of their own dams and scorching the earth before the invaders.

DAVIES' VOICE (OVER SCENE):
The Russian people will defend their cities. They will fight in their streets, in their forests, behind the German lines and over them in the air. They will scorch the earth and level their vast projects . . . but they will yield nothing to the invader but death.

305. CLOSE-UP SECOND ISOLATIONIST

SECOND ISOLATIONIST (sarcastically):
And I ask you, what business is all this of ours? No nation is threatening us.

306. AN AUDIENCE LISTENING

SECOND ISOLATIONIST'S VOICE:
Would you tell me how any aggressor could possibly molest our country—a country that by the blessing of Providence is isolated from attack by two vast oceans?

307. MED. SHOT DAVIES

DAVIES:
As I read of beleaguered Moscow and Leningrad and of Germany striking into the depth of Russian industries, then I say to myself and I say to you—

308. STOCK SHOT AN IMMENSE AUDIENCE
(MADISON SQUARE GARDEN OR SIMILAR HALL)

DAVIES' VOICE:
"There, but for the grace of God, goes America."

There *would* go America if we listened to these isolationists and defeatists who still believe that America can be safe as an island of Christian individualism in a sea of totalitarian dictatorship.

309.   FULL SHOT   CONGRESSIONAL COMMITTEE MEETING

FIRST ISOLATIONIST CONGRESSMAN (speaking to the others):
> I say, gentlemen, we can not only do business with Hitler, but we can make a nice profit doing so.

SECOND ISOLATIONIST CONGRESSMAN:
> And I say the same about Japan. Let's keep her happy, and we'll keep a good customer.

310.   MED. SHOT   DAVIES SPEAKING BEFORE OUTDOOR AUDIENCE

DAVIES (heatedly):
> We send our sympathy to China, but our oil and scrap iron to Japan!

311.   CLOSE SHOT   FOURTH ISOLATIONIST

FOURTH ISOLATIONIST:
> Let Russia and England come to terms with Germany.

312.   MAP OF EUROPE
The Nazi invasion of Russia reaches its farthest limit. Suddenly confettilike flakes fall over the gray map. Winter has come.

FOURTH ISOLATIONIST'S VOICE (OVER SCENE):
> What have they to gain by continuing a hopeless fight?

313.   MED. CLOSE SHOT   DAVIES

DAVIES:
Russia is the world's last rampart against Fascist slavery. Russia will hold that rampart!

At this point the conflicting voices become more and more intense and the shots more rapid.

314.   CLOSE SHOT   FIFTH ISOLATIONIST

FIFTH ISOLATIONIST:
Russia has no chance . . .

315.   CLOSE SHOT   SIXTH ISOLATIONIST

SIXTH ISOLATIONIST:
It's going to be Hitler's Europe and I say what of it!

316.   MED. SHOT   DAVIES
alone in a hotel room, writing furiously on a speech. Lines of fatigue are deepening on his face.

ISOLATIONIST'S VOICE (OVER SCENE):
Let's stop butting our heads against a stone wall.

317.   CLOSE SHOT   FIRST ISOLATIONIST

FIRST ISOLATIONIST:
That's why I prefer . . .

318.   STOCK SHOT   RUSSIAN CIVILIANS LYING DEAD IN THE SNOW

FIRST ISOLATIONIST'S VOICE (OVER SCENE):
. . . a negotiated peace to a complete victory by either side.

319.   CLOSE SHOT   DAVIES

DAVIES:
You can't negotiate with evil . . .

320. FULL SHOT AUDIENCE

ISOLATIONIST'S VOICE (OVER SCENE):
   This conscription bill is unconstitutional . . .

321. MED. SHOT SECOND ISOLATIONIST

SECOND ISOLATIONIST:
    . . . It takes away our rights as Americans.

322. CLOSE SHOT THIRD ISOLATIONIST

THIRD ISOLATIONIST:
   No one to my knowledge . . .

323. STOCK SHOT SUBMARINE PERISCOPE
rising and racing through the water toward the CAMERA.

THIRD ISOLATIONIST'S VOICE:
    . . . is so foolhardy as to attack this great nation.

324. CLOSE SHOT DAVIES
his voice rising in intensity.

DAVIES:
   Let's not delude ourselves. No one is safe as long as
   the power-crazed rulers of Japan and Germany are
   loose in the world.

325. STOCK SHOT UNIDENTIFIED BOMBING PLANES
in the far distance, flying toward the CAMERA.

FIRST ISOLATIONIST'S VOICE (OVER SCENE):
   Of all the Asiatic people . . .

326. MED. CLOSE SHOT FIRST ISOLATIONIST

FIRST ISOLATIONIST:
    . . . the Japanese are the most nearly like us. They
   have enough to do on their continent. They want
   no trouble with us. Why, they have actually gone to

the length of Clippering a special envoy over here to talk peace!

The speaker's upraised arm starts down to pound home his point. As the clenched fist descends, it becomes a bomb that envelops the whole scene, obliterating the speaker. The sky is full of bombs and flashes of fire as they strike warships and docks and landing fields. Without mentioning the name Pearl Harbor, we recognize the scene of the attack and catch a glimpse of the emblem of the rising sun on one of the attacking planes.[73]

DISSOLVE TO:

327.   STOCK SHOT   ESTABLISHING WASHINGTON AIRPORT

328.   LONG SHOT   AT PLANE
as passengers are leaving transport. A group of people are waiting—reporters, news photographers, Soviet officials in uniform, etc. There is a shout of welcome from them as Ambassador and Mrs. Litvinov appear from the plane. She smiles and he waves his hand. As Litvinov comes through the gate he is met by Davies. They grasp each other's hands warmly.

DAVIES:
Welcome to your new post, Mr. Ambassador.

LITVINOV (laughing):
Ah, yes, the tables are turned . . . It is good to see you.

DAVIES:
Maxim, you're coming right up to my house. Marjorie and I want you to have your first meal in Washington with us.

LITVINOV:
That is very kind.

The CAMERA TRUCKS with them as they start to walk down the runway.

LITVINOV (continuing):
Well, my friend, it has come. You, too, are at war.

DAVIES:
It's a terrible thing, but since it had to come, thank
God we're on the same side . . . the right side.
DISSOLVE TO:

329–31. OVER THE FLAGS   MAP ROOM
PANNING PAST the flags of the United States, Great Britain, Russia, China, and all those of the United Nations,
then to the huge planning table with its map of the
world.

DAVIES' VOICE:
And now, united among ourselves, and together
with Great Britain, Russia, China, and all free nations, we face our next mission—an even greater
mission—[74]

332.   CLOSE SHOTS   ON THE MAP
featuring Germany and Japan as the objectives.

DAVIES' VOICE:
—first and foremost is the task of winning this war.
With full faith in the outcome, we shall not fail or
forget those gallant people who first met the blazing
fury of the Nazi hordes . . .

333.   SERIES OF STOCK SHOTS OF FURIOUS FIGHTING
as the Nazi blitzkrieg smashes into Russia, tanks,
planes, and men; sweeps on to within ninety miles of
Moscow before it is jolted to a stop by the terrific defense of the Red Army, and then thrown back in defeat
by the great counteroffensive.

DAVIES' VOICE:
Never in history have there been such masses of
men and mechanized power as those which Hitler
hurled over the borders of the Soviet Union, in vio-

lation of the pledged honor of his government and his people. In brutal waves of blood the juggernaut of Germany rolled in high speed, scorching the earth on the road to Moscow. The jubilant Führer proclaimed his greatest victory: "The Red Army is annihilated!" But the wind of his boasts reaped a whirlwind of disaster. At the gates of Moscow and Leningrad, on the frozen fields of the Ukraine, and within the shambles of Stalingrad the Russian people stood firm in the crisis of our darkest hour. With millions of lives they paid for precious time. Time for America to rearm the United Nations. Time for Great Britain to reform her lines. Time for the Fascist tide to shatter its strength against the iron wall of human freedom!

334. FINAL SEQUENCE

As the last SHOT in the preceding MONTAGE, we see the Nazi army in Russia in headlong retreat. Now for smooth continuity we match this SHOT's general effect with a SHOT of our own, showing German infantrymen retreating through a gray fog or ground mist, twenty or thirty men in ragged formation, partly obscured by the fog. The sounds of battle continue faintly in the distance.

DAVIES' VOICE:

And now slowly but surely the tide of evil forces recedes across the earth, leaving in its wake the next great task of rebuilding a free world . . .

Now the German soldiers are swallowed up in the fog as they move on out of the scene, and for a few feet the screen reveals only the swirling fog, mixed with the smoke of battle. It slowly begins to lift and dispel during the following commentation.

DAVIES' VOICE:

In faith and justice to the heroes of all nations who have given their lives in this, the people's war . . .

The fog has now blown away and we see the bleak corner of a Russian battlefield, covered with swirling snow. Row on row of plain wooden crosses mark the graves of the Russian dead, and a Soviet sentinel is standing guard over them, holding his bayoneted rifle with its butt against the ground.

DAVIES' VOICE:
—we, the living, say to you: Wherever you may hallow the ground in which you lie—

335. CLOSE SHOT   THE RUSSIAN SENTINEL
with the rows of crosses visible beyond him in the snow. The plain Russian soldier with his strong, simple face is partly transparent, the dead sentinel of the Russian dead.

DAVIES' VOICE:
—whether beneath the snows of Russia—
LAP DISSOLVE TO:

336. CLOSE SHOT   A BRITISH SENTINEL
A plain soldier of Britain, wearing his sun helmet in the blazing sun of North Africa, is standing exactly as was the Soviet sentinel, and beyond him in the sands we see the rows of crosses of the valiant British dead.

DAVIES' VOICE:
—the desert sands of Africa—
LAP DISSOLVE TO:

337. CLOSE SHOT   A CHINESE SENTINEL
repeating the composition exactly as above, against a Chinese field with crosses.

DAVIES' VOICE:
—the ancient soil of ravaged China—
LAP DISSOLVE TO:

338. CLOSE SHOT   AN AMERICAN SENTINEL
A young soldier or marine, standing as were the others,

in his helmet and with grounded rifle, against a background of jungle and sea, his face and body partly transparent.

DAVIES' VOICE:

—or beneath the deep green jungles of Guadalcanal—know you all that we, the free men and women of the earth, will never again permit that you shall have died in vain . . .

As the soldier looks up slowly toward the sky, we

PAN UP TO:

339.   LONG SHOT   THE SKY

Slowly the clouds of war sweep away to reveal the bright sky of a new day and a new world, and CAMERA REMAINS on this inspiring symbol to the end, as the music builds powerfully with the closing words, spoken with great and moving sincerity.

DAVIES' VOICE:

And to you, the unborn generations yet to come, we pledge that whatever else our victory shall bring, it will first and forever make an end of war—so that you to whom the great future belongs, shall be able to live, not as fighting beasts, but with the spirit of God in your souls—free, happy, and secure in an everlasting peace.[75]

FADE OUT

THE END

Notes to the Screenplay

1 Scene 1 is omitted in the release print. Instead, Davies himself introduces the film, after this rolling title:

We have the honor to present the former Ambassador from the United States to the Soviet Union, the Honorable Joseph E. Davies, who will address you prior to the showing of a film made from his important book, *Mission to Moscow*.

In the picture itself, Mr. Walter Huston portrays Mr. Davies during those vital years encompassed in his now significant report to this nation. And now, Mr. Davies:

DAVIES: When I was your ambassador in Russia I little expected to write *Mission to Moscow*—much less to see it projected on the screen. But, when Germany attacked Russia, the Soviet Union became one of the nations fighting Hitler. And it was a desperate hour. If Hitler were to destroy the Red armies and to smash the Soviet Union, the three aggressor nations would dominate Europe, Asia, and Africa. The riches of these three continents and the enslaved labor of three quarters of the population of the world would be harnessed to conquer the rest of the earth. The Americas would be next—us. Unity among the forces fighting Hitler was vital. Nothing, as I saw it, was more important than that the fighting nations should understand and trust each other. There was so much prejudice and misunderstanding of the Soviet Union, in which I partly shared, that I felt it was my duty to tell the truth about the Soviet Union as I saw it for such value as it might have.

If I were down there in the audience with you, there are certain things that I would want to know about the man who is telling the story, so that I could assess the reliability of his judgment, and his bias or his lack of bias. Those things about me you're entitled to know. I would want to know them if I were you. Well, they're very simple. My people were pioneers; they came to New Orleans in a sailing ship.

I was born in Wisconsin, educated in the public schools, graduated from the University of Wisconsin, and went to Washington as one of Woodrow Wilson's young men. My religious convictions are basic. My sainted mother was an ordained minister of the Gospel. I think that I am peculiarly the product of our great country and its free institutions and its opportunities in a competitive society of free enterprise. I came up the hard way and I'm glad of it. I have a deep conviction and a firm faith that that system and our form of government is the best that the world has yet produced for the common man. But while in Russia I came to have a very high respect for the integrity and the honesty of the Soviet leaders. I respected the honesty of their convictions and they respected mine. I also came back with a firm conviction that these people were sincerely devoted to world peace and that they and their leaders only wanted to live in a decent world as good neighbors in a world of peace.

That peace has not yet been won. If unity, mutual understanding, and confidence in each other was necessary to win the war, it is still more necessary to win the peace. For there can be no durable peace without an agreement among those nations that have won the war that they will project that peace, maintain that peace, and protect that peace. That is why I wrote *Mission to Moscow*. That is why I am deeply grateful to those fine patriotic citizens the Warner Brothers, and to their great organization of dramatists, artists, and technicians who have projected this book upon the screen for you, my fellow citizens of the Americas and for you my fellow free men of the world. I thank you.

2 In scene 2 the inscription on the inkwell is omitted. As the hand writes, Davies (voice-over) begins, "Without prejudice or partisanship . . ."

3 Italy's Benito Mussolini invaded Ethiopia in October 1935. The League of Nations refused even economic sanctions as one League member used force to conquer another League member (the most obvious violation of the principle of collective security).

4 Laval was French premier in 1935 and met with British Foreign Secretary Sir Samuel Hoare to arrange to give Ethiopia to Mussolini—evidence of what England and France actually proposed to do about the spread of fascism. Laval does not appear in the film.

5 Paul Van Zeeland, Belgian political leader and president of the League of Nations.

6 Instead of this montage the film uses a montage from Leni Riefenstahl's *Triumph of the Will* plus the sounds of "Deutschland Über Alles." Hitler addresses young supporters amidst a sea of

heiling arms, and at Nuremberg's *Luitpoldhain* he places a wreath to honor the war dead.

7 Scenes 27–29 were omitted. Scenes 30–35 were reinserted as follows:

DAVIES (voice-over): Like other Americans I was only vaguely aware of those ominous events. During that summer, my family and I were spending our vacation at our camp on the St. Regis Lake in the Adirondack Mountains. On this particular day, my wife, my daughter, and I were getting ready for a camping trip over the lakes and deep into the mountains.

Mr. and Mrs. Davies and Emlen are loading supplies into a small boat moored along the lakeshore.

MRS. DAVIES: Joe, are you sure we have enough food to last four days?

DAVIES: There will be fish, my dear. Nice, fat lake trout fried over the campfire with bacon.

FREDDIE: Mr. Davies!

EMLEN: Oh, Daddy, here comes Freddie. Don't you dare let anything come up to ruin our trip now.

DAVIES: I suppose I forgot the screwdriver.

FREDDIE: No, sir. There's a telephone call from Washington.

DAVIES: It's the same thing.

FREDDIE: No, sir, it's Mr. Beebe in your office. He says there's a case coming up in the Supreme Court and they want you to try it.

DAVIES: Well! Very interesting. All right, you go back and tell them I'm so deep in the Adirondacks that it would take even Edgar Hoover and Henry Morgenthau to find me. Push us off—will yuh? Everything in, Marjorie?

MRS. DAVIES: Everything's in but you, dear.

EMLEN: Watch out for the tackle, Daddy. Don't step on it.

FREDDIE: Have a nice time.

MRS. DAVIES: Good-bye, Freddie.

DAVIES: Good-bye, Freddie.

EMLEN: If anybody calls for me, Freddie, tell 'em I'm opening sardine cans for Daddy!

RAYMOND: Mr. Davies, Mr. Davies! Mr. Davies!

MRS. DAVIES: Don't you think Raymond announces a bit loudly for a butler?

DAVIES: Five years I've been tryin' to take this vacation and now, by Godfrey, I'm gonna take it.

RAYMOND: I've gotta tell him, Freddie. It can't wait.

FREDDIE: Who wants him?

RAYMOND: Come on, help me with the canoe.

FREDDIE: Sure, I'll help you if you think it'll do you any good.

MRS. DAVIES: Oh, Joe. He's getting in the canoe.

EMLEN: And Freddie is coming with him.

DAVIES (grins and keeps on rowing): He'll have to catch us first. Dip your oars, me lads.

EMLEN: Daddy, row harder. Here they come. Oh. (Sighing.)

Full shot of the boats in the distance. The canoe slowly gains on the one in front of it. Cut to Davies boat, now drifting on the oars; the race is over. The canoe skims into the shot.

RAYMOND: Mr. Davies, you've got to come back.

DAVIES: Freddie, didn't I tell you that I wouldn't give up this trip for anything or anybody?

RAYMOND: Yes, sir. But this fella sounded kind of important.

DAVIES: Nobody's that important. I don't care if it's the president of the United States. Go back and tell 'im I'm busy.

RAYMOND: But, Mr. Davies, it *is* the president.

DAVIES: I don't care if it's the— Huh . . . ? Well, that's different.

The family look at each other in mute astonishment. Dissolve to scene 36.

8 Roosevelt did not usually permit impersonations of himself or of his voice on radio or in films. As a special concession, the White House granted an exception with the proviso that the actor remain off-camera. The audio mix was poor; as a result, Roosevelt seems to boom forth his ideas in what purports to be an intimate meeting of two old friends. (He was also impersonated—and by the same actor, Captain Jack Young—in *Yankee Doodle Dandy*, released in 1942.)

9 At this point in the Caldwell screenplay there was some comic dialogue about Emlen's taking along skis and snowshoes; Marjorie "digs out an enormous ice cream freezer and sighs with relief." Both Joseph and Marjorie Davies strenuously objected to this touch so it was dropped. In fact, however, the Davies did ship enormous amounts of frozen food to Russia because they feared they could not buy what they liked.

10 In other words, whether they are a Communist nation.

11 We recognize the group as Jewish. In the film the guards do not eat knackwurst while the refugees "watch hungrily."

12 The boys are singing "Unsre Fahne flättert uns voran," the official song of the Hitler Youth.

13 A hint that Nazi Germany may be working with conspirators inside the Soviet Union to overthrow Stalin.

14 The children sing "Unsre Fahne flättert uns voran."

15 The dialogue was changed to make the conversation more idiomatic. Davies takes charge in good German—the stereotype of the diplomat fluent in numerous languages.

16 A broad hint of Hitler's forthcoming attack on the Soviet Union in 1941. The film again and again makes the coming of World War II seem inevitable. In the Caldwell treatment of August 4, 1942, the German businessman says: "It will soon be our time to control the tobacco of the world. Then it will be the English who will have to smoke vile cigarettes, not us Germans."

17 Scene 67A was omitted. Crowd reaction shots from *Triumph of the Will* were added to scenes 68 and 76–80, and in the release print scenes 76–80 precede 68–75A.

18 Horace Greeley Hjalmar Schacht, Reich economics minister (acquitted at the Nuremberg trials in 1946). The Schacht scene is not clear. We never understand the visual significance of a mural behind Schacht's desk depicting a factory, nor is the significance of a factory model apparent. In the Caldwell treatments Davies and Schacht visit Minister of Propaganda Joseph Goebbels. In the Koch screenplay of October 6, 1942, Schacht calls Goebbels. In the end Schacht emerged as a more sympathetic character who genuinely responds to Roosevelt's disarmament plan (the one "good" Nazi), but the visuals are suited to a characterization of Schacht as proponent of armament plants. Schacht's unusual name is explained by the admiration of his father (who spent seven years in America) for the 1872 Democratic presidential candidate.

19 Roosevelt's promise to Latin America in 1933 that the United States would replace military intervention with true friendship.

20 William Edward Dodd, American ambassador to Germany.

21 Joachim von Ribbentrop, minister of foreign affairs; signed the Nazi-Soviet nonaggression pact in August 1939; was convicted at the Nuremberg trials and hanged. In the film this scene is played less broadly. Von Ribbentrop does not "laugh again at the colossal joke" nor does he "roar with laughter." Scene 75A is not in the film.

22 Philip Faymonville was extremely pro-Soviet, to the detriment of his career, between August 1939 and June 1941. During the war he supervised Lend-Lease in Moscow.

23 This sentence is not in the film.

24 Davies adds, "Marjorie, real food!" We see a banquet suggesting visually that everyone in Russia has more than enough to eat.

25 We see a sturdy girl, a more believable image. Freddie is played by George Tobias, who specialized in comic roles.

26 In the film he is identified as public prosecutor instead of procurator general. Andrei Vyshinsky is played by Victor Francen, replete with beard (in real life he never wore one) and a demeanor suggesting one who brooks no opposition. He took a leading role in the purge trials.

27 Untrue. The Soviet Union was deeply suspicious of all foreign diplomats and tried to ensure that nobody saw much of anything.

28 Such heavy-handed praise made some believe the film was a campaign document for the president's reelection.

29 Gross stereotyping of Chilston (played by Lumsden Hare). By seeing the French, British, and Polish ambassadors play pool we sense how little they are learning about the "facts" of the Soviet experiment. No wonder Davies decides not to take their cynical advice.

30 Following this scene in the film is a newsreel-style montage of Davies traveling around the Soviet Union to make his own inspection of Russian industry. It opens in a train compartment with a male secretary taking dictation:

DAVIES (voice-over): The Honorable Secretary of State. Finding so many divergent views in Moscow relative to the internal strength of the Soviet Union, I decided to take a trip and see for myself. When I explained my purpose to Premier Molotov, he was most helpful in arranging for me to go where I pleased and to find out the facts without any official guidance.

Dissolve to stock shot of Kharkov.

DAVIES (voice-over): My first stop was at Kharkov, an important industrial city as large as Pittsburgh . . .

Dissolve to stock shots of a modern tractor plant using conveyor belt and line assembly system (similar to the Ford plant at River Rouge, Detroit).

DAVIES (voice-over): . . . where we inspected a modern tractor plant employing twelve thousand people and producing thirty-seven thousand tractors a year.

To vary the narration, the following question-answer device was inserted. Although we do not necessarily see Davies, the answers to his questions come from various workmen or foremen whom the camera picks up in the course of its travels.

DAVIES (voice-over): When was this factory built?

SHOP FOREMAN: It was constructed under the first five-year's plan with the help of engineers from United States, France, and England. Most of the machinery is American.

DAVIES (voice-over): The facts and figures of their output are astonishing for a nation which, almost overnight, sprang from the Middle Ages into modern methods. But despite their great progress, it was my impression that the efficiency of their skilled labor was not yet up to our standard.

Dissolve to set stock shot of technical director's room covered with graphs and charts.

YOUNG WOMAN IN CHARGE: These are production records, Mr. Davies. We keep experimenting to find ways to increase our efficiency. Close shot of a table where a small model of a tractor runs mechanically a distance, then comes to a stop.

DAVIES: Well, what kind of a tractor is this? It looks different from the rest.

YOUNG WOMAN: Yes, Mr. Davies. The reason is this: it can easily be converted—so.

Her hand reaches into the shot, clamps a hood over the tractor, which suddenly becomes a tank. Dissolve to:

DAVIES (voice-over): On my way through the Ukraine, I passed many divisions of the Red Army on maneuvers. Even to a civilian observer this force looks impressive. It's an army on wheels and on wings, and in my opinion it is greatly underestimated by the rest of the world powers. Near the great Dnieper Dam (stock shot), at present the largest source of hydroelectric power in the world, we examined a huge steel plant which employs nine thousand men. Its open hearth steel capacity was 440,000 tons, which compares favorably with our own mills in Gary.

Dissolve to Davies walking in factory with young director.

DAVIES: Yeah, it's really quite amazing. How long were you in America?

YOUNG DIRECTOR: I spent a year in Detroit and Pittsburgh studying your methods and equipment, Mr. Ambassador. We believe our plant here combines the best features of both.

DAVIES: You're pretty young to run a plant like this. How'd yuh get the job?

YOUNG DIRECTOR: Bodje moi! Like anyone else! I worked for it! Watch it, Mr. Davies!

Stock shot of train (from new angle). Superimpose the background of an oil-producing section of the country—hundreds of derricks and oil-drilling machinery (available in our local fields).

DAVIES (voice-over): Then south to the Caspian Sea, where we inspected the oil fields at Baku, producing seven per cent of the country's supply.

DAVIES: Your equipment's pretty well worn out.

WORKMAN: We are trying to replace it as fast as we can. But our country needs so much oil, the supply cannot keep up with demand.

WORKMAN (voice-over): Beside, our government is storing up oil reserves in case comes war.

DAVIES (voice-over): Every plant, every industry is prepared for quick conversion to a wartime basis, and some we saw are not waiting too long.

Dissolve to stock shot of a huge oil-refining plant. Dissolve to interior of the plant. Davies and an American engineer are walking through an area filled with oil-refining machinery.

DAVIES: I certainly didn't expect to find an American engineer here.

ENGINEER: They hired me two years ago, sir, to give 'em advice on installations, and am I anxious to get back to Texas!

DAVIES (laughing): Homesick, huh?

ENGINEER: I'd give a carload of caviar for just one good hot dog.

Studio shot. By this time they are at the end of a factory interior. The engineer pauses, looks around to see that no one is close enough to overhear, then speaks in a low voice.

ENGINEER: Would you mind stepping up here to my office for a moment, sir? It isn't that I particularly want to get back to the States, Mr. Ambassador. In many ways I like it here. These are fine people and they're good at their jobs, too, most of them.

DAVIES: Yeah?

ENGINEER: Sit down, Mr. Davies.

DAVIES: All right to smoke in here?

ENGINEER: Sure. Something is happening in this country that I don't fully understand. There's always a few who seem to be working against the rest.

DAVIES: How do you mean?

ENGINEER: Thank you, sir. Oh, they forget to fill a crankcase or turn the wrong valve, and it takes us a good couple o' months to repair the damage. Production goes to pot. From what I hear, this happens in more places than in the airplane industry.

DAVIES: Sabotage, huh?

Engineer nods. The montage continues with shots of activity at a coal mine, a machine shop, and a farm and ends back in the train compartment.

DAVIES (voice-over): In the great Don Basin, I saw for myself the wealth of Russia's coal resources. I went down into the mine and talked with the workers. Much to my amazement, I discovered that thirty per cent of them were women.

WOMAN WORKER: Excuse me, Mr. Davies. Is it true that in America the women are not allowed to do work like this?

DAVIES: Well, there's no law against it, but we don't like to put them underground until we have to. (Woman laughs.)

DAVIES (voice-over): In Odessa, one of the largest Black Sea ports, I visited some of their machine shops. Again I felt a sense of haste, of pushing production to the limit.

DAVIES: My friend, you seem to enjoy hard work.

WORKER: Pochemu net? [Why not?] Of course, if you work hard, you make more money.

DAVIES: I thought all the profits went to the State.

SECOND FOREMAN: Only a fixed amount. Anything we can produce above that belongs to all of us who works in the factory, in addition to our wages.

DAVIES: Well, I hope I'm not speaking out of turn, but isn't that way of encouraging initiative a slight departure from your original theory?

SECOND FOREMAN: Perhaps, Mr. Davies. But what is it a theory except a means to the end? The greatest good for the greatest number of people.

DAVIES: Not a bad principle. We believe in it, too.

DAVIES (voice-over): The valley of the Dnieper River is one of the most fertile districts in the world. Most of these farms are cooperative, with over six hundred men and women working together on a unit of five thousand acres. Again, as in industry, the workers are entitled to divide the profits over and above the government's share. My conclusion, based on all I have seen and heard in the course of this trip is this: In spite of many mistakes, some inefficiency and even division among themselves, probably inevitable in any great change, I am convinced this nation's aware of its destiny and is making itself ready for whatever lies ahead.

Because revisions in the script often caused irregularities in the numbering of scenes, I have supplied numbers for the next two scenes—and elsewhere in the screenplay, as indicated by brackets—in order to restore sequence.

31 The scene opens with Freddie stepping out of his car and looking at the car behind his in the driveway.

FREDDIE (voice-over): Don't you Gay-Pay-Ooers ever get any sleep? (To attendant at door.) Good morning, Spadebeard.

ATTENDANT: Hello, Freddie. Kak podjivaete. [How-do-you-do?]

FREDDIE: Da, da.

Cut to interior of house where Mrs. Davies stands before mirror.

DAVIES: Marjorie, you look like the pictures of Catherine the Great in that outfit.

MRS. DAVIES: Oh, good heavens! And here am I about to call on the wife of a commissar.

Freddie's dialogue is a light-hearted reference to the fact that Davies and his family were always followed by secret police. To be correct, the reference should be to the KDVD, the People's Commissariat of Internal Affairs, as the GPU was officially renamed in 1934.

32 Apparently this reference to bugging was cut from the Russian version of the film. Koch's story outline of September 4, 1942, dealt with bugging immediately following the purge trial, as follows: "Next scene—the Kremlin. There we find Litvinov, Molotov and Kalinin listening to a record on the play-back for the dictograph machine. We are amazed to find this is a recording of the conversation we just heard between the diplomats during the recess of the trial. When they turn the record off, they discuss Davies favorably. They are convinced that he is a man whom they can trust."

33 The rest of scene 105A is not in the film. Scenes 111–14 were shot on April 15, 1943, less than two weeks before the film's release. Davies insisted on this to please his wife, who wanted audiences to know that she had been a successful businesswoman.

34 In the film the stock footage of crack Russian ski troops comes early in scene 115C, and the dialogue involving Grosjean and Emlen is abbreviated.

35 The film opens the ball scene with guests arriving outside and then cuts inside where Mrs. Molotov and three men (including Vyshinsky, to reintroduce him visually) come into the scene. "Do you commissars ever have time left for your private life?" she asks. Vyshinsky replies that they go fishing—"at parties like this." Cut to Davies and Molotov.

36 Our first introduction to one of the men to be tried in the purge trial

sequence. Tukhachevsky was the highest-ranking military man to be killed by Stalin. He was shot after a secret trial in June 1937.

37 A heavy-handed visual device. The "three stooges" stand together as an unsavory trio.

38 Chilston looks to be a born bumbler. His wife has a dowdy look. Such touches outraged the English when the film was shown widely in 1943 to promote wartime solidarity among America, Russia, and Britain.

39 Chilston's reference to the experiment against human nature and the reference to Mrs. Litvinov's being of English origin (she was) are not in the film.

40 The first part of scene 126A is not in the film.

41 Played by a Chinese actor, Peter Goo Chong, in broad fashion. In his book Davies describes Shigemitsu as "lame—a very able man." In the film we see a stock character with enormous glasses. The camera picks up the reflection off the lenses to suggest his inscrutable nature. He comes off a poor second in every conversation at the ball, in keeping with wartime anti-Japanese stereotypes.

42 The film adds the following dialogue:
SHIGEMITSU: Our young people prefer other forms of sports.
TANYA: Yes. I have seen some recent pictures of them, from China.
Tanya refers to the Japanese bombing of Chinese civilians in 1937.

43 This scene is visually unsuccessful for we do not remember von Ribbentrop as the person Schacht spoke to on the phone in scene 73. His appearance here hints at the Nazi connection with the "three stooges" who are fifth columnists.

44 Another obscure visual reference. The remark refers to Mussolini's sending of troops and material to aid Franco in the Spanish civil war, a touch that loses its effect in part because a montage from *The Triumph of the Will* replaced the references to Spain that were to have been used in scene 26.

45 Scene 135 is not in the film.

46 The script now links American isolationists—who hoped America could stay out of a European war—with European appeasers who, in the person of British Prime Minister Neville Chamberlain, gave away much of Czechoslovakia to Hitler at Munich in September 1938. This is guilt-by-association, and a straight lecture to the audience. Fifth columnists in Madrid, saboteurs inside Russia, American isolationists, appeasers—all are equally guilty.

47 As the camera moves to Litvinov's office, it catches, in a medium close-up, Yagoda, Radek, and Bukharin standing next to a bust of

Lenin. This visual transition reminds us that these three traitors have something to do with what Krestinsky is going to report. The bust of Lenin reminds us that these three are traitors to the revolutionary idealism of Lenin.

48 Limited front lighting accentuates the sinister aspect of the dialogue. It is unseen saboteurs at work, we conclude.

49 The dialogue that follows was changed and extended in this way:
SHIGEMITSU: Please tell your president that Japanese plans for a new order in Asia contemplate no interference in the Philippines, Hawaii, or any American possession. The present war was forced upon us by the hostility of China.
DAVIES: As ambassador, I will convey your message to my president. But, er, between ourselves, Mr. Shigemitsu, the suggestion that Japan had to defend herself against China is pure bunk.
He turns and walks away, the Japanese ambassador staring after him. The camera pans with Davies, who walks into the White Room. He passes Bukharin speaking with von Ribbentrop.
VON RIBBENTROP: . . . I'm leaving at midnight, Bukharin. I'll stop at your apartment on my way to the airport.
BUKHARIN: Very well, I'll expect you.
VON RIBBENTROP: Au revoir.
BUKHARIN: Au revoir.
SHIGEMITSU (coming into scene): What is bunk?
BUKHARIN: Bunk? I don't know.
   This dialogue makes three points. Viewers in 1943 know all about the Japanese sneak attack on Pearl Harbor, December 7, 1941, so the reference to the "hostility of China" is a device for showing how villainous the Japanese are. The reference to bunk is a much-loved wartime tale. The test of an enemy agent's English is whether he knows slang (of course the audience knows what bunk means). The conversation between Bukharin (traitor) and von Ribbentrop shows visually that the Nazis are working with Soviet fifth columnists.

50 After this we cut to a noisy cafe where Radek is enjoying himself with friends when the police come and arrest him. The most controversial part of the film was the decision, for good dramatic reasons, to compress a series of purge trials into one, thus necessitating the arrest of everyone at the same time. This decision had already been made in the Caldwell treatment of August 21, 1942, where Bukharin, Rykov, Yagoda, Tukhachevsky, Krestinsky, and Rakovsky were all tried together. Koch claims the series of arrests in the release

print suggests the reality of Stalinist terror, but this is not apparent
visually.

51 Scene 160 contains two significant additions, both visual. First,
there is stock footage of Fritz Kuhn, the American Nazi *Bund* leader,
at a 1939 rally at Madison Square Garden:

GERMAN VOICE: Sieg Heil, meine lieben Freunde. Communism
is unmasked before the world!

DAVIES (voice-over): No, this is not Germany. It is a *Bund* meeting in
New York City, where Americans were brutally beaten for dar-
ing to interrupt the Führer's friend.

Dissolve to this exchange:

FIRST WORKMAN: Yuh see this? (Cut to newspaper cartoon of Stalin
as butcher.)

SECOND WORKMAN: The Kremlin butcher.

52 Before continuing with this dialogue some additional evidence of
the Nazi conspiracy is offered. Sokolinikov, who identifies himself
as assistant to the commissar of foreign affairs, testifies that the
German army agreed to pay "250,000 marks annually as a subsidy."

53 At this point Tukhachevsky testifies that what Bukharin has said
about him is true—that though a marshal of the Red Army, he
plotted to overthrow Stalin. The statement is completely untrue.

54 The critical moment in the testimony of Bukharin (superbly played
by Konstantin Shayne). Here he offers a reasonable, and patriotic,
explanation for condemning himself to be shot. In the Caldwell
treatment of August 21, 1942, he was merely a stock villain who, for
example, tells Vyshinsky, "Leave me out of this."

55 The clumsy dramatic device of linking the purge conspirators with
Trotsky in exile (scenes 193–95) is omitted from the film. The
Caldwell treatment of August 21, 1942, cut to the "interior of Hitler's Hideaway in Bavaria" with "Hitler, von Ribbentrop, Goebbels, Hess, and Trotsky . . . seated in Hitler's library." The
dialogue was at best awkward:

HITLER: We are not ready for this turn of affairs. You have completely bungled the work you were supposedly directing with
judicious ability. That forces us to withdraw our hand completely for the present. That means Russia will be able to build
up its army and augment its supplies of war materials. You are
trying to force us to act in Russia before we are ready!

TROTSKY: No, no, Herr Hitler. This is all an unfortunate accident.
You know I am in perfect accord with your plans.

56 The stock footage does not match. Compare the shape of the planes seen overhead with that from which the parachutists leap.

57 The rest of scene 199A is cut, as are scenes 200–203.

58 This scene takes place in the Litvinov dacha. In the Koch outline of September 6, 1942, at this point he planned a series of flashbacks to Litvinov's youth as a device for justifying the revolution of 1917: "Litvinov, as a young boy of 15, asks for food at his landlord's house. He is struck with a whip and kicked out into the mud."

59 Scenes 207–12 are not in the film. Instead Davies visits various European capitals—a visual letter, beginning with Poland and Paderewski. Apparently the use of this famous Polish pianist, long out of power, was based on the idea that no other Polish leader would be familiar to most viewers. Davies also visits Austria, Yugoslavia, France, and Holland.

60 One of Roosevelt's few pre-1939 speeches about foreign affairs was his so-called Quarantine Address, delivered in Chicago, October 5, 1937. It is improbable that any report Davies sent back from Europe was the catalyst for the president's speech, though as Koch indicated in his outline of September 6, 1942, "We imply the president's warning now as a direct consequence of the events we have shown through the eyes of Davies." The voice of the president is again an impersonation. Scenes 213–14B are not in the film; it picks up the speech at scene 214C.

61 Scene 221 is not in the film. Scene 222 contains stock footage of Stalin watching the military parade.

62 The first part of the Davies-Rosso dialogue was cut from scene 232.

63 Most of the dialogue in scenes 234B and 234E was cut. "The American people," Davies says to the Chinese ambassador, "have been greatly shocked by the recent atrocities at Shanghai and the *Panay* incident." The reference is to Japanese bombing of Chinese civilians and the sinking of the American gunboat the *Panay* by the Japanese in December 1937. The scene somehow suggests that Stalin is helping the Chinese, though the Soviet Union did not declare war on Japan until August 1945.

64 On August 23, 1939, Hitler signed a nonaggression pact with Russia. Here Davies offers a justification for such a move.

65 A series of neutrality acts, the first passed in 1935, prohibited America's sending arms to either side in event of war.

66 We see Churchill in a stock shot after seeing his look-alike; we saw Stalin in stock footage before his look-alike appeared. Only

Roosevelt fails to appear in stock footage or more than fleetingly in a look-alike capacity.

67 Scene 257 is not in the film. The problem was the necessity of admitting the German-Soviet pact, a major reason for so many Americans' distrusting Stalin. A studio shot shows Davies and his wife on board ship. The moon is out:

MRS. DAVIES: Oh, there you are! I've been looking all over for you.
DAVIES: Have you?
MRS. DAVIES: What's the matter?
DAVIES: This radiogram came a few minutes ago.
MRS. DAVIES: "Dear Mr. Ambassador. Our worst fears are realized. This afternoon a nonaggression pact was signed between Germany and the Soviet Union." Then it's happened.
DAVIES: Hitler's closed his eastern door. God help the rest of us. I feel as though everything the Boss has sent me over to do has gone out the window, that I've accomplished nothing.
MRS. DAVIES: Oh, don't talk like that, Joe. You did everything you could possibly do. And, anyway, there's still a chance our government can do something.
DAVIES: That's right. Anyway, I'm glad we're going back home.

68 The animation shows only Hitler's march from the west, though the Soviet Union moved from the east at the same time.

69 Scene 287 was omitted, and the dialogue for scenes 283–92 was shortened.

70 In March 1941 Congress passed the Lend-Lease Act, which permitted the sending of war materiel to any country fighting Hitler. Roosevelt's decision to send aid to Russia in November 1941 was politically risky since so many believed Russia would be quickly defeated.

71 Emlen and Bob Grosjean were cut from this scene, and the dialogue was changed slightly.

72 Scene 299 precedes 295 to establish Davies' speaking tour.

73 Scenes 306–308, 311–13, and 326 are not in the film. The dialogue is reworked to refute objections about the Soviet Union. Davies speaks from what purports to be Madison Square Garden. Hecklers ask questions, such as why Stalin invaded America's friend, Finland, in 1940:

ELECTRICIAN: What's he in such a sweat about? We got a couple o' oceans, ain't we? (Crowd applauds.)
DAVIES: As I read of the millions of Russians dead, their countless

towns which lie in ruins, then I say to myself and I say to you, "There, but for the grace of God, goes America." There would go America, if we listen to the isolationists and defeatists who still believe that America can be safe as an island of Christian individualism in a sea of totalitarian dictatorship! (Crowd applauds.)

FIRST HECKLER: How do we know that we can trust Russia?

MAN: Sit down!

SECOND HECKLER: Yeah! How about poor little Finland?

DAVIES: This gentleman has asked a question, "How about Finland?" My friend, you've only heard one side of the story. I'll tell you the other.

THIRD HECKLER: I suppose you're gonna tell us she attacked Russia!

DAVIES: Russia knew she was going to be attacked by Hitler so the Soviet leaders asked Finland's permission to occupy strategic positions to defend herself against German aggression. She offered to give Finland twice as much territory in exchange, but Hitler's friend Mannerheim refused and the Red Army moved in. That's why, my friend. (Crowd applauds.)

SECOND MAN: I wonder why these things have been kept from us.

FOURTH HECKLER: What about Russia's air force? One of our aviation experts says their planes are all obsolete.

DAVIES: The gentleman you mention saw only what Russia wanted him to see. Russia has a powerful air force and is ready to defend herself against any aggressor.

FIFTH HECKLER: Why did Stalin make a deal with Hitler?

DAVIES: For self-protection! He was left standing alone against Hitler and he stalled because his army wasn't ready!

SIXTH HECKLER: What'd Russia ever do for us?

DAVIES: Russia has given us time!

SEVENTH HECKLER: Time! Time for what? No nation is threatening us! (December 7, 1941, superimposed over Japanese flag.) We're at peace!

74 As is so often the case, there was much argument about the ending of the film. As late as February 6, 1943, scene 331 cut to Davies at his desk "where we see an opened book which now closes before our eyes. The book is *Mission to Moscow*." The scene was not in the film, but the dialogue was retained ("And now, united among ourselves . . .").

75 Scenes 334–39 are accompanied by a chorus singing "You are your brother's keeper." The final voice-over actually ends as follows:

"And to you, the unborn generations yet to come, we pledge to work for a new world with justice and equality for all, to restore the dignity of man as an individual and not as a slave to any state or master, so that you, to whom the great future belongs, shall be able to reply as we have not, to the old angry cry of Cain, 'Am I my brother's keeper?' with the answer, 'Yes, you are!'" Chorus sings, "You are, yes, you are, you are your brother's keeper, now and fore'er, you are—"

In Koch's outline of September 6, 1942, he thought of ending "perhaps on the famous toast of Stalin to President Roosevelt: 'To President Roosevelt in his leadership of a peace-loving nation that is now engaged in the struggle of the democracies against fascism. May God help him in his most difficult task.'" Koch wanted the following ending, but was overruled by Davies and Buckner:

Full shot of a devastated Russian farm (to be broken up into other shots at the discretion of director). A burned-down house, scorched trees and the shell-pocked earth bear mute witness to recent battle. But already the peasant family—those members too young or too old for combat—are reclaiming their own. Out of the ruined foundation, an old woman digs up a bag of buried seeds, while her daughter gathers some charred cooking utensils and some pathetic fragments of furniture that have withstood the flames. Outside the foundation, the grandfather and his grandson have joyfully rescued a small handplow. In an exuberant gesture of defiance, the boy takes the plow in his hands. As the rest of the family look on, he presses its sharp edge into the ground and plows a furrow straight toward the camera. Larger and larger grow plow and furrow, against an immense span of sky, and the clean earth surges in a cleft wave over the broken land, burying in its wake a steel helmet, the iron fragments of shells and a broken cannon wheel. On the final words the plow, now filling the screen, becomes our symbol poised before the camera. Then the plow begins to move away from the camera and sweeps forward in silhouette against a brightening sky. Over this shot the music swells to a triumphant proclamation that peace and good will is man's final conquest of the earth.

Production Credits

Directed by	Michael Curtiz
Produced by	Robert Buckner
Screenplay by	Howard Koch
From the book by	Joseph E. Davies
Music by	Max Steiner
Director of Photography	Bert Glennon, A.S.C.
Film Editor	Owen Marks
Art Director	Carl Jules Weyl
Sound by	Oliver S. Garretson
Special effects by	Roy Davidson and
	H. F. Koenekamp, A.S.C.
Montages by	Don Siegel and
	James Leicester
Set decorations by	George James Hopkins
Technical Adviser	Jay Leyda
Ballet staged by	Leroy Prinz
Gowns by	Orry-Kelly
Make-up Artist	Gordon Bau
Musical Director	Leo F. Forbstein
Orchestral arrangements by	Bernard Kaun

Released: April 30, 1943
Running time: 123 minutes

Cast

Joseph E. Davies	Walter Huston
Marjorie Davies	Ann Harding
Maxim Litvinov	Oscar Homolka
Freddie	George Tobias
Molotov	Gene Lockhart
Emlen Davies	Eleanor Parker
Paul Grosjean	Richard Travis
Major Kamenev	Helmut Dantine
Vyshinsky	Victor Francen
Von Ribbentrop	Henry Daniell
Ivy Litvinov	Barbara Everest
Winston Churchill	Dudley Field Malone
Krestinsky	Roman Bohnen
Tanya Litvinov	Maria Palmer
Colonel Faymonville	Moroni Olsen
Loy Henderson	Minor Watson
Kalinin	Vladimir Sokoloff
Dr. Botkin	Maurice Schwartz
Chinese ambassador	Lee Tong Foo
Spendler	Jerome Cowan
Schacht	Felix Basch
Timoshenko	Kurt Katch
Haile Selassie	Leigh Whipper
Lady Chilston	Kathleen Lockhart
Mrs. Molotov	Frieda Inescort
Judge Ulrich	Frank Puglia
Grinko	John Abbott
Stalin	Manart Kippen
Mrs. Churchill	Doris Lloyd
Von Schulenberg	Frank Reicher
Yagoda	Daniel Ocko
Bukharin	Konstantin Shayne
Tukhachevsky	Ivan Trisault

Cast

Shigemitsu	Peter Goo Chong
Lord Chilston	Lumsden Hare
Grzybowski	Alec Caze
Coulondre	John Wengraf
Franklin Roosevelt	Captain Jack Young
Maid	Virginia Christine
Dancers in ballet sequence	Cyd Charisse
	Michael Panaieff

Appendix

The fifteen documents that follow contain supporting evidence about the making of *Mission to Moscow* and its reception, both in America and abroad. Documents 1 and 2 come from Davies' book, *Mission to Moscow*. The first describes his personal meeting with Stalin, which was depicted, without change of emphasis, in the film. The second shows that in 1938 Davies had mixed feelings as to the guilt of the purge victims, including Bukharin. Not so in the film, where much of the insistence on absolute guilt comes from the second part of document 2, "Fifth Columnists in Russia: A Study in Hindsight—1941." Document 3 appeared in a pro-Trotskyite American newspaper and indicates that in 1937 Davies was much less enthusiastic about Stalin than document 1 would have us believe.

The next five items discuss the film's production. Documents 4 and 5 show that Davies reported to Roosevelt about the film and that the president knew what was happening. We also see what Davies thought about the appearance of Walter Huston. In document 6 Howard Koch describes Davies' role in changing the opening of the film. Document 7 contains two extensive letters from the film's producer, Robert Buckner, relating to script changes, the film's political implications, and Davies' role. Document 8 is significant given the critical outcry against the film, once released. The Office of War Information's own censor approved the film exactly as it stood and saw nothing wrong with its political content. Documents 9 and 10 show the positions of pressure groups who attacked or defended the film in the United States at the time of release.

Documents 11, 12, and 13 relate to the reception of the film within the Soviet Union. Document 11 was sent from Moscow; Davies reports that Stalin loved *Mission to Moscow*. The exact opposite is stated in document 12, though in May 1943 Ambassador Standley had already been recalled and was bitter toward Roosevelt for having sent Davies as a special messenger. Document 13, from February 1946, describes the distribution of American feature films within the Soviet Union, 1939–45.

Documents 14 and 15 relate to *Mission to Moscow*'s impact in 1947, when many feared that Communists had taken over Hollywood. Document 14 is a 1942 letter from Jack Warner stating that he has read the controversial section of the manuscript dealing with the purge trials and considers it "excellent." Document 15, from 1947, shows Warner claiming under oath that he never knew what was in the script. Robert Stripling, who asks the questions, was the chief investigator for the House Committee on Un-American Activities.

1. Davies' Meeting with Stalin: 1938

Well, after I had left President Kalinin's office and gone to the Premier's apartment—and within a very few minutes after sitting down at the desk—I was perfectly amazed and almost struck dumb with surprise to see the far-end door of the room open and Stalin come in alone. I had not the remotest idea it was going to happen. In the first place, he is not the head of the state, and it is his purpose and theirs, apparently, to keep him apart from the state, and, as you know, no diplomat ever sees him officially or otherwise in a personal way. In fact, he avoids any such meeting. So closely has he been shielded from the public that it has almost become a historical event when he receives any foreigner.

Well, when he came in, of course, I stood up and approached him. He greeted me cordially with a smile and with great simplicity, but also with a real dignity. He gives the impression of a strong mind which is composed and wise. His brown eye is exceedingly kindly and gentle. A child would like to sit in his lap and a dog would sidle up to him. It is difficult to associate his personality and this impression of kindness and gentle simplicity with what has occurred here in connection with these purges and shootings of the Red Army generals, and so forth. His friends say, and Ambassador Troyanovsky assures me, that it had to be done to protect themselves against Germany—and that some day the outside world will know "their side."

Joseph E. Davies, *Mission to Moscow* (New York: Simon & Schuster, 1941), pp. 356–57. Copyright © 1941, 1969 by Eleanor Davies Ditzen, Rahel Davies Broun and Emlen Davies Grosjean. Reprinted by permission of Simon & Schuster, a Division of Gulf & Western Corporation.

2. The Meaning of the Purge Trials: 1938 vs. 1941

SO-CALLED BUKHARIN MASS TREASON TRIAL
NO. 1039   *Moscow, March 17, 1938*
TO THE HONORABLE THE SECRETARY OF STATE

Confidential

Appendix

Sir:

I have the honor to report that this confirms cable sent in confidential code with reference to the judgment of the court in the so-called Bukharin mass treason trial.

Paraphrase of the cable is as follows:

On March 13, 1938, at approximately five o'clock in the morning, all of the defendants in the trial were adjudged guilty and the sentences were imposed. Three of the defendants were condemned to imprisonment and the remainder to death through shooting. Eight of the most prominent former members of the Soviet government, including a former premier, six former cabinet officers, one of the most prominent party leaders and member of the Politburo, and also a former president of one of the constituent republics were among those condemned to be shot. Condemned to imprisonment were a former Ambassador to England and France, a former Counselor of the Soviet Embassy in Berlin, and one famous heart specialist.

Notwithstanding a prejudice arising from the confession evidence and a prejudice against a judicial system which affords practically no protection for the accused, after daily observation of the witnesses, their manner of testifying, the unconscious corroborations which developed, and other facts in the course of the trial, together with others of which a judicial notice could be taken, it is my opinion so far as the political defendants are concerned sufficient crimes under Soviet law, among those charged in the indictment, were established by the proof and beyond a reasonable doubt to justify the verdict of guilty of treason and the adjudication of the punishment provided by Soviet criminal statutes. The opinion of those diplomats who attended the trial most regularly was general that the case had established the fact that there was a formidable political opposition and an exceedingly serious plot, which explained to the diplomats many of the hitherto unexplained developments of the last six months in the Soviet Union. The only difference of opinion that seemed to exist was the degree to which the plot had been implemented by different defendants and the degree to which the conspiracy had become centralized.

I have the honor to be, Sir, respectfully yours,

Joseph E. Davies

FIFTH COLUMNISTS IN RUSSIA.
A STUDY IN HINDSIGHT—1941

NOTE: Although this was written after the German invasion of Russia in the summer of 1941 it is inserted here because this seems the logical place to illustrate how the treason trials destroyed Hitler's Fifth Column in Russia.—J. E. D.

Passing through Chicago, on my way home from the June commencement of my old University, I was asked to talk to the University Club and combined Wisconsin societies. It was just three days after Hitler had invaded Russia. Someone in the audience asked: "What about Fifth Columnists in Russia?" Off the anvil, I said: "There aren't any—they shot them."

On the train that day, that thought lingered in my mind. It was rather extraordinary, when one stopped to think of it, that in this last Nazi invasion, not a word had appeared of "inside work" back of the Russian lines. There was no so-called "internal aggression" in Russia co-operating with the German High Command. Hitler's march into Prague into 1939 was accompanied by the active military support of Henlein's organizations in Czechoslovakia. The same was true of his invasion of Norway. There were no Sudeten Henleins, no Slovakian Tisos, no Belgian De Grelles, no Norwegian Quislings in the Soviet picture.

Thinking over these things, there came a flash in my mind of a possible new significance to some of the things that happened in Russia when I was there. Upon my arrival in Washington, I hastened to reread my old diary entries and, with the permission of the State Department, went through some of my official reports.

None of us in Russia in 1937 and 1938 were thinking in terms of "Fifth Column" activities. The phrase was not current. It is comparatively recent that we have found in our language phrases descriptive of Nazi technique such as "Fifth Column" and "internal aggression."

Generally speaking, the well informed suspected such methods might be employed by Hitler; but it was one of those things which many thought just couldn't really happen. It is only within the last two years, through the Dies Committee and the F.B.I., that there have been uncovered the activities of German organizations in this country and in South America, and that we have seen the actual work of German agents operating with traitors in Norway, Czechoslovakia, and Austria, who betrayed their country from within in co-operation with a planned Hitler attack.

These activities and methods, apparently, existed in Russia, as a part of the German plan against the Soviets, as long ago as 1935.

It was in 1936 that Hitler made his now famous Nuremberg speech, in which he clearly indicated his designs upon the Ukraine.

The Soviet government, it now appears, was even then acutely aware of the plans of the German high military and political commands and of the "inside work" being done in Russia, preparatory to German attack upon Russia.

As I ruminated over this situation, I suddenly saw the picture as I should have seen it at the time. The story had been told in the so-called treason or purge trials of 1937 and 1938 which I had attended and listened to. In re-examining the record of these cases and also what I had written at the time from this new angle, I found that practically every device of German Fifth Columnist activity, as we now know it, was disclosed and laid bare by the confessions and testimony elicited at these trials of self-confessed "Quislings" in Russia.

Joseph E. Davies, *Mission to Moscow* (New York: Simon & Schuster, 1941), pp. 271–74. Copyright © 1941, 1969 by Eleanor Davies Ditzen, Rahel Davies Broun and Emlen Davies Grosjean. Reprinted by permission of Simon & Schuster, a division of Gulf & Western Corporation.

3. Davies' Fears about Stalin: 1937

A letter from Ambassador Davies to Eugene Lyons. It was dated October 16, 1937, and was written from the U.S. Embassy in Moscow. Its occasion was Davies' reading of *Assignment in Utopia*, Lyons' documented indictment of the Stalinist regime as a cynical, totalitarian dictatorship over the Russian people. . . .

My dear Mr. Lyons:
You have written a very remarkable book. I was so fascinated by it that I could not lay it down until long in the night and, in fact, until I had read its first 300 pages. I do not think I could say anything more commendatory than that.
As a human document I find it fascinating. Your first chapter outlining conditions in the East Side of New York and the natural mental reactions which those conditions induced commanded my sympathy and complete understanding, and further on the frankness and elucidation with which you describe the evolution of your thought are most remarkable. It is a fine piece of writing. I greatly honor and respect the intellectual honesty, candor, and courage which the book discloses. . . .
You have written an extraordinary book. I predict for it a great success. Personally I found the greatest of interest and value in its pages. It contributed substantially to my perspective.
I am looking forward to meeting you personally, for there are many things that you write of that I should like to have the benefit of further discussion with you upon.
With assurance of my esteem, I am, very truly yours,
(Sgd.) JOSEPH E. DAVIES

Ex-Ambassador Davies supervised the Warner Bros. film production of his book, *Mission to Moscow*. The movie was a flagrant distortion of the text of the book, but Davies gave unqualified approval to the Hollywood production preceding its release to American audiences.

Eugene Lyons was one of the leading critics of the "totalitarian propaganda" and "fraudulent history" embodied in the Kremlinized screen version. His series of critical articles, and his review in the *American Mercury*, were among the most substantial contributions of the liberal-labor democratic "opposition."

Matthew Low, "A Page That Joseph Davies Forgot." Reprinted with permission from *The New Leader*, June 26, 1943.

4. Davies Reports to Roosevelt about the Film

I had a conference with the President today with reference to his plans for the War Relief Control Board. . . . When I was there, he received a message which had just come from the Russian Embassy by special messenger. After he read it, he turned it over to me and said: "Read it, Joe." It was a personal message from Stalin which Ambassador Litvinov had just sent over. It was very interesting. . . . We discussed the Stalin-Churchill situation and gave him copy of my memo to H. H[opkins].

He asked how "Mission to Moscow" was going, and I told him that it had now been translated into seven different languages; transcribed into Braille in the United States, and into Braille in England (for the blind); it was published in eleven different countries; that the Australian Minister Designate to Moscow, who was passing through, advised me that the book had made a sensation in Australia and was far and away the best seller. He asked me how the cheaper editions were going. I explained to him that I did not wait for the complete run on the $3.00 edition, but with the cooperation of the publishers had arranged for a $1.49 edition, and had now arranged for 25¢ edition, and that the publishers were getting out a million and a half copies immediately. I also told him that "Mission to Moscow" now leads, according to the Book Trade Magazines, as the "best seller" on repress and had displaced "Berlin Diary." He kidded me about going out to Hollywood to have the picture filmed.

While I was there, Secretary Hull came in for his appointment and when the President asked if "Marjorie" was going with me, I told him: "Of course," and Secretary Hull then said that Mrs. Hull was very devoted to Mrs. Davies and admired her very much.

Diary of Joseph Davies, November 20, 1942, Box 12, Joseph E. Davies, Papers,

Manuscript Division, Library of Congress, Washington, D.C. Reprinted by permission of Eleanor Davies Ditzen and Emlen Davies Evers.

5. Davies in Hollywood

Spent the day at Warner Bros. It is a magnificent plant—one of the best in the world, I understand.

Had lunch with the entire executive staff, as well as Colonel "Jack," and Mr. "H.M." It was a very pleasant occasion.

I saw the first scene in the shooting of "Mission to Moscow". It was the scene between the Ambassador and Spendler, the young attache who reported the alleged microphones discovered in the Italian Embassy and kept urging that we have our premises searched.

Much impressed with Curtiz, the director. Too bad I didn't see him last summer.

Huston is a splendid actor but apparently refused to make himself up to resemble in any way the personality he purports to represent. That is not important, except that it makes a distinction between the other characters who are impersonated physically by resemblances.

Marjorie and I spent the evening in a very pleasant bungalow and played gin-rummy.

Diary of Joseph Davies, November 23, 1942, Box 12, Joseph E. Davies Papers, Manuscript Division, Library of Congress, Washington, D.C. Reprinted by permission of Eleanor Davies Ditzen and Emlen Davies Evers.

6. Davies in Hollywood

About midway through the shooting Ambassador and Mrs. Davies, along with their entourage, arrived at the studio. Everyone was a little nervous, wanting to make sure that the right things would be said to an author who was protected by an excellent contract. Harry Warner himself piloted the party down to the stage, where the prop man displayed properly named chairs for the distinguished visitors.

The trouble started on the first day. Mr. Davies looked over the actors, looking longest at Walter Huston, who was playing the ambassador. Finally, when Curtiz sidled up to him, Mr. Davies spoke his mind.

"There's one thing I can't understand. You've made an effort in casting and makeup to have all the other characters resemble the originals—Roosevelt, Kalinin, Churchill, Litvinov. But Mr. Huston doesn't look like me."

"But, Mr. Davies, all these other people are well-known men."

(A horrified silence except for a slight giggle from one of the crew.)

"Why, what do you mean?" Davies replied. "I'm well known. I have thousands of friends." . . .

Finally a compromise was worked out: Mr. Davies would be permitted to appear on the screen as himself at the opening of the picture. For this prologue he wrote his own speech. When I read it, I was dismayed. In essence it was a long, drawn-out statement to assure the audience that, in spite of the favorable things about the Soviet Union noted in his book and in the film, he was a true-blue capitalist who believed in free enterprise, the pioneer spirit, motherhood, and apple pie.

Howard Koch, *As Time Goes By* (New York: Harcourt Brace, 1979), pp. 125–26.

7. The Producer's Viewpoint

(1) It was Mr. Davies who insisted upon Erskine Caldwell as the screenplay writer for *Mission to Moscow*. This was against the wishes of · both Mr. Jack L. Warner, chief executive of the studio, and myself as the producer. And our objections were based purely upon professional, not personal, reasons. Davies' book was almost totally unsuited for translation to the screen for the general public, presenting an extremely difficult job for even the most expert screen writer; and Caldwell was not experienced as a writer for the screen. But because Davies knew him when he was the ambassador in Moscow and when Caldwell was visiting there as a journalist, Davies pressed for his services. It soon proved to be a mistake and a waste of time and money. I liked Caldwell personally but his work and analysis of the problems was quite unacceptable. He was well paid and excused, and his work on the screenplay was unusable, even by Davies' admission.

(2) It was Jack Warner's decision to use Michael Curtiz as the director. His strong recommendation, after many discussions with me and others, persuaded Davies to accept him. Davies wanted a "bigger" name, but after Caldwell's failure Davies was less demanding with his recommendations. I had worked with Curtiz on several successful films previously, and Warner felt we could solve the many problems between us. Curtiz, a Hungarian and totally unpolitically educated, had a great talent for graphic effects, but never any real understanding of the issues involved in *Mission to Moscow* (the book). Even after the script

was finally written and approved Curtiz had to be reminded almost daily of the meaning of the events he was directing. The fact that he succeeded in making the film fairly clear to the average person is a tribute to Curtiz's instinctive abilities as a director.

(3) Ivy Low Litvinoff was never in Hollywood during the production of the film, to the best of my memory. I met her first at Davies' (or rather Mrs. Davies') lodge in the Adirondacks some months prior to the start of the film's production, when she was a guest there with Litvinoff, and when I was called there to consult with Davies as to how the book might be handled for films. Mme. Litvinoff was a delightful person, witty and wise and a help to me with Davies and Mrs. Davies, who were understandably somewhat less objective about the matter—i.e., both the facts and filming requirements involved.

(4) I did not believe that the victims of the so-called Purge Trials were guilty as charged, nor did the majority of the foreign correspondents, as you undoubtedly are aware. I am convinced that Stalin framed them and I read everything possibly available on the subject, before and long after the film was made. In fact I had a rather violent argument with Davies on this subject when time came to film the trial scenes. An ambiguity about the guilt or innocence had been purposely suggested by Davies when the script was being written, but when time came to shoot the scene and the guilt or innocence had to be made specific, Davies insisted upon the guilt. I went to the brothers Warner and told them I felt that a great historic mistake was being made. They called a meeting with Davies and myself to settle the point, and Davies made one of the most beautiful poker-play bluffs I have ever witnessed. Instead of answering our questions he asked how much the film had cost to that point. I had the figure at hand, just under one million dollars. Davies said: "All right, let's say one million as a round figure. I will give you the million here and now and will take over the negative of the film from you." He took out a checkbook and pen and prepared to write the check. I don't think he ever would have done so, but the Warners and I knew that with Mrs. Davies' money behind him he could have paid such a sum. The Warners were tempted to call his bluff but they didn't at last, and Davies won his point that the Purge Trials would "make clear" that the victims were guilty as traitors and Trotskyites. At this decision I offered to resign as the producer but Warner would not let me. From this point on relations between Mr. Davies and myself were understandly strained.

(5) I did not fully respect Mr. Davies' integrity, both before, during and after the film. I knew that FDR had brainwashed him, and the

Warners as well, into making the film; as FDR said in a meeting at the White House: "to show the American mothers and fathers that if their sons are killed in fighting alongside Russians in our common cause, that it was a good cause, and that the Russians are worthy allies." This statement was relayed to me by Harry Warner, head of the studio, who was present when FDR spoke in front of Davies, Litvinoff, Harry Hopkins and others. Davies and Mrs. Davies were in Hollywood throughout the film's production, as guests of the Warners, at the Beverly Hills Hotel. They had a say in the approval of Walter Huston, Ann Harding and other actors, and in most of the stage sets. Personally, they were a general nuisance rather than helpful; Davies especially. He was a pompous, conceited, arrogant man with greater political ambitions than his abilities justified. . . . It is now common historical knowledge, of course, that Stalin brainwashed him completely.

I could write you at much greater length about the history of the film's production, the strong exceptions I had to many scenes upon which Davies insisted. Howard Koch was a capable screenwriter, following orders, but with no clear knowledge or convictions of the truth or falsity of the issues involved. I take no pride in this film except in the quality of the physical production. It was an expedient lie for political purposes, glossily covering up important facts with full or partial knowledge of their false presentation. This is my sincere opinion. And you are undoubtedly aware that no one was more amused by it than Stalin and Molotov and the others when they screened the film in the Kremlin. This is a recorded fact. They had every reason to find it hilarious.

However many scripts Caldwell wrote, and I can only recall the contracted revisions of his first draft, his screenplay was obviously unacceptable to the studio, to me as the producer, and to Curtiz the director. Otherwise he would not have been replaced. Davies himself made no argument about this when faced with our united opinions. Caldwell did his best, and Davies' book was a ponderous mass of ungraphic details which would have stumped almost any writer. . . .

Koch had no way of knowing Davies well, since he saw relatively little of him, especially during the production. I, on the contrary, saw Davies practically every day, either in my office at the studio, on the sets, or at Davies' bungalow at the Beverly Hills Hotel. Also, I spent a week with Davies, his wife, Maxim Litvinoff and Mme. Litvinoff, at the Davies lodge in the Adirondacks, prior to the production. Koch came to join me there for the final days of those conferences. A very amusing story could be written about that week, with Mrs. Davies masterminding the procedures, and the Litvinoffs' amusement at our opulent surroundings and service. I had two private chats with Litvinoff during that week which were quite revealing about the Davieses' time in Moscow, but of course the old Bolshevik was too diplomatic to answer all my questions outright. A year or two after the film was released I ran into Ivy Litvinoff on 5th Ave. in New York, and we had an interesting conversation about our experiences with the Davieses and the eventual film. She told me that Stalin and the Comintern members were "vastly amused" by the film and especially by the American actors who imitated themselves. Davies had told me they thought it was "great," and so they might have said, of course. But evidence to the contrary, i.e., the truth of the film's merits—both as to its historical accuracy and as a film per se—are, in my opinion and that of many others, rather overwhelming. I certainly take no pride in it as the producer. . . .

Davies was variously helpful or a damn nuisance, with his final OK of everything in his contract. Curtiz, who had a notoriously short temper on the set, was often furious with Davies' petty objections, and I had to restrain him on several occasions, although I shared his feelings.

Now to answer your questions: it was definitely Davies who inserted the insinuation that Finland was not actually invaded by the USSR. I recall questioning him about this point at the time, for it was then general knowledge or feeling that the opposite was true; but Davies insisted that he had "privileged knowledge" of the facts of the case, and I had no way of contradicting him. Davies was often prone to pulling this mysterious inside knowledge to silence us.

I cannot recall any Soviet Russians being in Hollywood when the film was shot; nor if the Soviet Embassy read the screenplay prior to production. Their right to do so was certainly not in our contract, but it may have been in a private agreement with Davies. I have no way of knowing, but I doubt if they read it.

I have no memory of a Jay Leyda's role in the film, but I do recall a technical adviser being employed at Davies' insistence. This was mainly to achieve some accuracy in set dressing, costumes, makeup, etc. This may well have been Leyda. But he did not participate in the casting of Bukharin or anyone else. Curtiz and I handled all of that, working from photographs of the originals and supervising all of the makeup and costume tests—a big and wearing job it was. And no, the technical adviser (Leyda or whoever) had no say or influence with his political views, at least not with me or Curtiz.

Mission to Moscow was not a financially successful film. It did not return its negative cost, although the publicity released by the studio insinuated otherwise. I could never obtain the exact figures (few ever can in any studio), but I had a good friend in the accounting department who confided to me years later that the film was a financial failure. Not a disaster, just that it never broke even. I can assure you that you'll never get any closer to the fact.

Of course Davies arranged for the film to be made. How can you possibly doubt it? I was present at conferences in Washington when this was made crystal clear by Davies, and confirmed by FDR to the brothers Warner in person.

Robert Buckner to Culbert, January 1 and January 14, 1978.

8. Government Censor Approves Completed Film

MISSION TO MOSCOW is a magnificent contribution to the Government's motion picture program as a means of communicating historical and political material in a dramatic way. As the picture unfolds the whole field of international relations, Axis intrigue and the shameful role of the appeasers of the Axis in the past decade is illuminated for us. The presentation of the Moscow trials is a high point in the picture and should do much to bring understanding of Soviet international policy in the past years and dispel the fears which many honest persons have felt with regard to our alliance with Russia. The clarity and conviction with which this difficult material is presented is a remarkable achievement for the screen and should do much to lay the "ghosts of fascist propaganda" which still haunt us and delay the forging of that international unity which is essential to the winning of the war and the peace. MISSION TO MOSCOW pulls no punches; it answers the propaganda lies of the Axis and its sympathizers with the most powerful propaganda of all: the truth. The possibility for the friendly alliance of the Capitalist United States and the Socialist Russia is shown to be firmly rooted in the mutual desire for peace of two great countries. The condition for world peace is shown to be the international unity of all the freedom-loving peoples of the world, without exception.

The producers of this picture are to be congratulated for the forthright courage and honesty which made its production possible. Not only is it a great contribution to the war program in itself but it may well affect Hollywood's war product. Especially remarkable is the use of documentary footage in this picture, not simply as material for transitional montage or a background for narration but as the very warp and woof of the story itself. The result is to give the picture as a whole the immediacy of a vivid personal experience. It is to be hoped that MISSION TO MOSCOW will have immediate release and the widest possible distribution. The picture presents no problems for the point of view of either domestic or overseas distribution.

Report, Hollywood Office, Bureau of Motion Pictures, Office of War Information, April 29, 1943, Box 1434, entry 264, Record Group 208, Office of War Information Records, Archives Branch, Washington National Records Center, Suitland, Md.

9. Attacking the Film

The current movie, "Mission to Moscow," raises a most serious issue: it transplants to the American scene the kind of historical falsifications which have hitherto been characteristic of totalitarian propaganda. A group of individuals concerned with this issue are therefore circulating the enclosed statement for signatures. It is being sent to several hundred liberals, labor leaders, historians, writers, and others most especially affected by the issues raised by "Mission to Moscow."

You are invited to add your signature, if you agree with the statement after having seen the film. The statement will be released to the press in two weeks. Please let us hear from you by May 21st at the latest.

INITIATING SIGNATURES

George S. Counts (Teachers College, Columbia U.)
Max Danish (Editor "Justice" ILGWU organ)
Max Eastman (Author, "Enjoyment of Laughter," etc.)
James T. Farrell (Author, "Studs Lonigan," etc.)
Harry D. Gideonse (President, Brooklyn College)
Sidney Hook (Dept. of Philosophy, N.Y. Univ.)
Horace M. Kallen (New School for Social Research)
Alfred Kazin (Critic, author of "The Ground We Stand On")
Dwight Macdonald (Editor "Partisan Review")
John McDonald (Editor "Film News")
A. Philip Randolph (President, Brotherhood of Sleeping Car Porters)
Jacob Rich (City Editor "Jewish Daily Forward")
Norman Thomas
Edmund Wilson (Critic, author "Axel's Castle," etc.)
W. E. Woodward (Historian, author "A New American History")

(Affiliations are given for purposes of identification only.)
Please address reply to Dwight Macdonald, 117 East 10th St., New York City.

The film version of *Mission to Moscow* is a political event to which no thoughtful American can remain indifferent. With this film Warner Brothers have produced in this country the first full-dress example of the kind of propaganda movie hitherto confined to the totalitarian countries. It is our considered opinion that *Mission to Moscow* falsifies history and glorifies dictatorship.

This super-production will be seen by at least fifty million Americans. It is presented not as a fictionalization, but as a documentary record of history. It shrewdly combines actual newsreel sequences with impersonations of Stalin, Roosevelt, Churchill and other leaders in such a way as to give it an almost irresistible air of authenticity. It also pretends to be based on the official reports to the U.S. State Department made by ex-ambassador Davies, who appears in person in a prologue to give it his benediction. *Mission to Moscow* will thus create, if successful, an impression in the minds of tens of millions of Americans that the methods of Stalin's dictatorship are nowise incompatible with genuine democracy.

It seems necessary, therefore, to speak out on this issue, and to invite others to make their voices heard. In doing so, we do not contest the right of Warner Brothers to issue *Mission to Moscow*. But we feel that we ourselves have the right, and the duty, to expose its falsifications.

We make three main charges:

1. *"Mission to Moscow" falsifies history and even distorts the very book on which it is based.*

One of the chief purposes of the film is to present the Moscow Trials of 1936–1938 as the just punishment of proved traitors. These trials were generally regarded, at the time they took place, as brutal travesties of justice. Most of the American press, like the rest of the civilized world, considered them to be frame-ups of Stalin's personal and political opponents. Only the loyal supporters of the Communist Party accepted the verdict of the Trials that Trotsky, Bukharin, Radek, Rakovsky, Kamenev, Zinoviev and almost all the other surviving leaders of the 1917 revolution had plotted to restore capitalism in Russia and to betray the nation they founded to Hitler and the Mikado. In 1937 a commission headed by John Dewey investigated the Trials, heard numerous witnesses, and published a two-volume report finding that the Trials were "frame-ups," the verdicts unfounded, and the whole procedure contrary to the principles of Soviet law which, like our own, does not regard confessions as a sufficient evidence of guilt. Since then, no evidence has been presented to substantiate the charges of the Russian Court or to refute those of the Dewey Commission. . . .

2. *"Mission to Moscow" glorifies the Stalin dictatorship and its methods.*

It may seem curious that Warner Brothers should be so anxious to re-educate the American public on the Moscow Trials, an issue long since past and one which might seem of interest today chiefly to those who are supporting Stalin's straight party line. The fact is that *Mission to Moscow* is not a record of current history; it is not even a film designed to arouse sympathy for the heroic resistance to Nazi aggression of the Russian people; it is quite simply official propaganda on behalf of the present government of Russia. It corresponds in every detail with what the Kremlin would like the American people to think about its domestic and foreign policies. It denounces Britain's appeasement of Hitler, but the appeasement of the Stalin-Hitler Pact is glossed over as . . . realism! It shows half the map of Poland in flames when Hitler attacks, but the other half, invaded by the Red Army appears unaffected. The invasion of Finland is presented as an anti-fascist action. Throughout the film, Davies-Huston reiterates his determination to consider both sides of every question, but the audience never gets a glimpse of the seamy side of Stalin's policies. Even the tapping of foreign embassies' telephones by the Secret Police is airily dismissed by Davies-Huston.

A Nazi film devoted to whitewashing the Blood Purge, the Reichstag Fire Trial and similar matters would use no other means than are employed in *Mission to Moscow*.

3. *"Mission to Moscow" has the most serious implications for American democracy.*

Throughout the film there is a deliberate confusion of Soviet and American policy, so that critics of the one at any time in the past few years are presented as necessarily opposing the other. The Kremlin and the White House are practically brought under the same roof. All opponents of Roosevelt's pre-Pearl Harbor foreign policy are smeared as either fascists or dupes of fascism; Congress is slanderously portrayed and President Roosevelt is correspondingly exalted as all-seeing and all-wise. These "amalgam" techniques, this deification of The Leader are methods hitherto more characteristic of totalitarian propaganda than of our own. . . . The Kremlin's values are not our values, its political methods are not our methods, and we are deeply disturbed by quasi-official propaganda designed to prove the contrary.

Form letter, Dwight Macdonald et al. to "Dear Friend," May 12, 1943, NAACP MSS, Manuscript Division, Library of Congress, Washington, D.C. Reprinted by permission of Dwight Macdonald.

10. Defending the Film

Those of us who believe there is no single thing more important today than conquering Fascism and winning the war, and who realize that this requires complete unity against the enemy, must do our share in bringing this unity about. For this reason we must likewise raise our voices against those who would endanger this unity.

The Warner Brothers film *Mission to Moscow* is an instrument for understanding and friendship between the Allies, but it is being attacked by some whose hatred of the Soviet Union is greater than their desire to win the war.

Will you join with us in a statement to the press defending the film from these attacks, an action which we believe is important to make? You have undoubtedly seen the film, but if not we can arrange for you to do so. . . .

The picture "Mission to Moscow" strikes a new note in films, and like most experiments has aroused criticism as well as praise. Here is a story which is not a drama but is intensely dramatic; it is not a newsreel but is full of dynamic news. Perhaps it might be termed a "Personal History" vividly presented. It gives the audience a close-up of Russia's fight for industrialization and a modern and mechanized agriculture, as seen through the eyes of the American Ambassador to Moscow, Joseph E. Davies, who spent more time in visiting Soviet factories and Collective Farms than did any of his colleagues. There is shown, too, Russia's fight against internal enemies and potential Quislings who gave such aid and comfort to Nazi invaders in other countries of Europe. A notable feature is the inclusion of authentic newsreel shots of a military parade in Moscow's Red Square which reveal impressively the discipline and precision of movement, the advanced technical equipment and mechanization that have enabled the Red Army to withstand Hitler's most desperate assaults. These and other factors will be a revelation to millions of Americans who had come to believe that the USSR was a welter of mud, blood and semi-oriental barbarism. . . .

It is an unfortunate thing that many well-intentioned and doubtless patriotic people are still unaware of the extent and subtlety of Nazi propaganda and of its ceaseless efforts to sow the seeds of disunion in the United Nations' front. . . . When Mr. Davies first went to Moscow those relations were bad. He did much to make them better. The Warner Brothers film shows how he did it, and far from being untruthful it gives a picture of truth.

Herman Shumlin et al. to Walter White, June 1, 1943, NAACP MSS, Manuscript Division, Library of Congress, Washington, D.C.

Appendix

11. Stalin Likes the Film

Dear H. M.:

. . . This hurried note is to tell you that at the dinner given in my honor at the Kremlin last night, the picture was shown to the guests in one of the great rooms of the Palace. The favorable and even enthusiastic comments by some of the living characters portrayed in the film would have given you a "kick." I wish you could have enjoyed it with me. The Marshal and Premier Molotov were generous in their praise of the picture.

Joseph Davies to Harry M. Warner, May 24, 1943, Box 13, Joseph E. Davies Papers, Manuscript Division, Library of Congress, Washington, D.C. Reprinted by permission of Eleanor Davies Ditzen and Emlen Davies Evers.

12. Soviet Response to the Film (Unfavorable)

Stalin entertained Davies at formal dinner in the Kremlin on Sunday night . . . notable for the absence of spontaneous cordialty or genuine good humor.

It was the dullest Kremlin dinner I have ever attended, and while an atmosphere of reserved friendliness on the part of the Russians prevailed most of them including Stalin appeared bored.

Molotov proposed the initial toast to American-Soviet solidarity and in laudatory terms greeted Davies as a real friend of the USSR who had greatly contributed to closer friendly relations between our two countries. Davies replied with a long oration on the horrors of war, the glories of Stalingrad, and the greatness of the Soviet armies, peoples, and leaders. He proposed that Stalingrad be left in ruins as a monument of the atrocities of the Germans and that the new city be erected five miles up or down the river. I felt that Davies overdid his attempts to impress the Russians of his sincerity and love for them and that his speech was much too long.

Shortly afterwards Davies proposed a toast to Litvinov who responded by commenting on Davies' fine work in helping the American people better to understand the Soviet Union. He stated that Davies was in effect also an envoy of the Soviet Union in Washington. . . . Before the dinner had terminated the guests were asked to come to the motion picture hall to see *Mission to Moscow*. All the Americans present who expressed an opinion to me felt that the film was received with rather glum curiosity and doubted if the Hollywood treatment of events described in Davies' book met with the general approval of the Russians. They successfully refrained from favorable comment while the film was being shown but Stalin was heard to grunt once or twice. The glaring discrepancies must have provoked considerable resentment among the Soviet officials present. Its object—flattery of everything Russian and the ill-advised introduction of unpleasant events in Soviet international history that I am inclined to think the Kremlin would prefer to forget—makes me believe that the Russians will not desire to give publicity to the film, at least in its present form. In any event I feel that the film will not contribute to better understanding between the two countries.

Telegram, Ambassador William Standley to Secretary of State, May 25, 1943, Box 68, President's Secretary's File, Franklin D. Roosevelt Library, Hyde Park, N.Y.

13. American Feature Films in the Soviet Union

The Chargé d'Affaires ad interim has the honor to report below certain findings and recommendations growing out of an examination of the Embassy's motion picture program.

Before discussing operations and recommendations, something should be said about the attitude of the Soviet Government and the Communist Party toward American motion pictures. It is the aim of the Soviet Government and of the Communist Party to direct the thinking of the Soviet population into a definite ideological pattern. To achieve this, it is necessary that the Government and the Party not only mold all Soviet expressions of opinion—the press, other publications, the radio and motion pictures—but also that they strictly control the entry into the Soviet Union of anything foreign likely to influence Soviet thinking.

American motion pictures fall within this latter category. Because the few American pictures which have been shown in the USSR have been tremendously popular and because the average American picture is in official Soviet eyes not only ideologically demoralizing, but also often tends to create pro-American sentiments, the Government and the Party are most wary of making available American motion pictures for public exhibition.

The American motion picture industry has until the autumn of 1945 (Department's instruction No. 839 of October 5, 1945) on two occasions during the war provided the Embassy with American films for showing at the Embassy and for examination by the Film Committee of the Council of People's Commissars with a view to their ultimate purchase. The Film Committee holds the pictures for several weeks or longer.

("Wilson" was in the possession of the Film Committee for some four months.) During the time that the pictures are in the possession of the Film Committee, they are shown to certain high officials and organizations including, we understand, the Kremlin. The USSR is perhaps the only country in which the Chief of State acts personally as principal movie censor. The Embassy has no information regarding the number of showings or size of audiences viewing the films during this period. After completion of these exhibitions, the films are returned to the Embassy or, in a few cases, purchased for public exhibition. . . .

The organizations on the "approved list" are named below together with the estimated number of exhibitions at each organization and the estimated total audiences: Foreign Office, 1—300; Soviet Information Bureau, 2—800; VOKS, 1—300; Red Army, 3—2500; Red Navy, 3—2500; Actor's Club, 2—800; Artists' Club, 2—800; Vaktangova Theater, 1—500; Red Army Theater, 1—500; Bolshoi Theater, 1—3000.

The popularity of American films and the restrictions placed on their exhibition inevitably means that there is considerable maneuvering on the part of organizations not included in the "approved list" to obtain loans of films. For the Department's strictly confidential information, the Embassy's Soviet employee charged with the distribution of films states that he has been offered bribes by various organizations desirous of borrowing pictures in the possession of the Embassy. He claims that these offers, have, of course, been refused. . . .

It seems to the Embassy, however, that the issues involved in the motion picture program for the USSR are more fundamental than questions of procedure. There would appear to be two basic issues. One is how the interests of the American film industry can be best served. The second is how American propaganda interests can best be served.

According to the Film Committee, during the years 1939–1945, inclusive, the Soviet Government purchased from the American film industry twenty-four American motion pictures—an average of three to four a year. Films purchased, according to this source, were: 1939—100 Men and a Girl; 1940—The Great Waltz; 1941—Champagne Waltz, Give Us This Night, Three Musketeers, In Old Chicago, Under Your Spell; 1942—(no picture purchases); 1943—Bambi, Mission to Moscow, Sun Valley Serenade, Edison, Battle for Russia, shorts: The Face of the Fuehrer, The Old Mill; 1944—The Hurricane, The Little Foxes, The North Star, Song of Russia, Charlie's Aunt; 1945—His Butler's Sister, Appointment for Love, Spring Parade, This Is the Army, Men in Her Life. . . .

The Embassy recommends that discrimination be exercised in turn-

Appendix

ing over films to organizations in the Soviet Union for exhibition. In the publication of *America* the material issued has been carefully selected. If broadcasting in Russian is undertaken, the programs will assumably be edited with a view to the peculiarities of the Soviet audience. Similarly, only expertly selected motion pictures should be made available for showing to Soviet audiences.

The reasons for such selection are well-founded. In the Soviet Union we start at a disadvantage in attempting to present a balanced exposition of the United States. Day in and day out the Soviet propaganda machine presents a derogatory picture of the United States. An absolutely proportional presentation of America's virtues and faults will not restore the balance. Compensatory weight on the side of favorable interpretation is necessary if the overall impression is even to approach a realistic exposition of American life. This is particularly true because the Soviets will themselves exercise such selection as they can with a view to supporting their own preconceived propaganda version of American reality. If our Government fails to exercise some selection over what is sent, it will therefore simply be aiding a foreign propaganda office to distort American reality for anti-American purposes. . . .

Lest the socially conscious elements in Hollywood be concerned that pictures with a social message be eliminated, it may be said that Soviet authorities are inclined to cast a jaundiced eye on the average American motion picture portraying social problems. This is so, not because they deny the existence of faults in American society, but because the Hollywood analysis of American social evils usually does not hew to the Marxist-Engelist-Leninist-Stalinist line. It will be noted that among the twenty-four pictures puchased, only one—Miss Hellman's "Little Foxes"—might be considered as freighted with social consciousness. But it was set in the nineteenth century, and the ideological content was entirely satisfactory from the Moscow standpoint.

John Paton Davies, "Motion Picture Program for USSR," to Secretary of State, February 18, 1946, No. 2449, 861.4061, Record Group 59, Department of State, National Archives, Washington, D.C.

14. Jack Warner Supports Film: 1942

I have read through the entire trial, and told Bob Buckner I consider this whole script excellent.

However, I feel that unless you step on it and get some of the script ready, Curtiz is going to catch up with you and will have nothing to shoot.

I will greatly appreciate it if you will make more speed on MISSION TO MOSCOW, as we certainly do not want to find ourselves with a Director who has nothing to shoot.

Jack Warner to Howard Koch, November 24, 1942, Howard Koch Collection, Wisconsin Center for Film and Theater Research, Madison, Wis. Reprinted by permission of the Wisconsin Center for Film and Theater Research.

15. Warner Defends Film against Pro-Communist Charges: 1947

(STATEMENT OF JACK L. WARNER)

It is a privilege to appear again before this committee to help as much as I can in facilitating its work.

I am happy to speak openly and honestly in an inquiry which has for its purpose the reaffirmation of American ideals and democratic processes. As last May, when I appeared before a subcommittee of this group in Los Angeles, my testimony is based on personal opinions, impressions, and beliefs created by the things I have heard, read, and seen. It is given freely and voluntarily.

Our American way of life is under attack from without and from within our national borders. I believe it is the duty of each loyal American to resist those attacks and defeat them.

Freedom is a precious thing. It requires careful nurturing, protection, and encouragement. It has flourished under the guaranties of our American Constitution and Bill of Rights to make this country the ideal of all men who honestly wish to call their souls their own.

I believe that I, as an individual, and our company as an organization of American citizens, must watch always for threats to the American way of life. History teaches the lesson that liberties are won bitterly and may be lost unwittingly.

We have seen recent tragic examples of national and personal freedoms destroyed by dictator-trained wrecking crews. The advance guards of propagandists and infiltrationists were scarcely noticed at first. They got in their first licks quietly, came into the open only when they were ready to spring the trap. Heedless peoples suddenly woke up to find themselves slaves to dictatorships imposed by skillful and willful groups.

I believe the first line of defense against this familiar pattern is an enlightened public. People aware of threats to their freedom cannot be victimized by the divide-and-conquer policies used by Hitler and his counterparts.

It is my firm conviction that the free American screen has taken its rightful place with the free American press in the first line of defense.

Ideological termites have burrowed into many American industries, organizations, and societies. Wherever they may be, I say let us dig them out and get rid of them. My brothers and I will be happy to subscribe generously to a pest-removal fund. We are willing to establish such a fund to ship to Russia the people who don't like our American system of government and prefer the communistic system to ours.

That's how strongly we feel about the subversives who want to overthrow our free American system.

If there are Communists in our industry, or any other industry, organization, or society who seek to undermine our free institutions, let's find out about it and know who they are. Let the record be spread clear, for all to read and judge. The public is entitled to know the facts. And the motion-picture industry is entitled to have the public know the facts.

Our company is keenly aware of its responsibilities to keep its product free from subversive poisons. With all the vision at my command, I scrutinize the planning and production of our motion pictures. It is my firm belief that there is not a Warner Bros. picture that can fairly be judged to be hostile to our country, or communistic in tone or purpose.

Many charges, including the fantasy of "White House pressure," have been leveled at our wartime production Mission to Moscow. In my previous appearance before members of this committee, I explained the origin and purposes of Mission to Moscow.

That picture was made when our country was fighting for its existence, with Russia as one of our allies. It was made to fulfill the same wartime purpose for which we made such other pictures as Air Force, This Is the Army, Objective Burma, Destination Tokyo, Action in the North Atlantic, and a great many more.

If making Mission to Moscow in 1942 was subversive activity, then the American Liberty ships which carried food and guns to Russian allies and the American naval vessels which convoyed them were likewise engaged in subversive activities. The picture was made only to help a desperate war effort and not for posterity.

The Warner Bros. interest in the preservation of the American way of life is no new thing with our company. Ever since we began making motion pictures we have fostered American ideals and done what we could to protect them.

Not content with merely warning against dangers to our free system, Warner Bros. has practiced a policy of positive Americanism. We have gone, and will continue to go, to all possible lengths to iterate and reiterate the realities and advantages of America.

Good American common sense is the determining factor in judging motion-picture scripts before they are put in production and motion-picture scenes after they are photographed. We rely upon a deep-rooted, pervading respect for our country's principles.

One of those American principles is the right to gripe and criticize in an effort to improve. That right to gripe is not enjoyed under communistic dictatorships. To surrender that privilege under pressure would betray our American standards.

Freedom of expression, however, does not, under our Constitution and laws, include a license to destroy.

We believe positive methods offer the best defense against possible subversive activities. In my previous testimony before a subcommittee of this committee, I stated certain people whom we let go were subsequently hired by other studios.

By no stretch of the imagination can that be construed as questioning the loyalty of other employers. The producers who hired the men we discharged are good Americans. There is no positive guide to determine whether or not a person is a Communist; and the laws of our land, which are in the hands of you gentlemen, offer no clean-cut definition on that point.

We can't fight dictatorships by borrowing dictatorial methods. Nor can we defend freedom by curtailing liberties, but we can attack with a free press and a free screen.

Subversive germs breed in dark corners. Let's get light into those corners. That, I believe, is the purpose of this hearing and I am happy to have had the opportunity to testify. . . .

MR. STRIPLING. Mr. Warner, in mentioning the pictures which you have produced, I noticed you did not mention Mission to Moscow.

MR. WARNER. What list are you referring to?

MR. STRIPLING. You referred to the pictures you have made.

MR. WARNER. Do you want me to read the list?

MR. STRIPLING. No; but we want to get to Mission to Moscow. Would you like to testify about that here, or do you want me to read your former testimony?

MR. WARNER. I would like to correct one error that I personally committed by not having the facts in Los Angeles. It is not a great error.

MR. STRIPLING. I ask, Mr. Chairman, that the witness be permitted to correct that statement when we reach it. Shall we proceed with your testimony on Mission to Moscow?

MR. WARNER. Very well.

MR. STRIPLING. Mr. Chairman, this is the testimony which was given in Los Angeles before the subcommittee regarding the picture Mission to Moscow.

Mr. Stripling to Mr. Warner:

MR. STRIPLING. Were you asked to make Mission to Moscow?

MR. WARNER. There is a correction I wish to make.

MR. STRIPLING. Let me read your first statement.

MR. WARNER. I just wish the record to show that I want to make a correction.

MR. STRIPLING (reading):

MR. WARNER. I would say we were to a degree. You can put it in that way in one form or another.

Is that what you want to correct?

MR. WARNER. I would appreciate if I could correct it.

MR. STRIPLING. Just that answer, or are there other answers?

MR. WARNER. No; it is on that point.

I would say we were to a degree. You can put it in that way in one form or another.

Then Mr. Thomas said: "Who asked you to make Mission to Moscow?" And I replied, "I would say the former Ambassador Davies."

That is not correct. Since making that statement I have gone over the authentic details of what occurred, and here they are in sequence.

On page 19 at the bottom that question was asked, and if you will go to page 22, you will find that I replied—well, it refers to who contacted us about making the film. I said:

At the time I can't remember if he contacted us, or my brother who was in New York contacted Mr. Davies. I can't say who contacted whom, but I know that we went ahead with it.

Here is the story of what occurred. My brother contacted Mr. Davies after reading Mission to Moscow as a best seller on the stands and in the newspapers. Mr. Davies stated, "There are other companies wanting to produce this book and I would be very happy to do business with you if you want to make it," or words to that effect. My brother made the deal with Mr. Davies to make it and it was at my brother's suggestion and not Mr. Davies'. I am rather surprised I said what I did, but I want to stand corrected, if I may.

MR. STRIPLING. All right, Mr. Warner. Now, I would like to read further, Mr. Chairman.

THE CHAIRMAN. Proceed.

MR. STRIPLING (reading):

MR. STRIPLING. Did Mr. Davies come to Hollywood to see you relative to the making of Mission to Moscow, or did you confer with him at any time about it in person?

MR. WARNER. I conferred with him in Washington and we made the deal in the East, in New York or Washington; I have forgotten which. But he did come here when the film was being produced, and he also acted in an advisory capacity throughout the making of the film. As a matter of fact, he appeared in a slight prologue of the picture.

MR. STRIPLING. Don't you consider very frankly that the film Mission to Moscow was in some ways a misinterpretation of the facts, or the existing conditions?

MR. WARNER. Of the time, you mean?

MR. STRIPLING. Yes.

MR. WARNER. In 1942?

MR. STRIPLING. In other words, certain historical incidents which were portrayed in the film were not true to fact?

MR. WARNER. Well, all I could go by—I read the novel and spoke to Mr. Davies on many, many occasions. I had to take his word that they were the facts. He had published the novel and we were criticized severely by the press in New York and elsewhere. As I remember, it was started up by this Professor Dewey from Columbia University. From what I read and heard, he was a Trotskyite and they were the ones who objected mostly to this film because of Lenin versus Trotsky—

MR. STRIPLING. That is Dr. John Dewey?

MR. WARNER. Yes. That is what I read. He made statements in the New York Times which were as long as the paper was, but as to the actual facts, if they weren't portrayed authentically—I never was in Russia myself and I don't know what they were doing in 1942, other than seeing the events of the battles for Stalingrad and Moscow, which we all saw in the films and read about. But I talked to Mr. Davies about that after we were criticized, and there is only one thing that happens which is a license, what we call condensation in the making of films. We put the two trials in one and the two trials were condensed because if you ran the two trials it would go on for 20 reels. I personally did not consider that film pro-Communist at the time.

MR. THOMAS. Now, it is 1947. Do you think it is pro-Communist now?

MR. WARNER. That I would have to think over. Let me pause for a minute and ask you a question or two, if you don't mind. You mean by saying that the type of scenes shown in that film today would that make the picture pro-Communist; is that it?

MR. THOMAS. You said in 1942.

MR. WARNER. It was made in 1942.

MR. THOMAS. You did not believe it was pro-Communist?

MR. WARNER. No. We were at war at that time.

MR. THOMAS. Now it is 1947. Do you believe it is pro-Communist?

MR. STRIPLING. Would you release the film now, in other words?

MR. WARNER. No; we would not release the film now.

MR. THOMAS. Why not release the film now?

MR. WARNER. Because of the way Russia is handling international affairs since the cessation of the war. I consider, in my opinion as an American, that they are advocating communism throughout the world and I am not in any shape, manner, or form in favor of anything like that. In fact, I despise and detest the very word.

MR. THOMAS. You say Mr. Davies got in touch with you. He was the first one to get in touch with you about the idea of producing this film; is that correct?

MR. WARNER. At the time I can't remember if he contacted us, or my brother who was in New York contacted Mr. Davies. I can't say who contacted whom, but I know that we went ahead with it.

MR. THOMAS. Did any other person in the Government contact either you or your brother in connection with producing Mission to Moscow?

MR. WARNER. Not to my knowledge; no.

MR. STRIPLING. What about the State Department?

MR. WARNER. You mean anyone in the State Department that asked us to make it?

MR. STRIPLING. Were they consulted in any way in this film, or did they consult with you?

MR. WARNER. I am trying to think hard who—

MR. STRIPLING. I am being very frank, Mr. Warner.

MR. WARNER. If you will give me a couple of minutes.

MR. STRIPLING. I will be very frank with you. The charge is often made and many statements have been made to the committee to the effect that Mission to Moscow was made at the request of our Government as a so-called appeasement or pap to the Russians; in other words, it was produced at the request of the Government. Now, is such a statement without foundation?

MR. WARNER. I see what you mean. No; it is not without foundation. That is why I am very happy you put it that way. In order to answer that question correctly, I would say there were rumors and many stories to the effect that if Stalingrad fell, Stalin would again join up with Hitler because, naturally, the way the stories were that far back, during the hardest days of the war, from what I could get out of it, is that the authorities in Washington who were conducting the war were afraid if Stalin would make up with Hitler they would destroy the world, not only continental Europe and Russia, but Japan and everything else. And we know what the scheme of things was, that the Japs and Germans were to meet in India or Egypt, I forget just which.

MR. THOMAS. Do you mean to say some of the Government officials in Washington informed you that they were fearful that Stalin might hook up with Hitler?

MR. WARNER. No; but that was the tenor of things. It would be pretty hard for me to say that someone told me that, but that was just the general feeling in Washington. Every time I would go there that would be it.

MR. THOMAS. Mr. Stripling asked a question that I don't think we have had an answer to yet.

MR. STRIPLING. Let me state further, Mr. Chairman, it has also been charged that this film had the tacit approval, if not the request, of the White House.

Mr. Warner, was there anything that occurred prior to the production of this film which led you to believe that the Government, the Federal Government, desired that this film be made as a contribution to the war effort? In other words, what I want to make clear, there is no desire on the part of the subcommittee to put you or your company on the spot for making Mission to Moscow but if it was made, as in other films, at the request of the Government as a so-called patriotic duty, you would have no other course to follow and you would naturally be expected to do so.

MR. WARNER. The general feeling as I found it in Washington was a tremendous fear that Stalin might go back with Hitler because he had done it before.

MR. THOMAS. No. What we want to get at is the reason, not the general feelings.

MR. WARNER. Yes; but I am just going to come back to that.

MR. THOMAS. All right.

MR. WARNER. The Russians were very discouraged and they figured that the United States was not going to back them up with lend-lease and so on and so forth in sufficient quantities to beat Hitler, which was very, very important to civilization, and the feeling was if a film could be made—and I imagine other things were being done—to assure the Russians and Stalin—

MR. THOMAS. Can't you be more specific. You say a feeling existed.

MR. WARNER. Yes.

MR. THOMAS. We want to know more about the specific thing, something more than just a general feeling. We want to know the persons in the Government who got in touch with you concerning the making of this film.

MR. WARNER. Well, I don't think Mr. Davies was in the Government then. He was then ex-Ambassador to Russia and almost everything was dealt through him.

MR. THOMAS. Did anyone in the State Department get in touch with you or not?

MR. WARNER. No. I don't know. Not to my knowledge. No one here or in New York.

MR. THOMAS. Did anyone in the White House get in touch with you?

MR. WARNER. No, not directly in touch; no, sir.

MR. THOMAS. Not directly in touch?

MR. WARNER. Do you mean did anyone in the White House say we should make the film for reasons along those lines?

MR. THOMAS. Directly or indirectly?

MR. WARNER. Well, as I understood at the time through Mr. Davies that he had contacted the White House and for all of the reasons I recited it was good for the defense and for the prosecution of the war to keep the Russians in there fighting until the proper time when the United States and Britain could organize, in other words, give us time to prepare.

MR. THOMAS. Let's have the date you started producing that film.

MR. WARNER. We started November 9, 1942.

MR. THOMAS. And you completed production when?

MR. WARNER. On February 2, 1943. It took a little under 4 months.

MR. STRIPLING. That is rather a quick production, isn't it?

MR. WARNER. No; that was about the usual length of time. They are usually 8 or 10 weeks.

MR. STRIPLING. From a commercial standpoint the film was not very successful, was it?

MR. WARNER. No; it was not exceptionally successful. It was not successful to any great degree. It did very good at first.

MR. STRIPLING. I mean from what I heard. In fact, there has been testimony it was not very successful.

MR. WARNER. No; I would not call it very successful. Commercially it wasn't exceedingly successful; no, sir.

MR. STRIPLING. Mr. Warner, there is one question which I think the subcommittee would like to have cleared up and I think that you as a studio executive could probably give them some information about it.

That testimony, Mr. Chairman, does not deal with Mission to Moscow.

I would like to skip over to the next page, which picks it up again [reading]:

MR. STRIPLING. If you had not been approached by Mr. Davies or by anyone in the Government indirectly it would have been very likely that you would not have filmed Mission to Moscow?

MR. WARNER. No; we would not.

MR. STRIPLING. I think the writers are the most important people in this investigation. I believe you mentioned Koch.

MR. WARNER. Howard Koch.

MR. WARNER. Pardon me, you missed some very important information here.

MR. STRIPLING. I am sorry.

MR. WARNER. You said the next page, and you skipped a page.

MR. STRIPLING. I am sorry, Mr. Warner, I did.

MR. WARNER. If you will go back to page 28 you will find it refers—oh, yes; at the bottom of page 27 [reading]:

MR. WARNER.—

this is myself speaking—

I was going to say something about that after I recited some of the chronological events of the war in order to confirm my feeling for the reasons that the Government was interested in the making of the picture. This is one of the reasons. I am not here to defend the Government because that is their business.

MR. THOMAS. We will be glad to have it.

MR. WARNER. When the Germans were halted at Stalingrad, that was one of the things Mr. Davies told my brother, that it was essential to keep the Russians in there—

Mr. Thomas said "pitching," and I replied:

***pitching to give our country a chance to arm, the Navy, the Army, airpower, and everything else, which we were not prepared for at the time, and of course history has told the story.

And I want to introduce the front pages of a New York newspaper, starting with the day following Pearl Harbor, December 8, 1941, right up to December 30, 1942, which gives a very vivid history of the process of the war by the Russians.

THE CHAIRMAN. How many pages are there, Mr. Warner?

MR. WARNER. I am going to read them.

THE CHAIRMAN. No. How many are there?

MR. WARNER. There are about 25—just papers.

THE CHAIRMAN. We will take that as an exhibit.

MR. STRIPLING. Is that the chronological statement which you gave to the committee?

MR. WARNER. It is, to one degree or another. And I have a copy of the chronological statement, too. I will give you another one, if you want.

MR. STRIPLING. Yes.

MR. WARNER. But this tells the story of Russia's distress, Russia getting beaten.

THE CHAIRMAN. We will be glad to receive those as an exhibit. Go ahead with the questioning, Mr. Stripling.

MR. STRIPLING. Now, Howard Koch wrote the script for Mission to Moscow?

MR. WARNER. Yes; he did.

MR. STRIPLING. Was Howard Koch one of those writers whom you subsequently dismissed?

MR. WARNER. Let us get it correct. I never dismissed anyone for any activity. His contract expired and we didn't renew his contract.

MR. STRIPLING. You haven't employed him since?

MR. WARNER. We didn't make a new deal with him.

MR. STRIPLING. Now, when the picture Mission to Moscow was made, were you aware that there were certain historical events which were erroneously portrayed in the picture?

MR. WARNER. I stated the only historical events that I know, by claim of many people—the press and public, in general—were the trials of the purge, or whatever they called it at the time in the book, which was condensed.

MR. STRIPLING. Mr. Warner—

MR. WARNER. I told you, I don't know if it was all correct or not.

MR. STRIPLING. Yes.

MR. WARNER. Mr. Davies was—

MR. STRIPLING. The point is this, Mr. Warner, that here was a picture which was produced and shown to the American people, and it was shown in other countries, I presume, was it not?

MR. WARNER. I think it was shown in England and several other countries.

MR. STRIPLING. It was also shown in Moscow, to Mr. Stalin?

MR. WARNER. In Moscow and to Stalin; yes.

MR. STRIPLING. Here is a picture, however, which portrayed Russia and the Government of Russia in an entirely different light from what it actually was?

MR. WARNER. I don't know if you can prove it, or that I can prove that it was. . . .

MR. STRIPLING. Well, is it your opinion now, Mr. Warner, that Mission to Moscow was a factually correct picture, and you made it as such?

MR. WARNER. I can't remember.

MR. STRIPLING. Would you consider it a propaganda picture?

MR. WARNER. A propaganda picture—

MR. STRIPLING. Yes.

MR. WARNER. In what sense?

MR. STRIPLING. In the sense that it portrayed Russia and communism in an entirely different light from what it actually was?

MR. WARNER. I am on record about 40 times or more that I have never been in Russia. I don't know what Russia was like in 1937 or 1944 or 1947, so how can I tell you if it was right or wrong?

MR. STRIPLING. Don't you think you were on dangerous ground to produce as a factually correct picture one which portrayed Russia—

MR. WARNER. No; we were not on dangerous ground in 1942, when we produced it. There was a war on. The world was at stake.

MR. STRIPLING. In other words—

MR. WARNER. We made the film to aid in the war effort, which I believe I have already stated.

MR. STRIPLING. Whether it was true or not?

MR. WARNER. As far as I was concerned, I considered it true to the extent as written in Mr. Davies' book.

MR. STRIPLING. Well, do you suppose that your picture influenced the people who saw it in this country, the millions of people who saw it in this country?

MR. WARNER. In my opinion, I can't see how it would influence anyone. We were in war and when you are in a fight you don't ask who the fellow is who is helping you.

MR. STRIPLING. Well, due to the present conditions in the international situation, don't you think it was rather dangerous to write about such a disillusionment as was sought in that picture?

MR. WARNER. I can't understand why you ask me that question, as to the present conditions. How did I, you, or anyone else know in 1942 what the conditions were going to be in 1947. I stated in my testimony our reason for making the picture, which was to aid the war effort—anticipating what would happen.

MR. STRIPLING. I don't see that that is aiding the war effort, Mr. Warner—with the cooperation of Mr. Davies or with the approval of the Government—to make a picture which is a fraud in fact.

MR. WARNER. I want to correct you, very vehemently. There was no cooperation of the Government.

MR. STRIPLING. You stated there was.

MR. WARNER. I never stated the Government cooperated in the making of it. If I did, I stand corrected. And I know I didn't.

MR. STRIPLING. Do you want me to read that part, Mr. Chairman?

THE CHAIRMAN. No; I think we have gone into this Mission to Moscow at some length.

MR. WARNER. I would like to go into it at great length, in order to make the Warner Bros.' position to the American public clear, as to why we made the film. You couldn't be more courageous, to help the war effort, than we. Certainly there are inaccuracies in everything. I have seen a million books—using a big term—and there have been inaccuracies in the text. There can be inaccuracies in anything, especially in a creative art. As I said, we condensed the trials—

U.S. Congress, House, Committee on Un-American Activities, *Hearings Regarding the Communist Infiltration of the Motion Picture Industry*, 80th Cong., 1st sess., October 20, 1947, pp. 9–11, 32–39. Footnotes referring to an appendix in the original document have been omitted. The testimony marked by ellipsis on p. 274 concerns a passage from Quentin Reynolds, *The Curtain Rises*.

Inventory

The following materials from the Warner library of the Wisconsin Center for Film and Theater Research were used by Culbert in preparing *Mission to Moscow* for the Wisconsin/Warner Bros. Screenplay Series:

Mission to Moscow, by Joseph E. Davies. New York: Simon and Schuster, 1941. 683 pages.

Treatment, by Erskine Caldwell. August 4, 1942. Annotated. Incomplete. 125 pages.

Treatment, by Caldwell. August 21, 1942. Incomplete. 122 pages.

Screenplay, by Caldwell. No date. Incomplete. 39 pages.

Story Outline, by Howard Koch. August 28, 1942. Incomplete. 9 pages.

Story Outline, by Koch. September 6, 1942. 18 pages.

Temporary, by Koch. September 29 to October 6, 1942. Incomplete. 41 pages.

Final, by Koch. October 15, 1942, to January 12, 1943. 181 pages.

DESIGNED BY GARY GORE
COMPOSED BY THE NORTH CENTRAL PUBLISHING CO.
ST. PAUL, MINNESOTA
MANUFACTURED BY INTER-COLLEGIATE PRESS, INC.
SHAWNEE MISSION, KANSAS
TEXT AND DISPLAY LINES ARE SET IN PALATINO

Library of Congress Cataloging in Publication Data
Main entry under title:
Mission to Moscow.
(Wisconsin/Warner Bros. screenplay series)
1. Mission to Moscow. [Motion picture]
I. Culbert, David Holbrook.
II. Mission to Moscow. [Motion picture]
III. Series
PN1997.M6184   791.43'72   80-5108
ISBN 0-299-08380-2
ISBN 0-299-08384-5 (pbk.)

The Wisconsin/Warner Bros. Screenplay Series, a product of the Warner Brothers Film Library, will enable film scholars, students, researchers, and aficionados to gain insights into individual American films in ways never before possible.

The Warner library was acquired in 1957 by the United Artists Corporation, which in turn donated it to the Wisconsin Center for Film and Theater Research in 1969. The massive library, housed in the State Historical Society of Wisconsin, contains eight hundred sound feature films, fifteen hundred short subjects, and nineteen thousand still negatives, as well as the legal files, press books, and screenplays of virtually every Warner film produced from 1930 until 1950. This rich treasure trove has made the University of Wisconsin one of the major centers for film research, attracting scholars from around the world. This series of published screenplays represents a creative use of the Warner library, both a boon to scholars and a tribute to United Artists.

Most published film scripts are literal transcriptions of finished films. The Wisconsin/Warner screenplays are primary source documents–the final shooting versions including revisions made during production. As such, they will explicate the art of screenwriting as film transcriptions cannot. They will help the user to understand the arts of directing and acting, as well as the other arts involved in the film-making process, in comparing these screen plays with the final films. (Films of the Warner library are available at modest rates from the United Artists nontheatrical rental library, United Artists/16 mm.)

From the eight hundred feature films in the library, the general editor and the editorial committee of the series have chosen those that have received critical recognition for their excellence of directing, screenwriting, and acting, films that are distinctive examples of their genre, those that have particular historical relevance, and some that are adaptations of well-known novels and plays. The researcher, instructor, or student can, in the judicious selection of individual volumes for close examination, gain a heightened appreciation and broad understanding of the American film and its historical role during this critical period.